THE FABER BOOK
OF
CHILDREN'S VERSE

also edited by Janet Adam Smith

*

THE LIVING STREAM:

An Anthology of Twentieth-Century Verse

THE FABER BOOK
OF
CHILDREN'S VERSE

compiled by

JANET ADAM SMITH

faber and faber

First published in 1953
by Faber and Faber Limited
3 Queen Square, London, W.C.1
First published in Faber Paperbacks 1963
Reprinted 1966, 1968, 1969, 1973, 1978 and 1983
Printed in Great Britain by
Redwood Burn Limited, Trowbridge, Wiltshire

ISBN 0 571 05457 9

CONTENTS

7

Contents

BEASTS AND BIRDS

Contents

CHILDREN

9

Contents

VICTUALS AND DRINK

Contents

SOME PEOPLE

FOUR COUNTRIES

KINGS, QUEENS AND HEROES

Contents

Contents

FAIRIES, NYMPHS AND GODS

WITCHES, CHARMS AND SPELLS

Contents

MARCH AND BATTLE

DIRGES, CORONACHS AND ELEGIES

Contents

MARVELS AND RIDDLES

VOYAGING AND TRAVEL

Contents

THE SEA

LOVE

Contents

GOD AND HEAVEN

17

Contents

EPIGRAMS AND REFLECTIONS

INTRODUCTION

I am assured that nobody objects to being called a child up to
the age of fourteen: and I have compiled this book with the
ages eight to fourteen mainly in mind. Among the younger
readers will be some children who have only lately learned to
read to themselves for enjoyment; among the older, children
who are reading *Macbeth* and the *Canterbury Tales* in school,
and discovering *Prufrock* and *Byzantium* outside. But the age
limits are not exclusive, and the book contains many poems
which have given much enjoyment when read aloud to four
and five year olds.

Certainly children between eight and fourteen have played
an important part in building up this book. They have sug-
gested poems for inclusion, and given their opinion on the
poems I suggested. I have also consulted a number of people
between the ages of fourteen and twenty-one, who not only
remember very clearly what poems they enjoyed as children,
but have decided opinions as to which of these have not
worn well in their memories. The final choice, and the
arrangement, is mine: but there is no poem in the book that
has not been liked by children—either by myself or other
elders when we were young, or by those who are children now.

I have grouped the poems by subjects, as this seemed to be
the most convenient and natural way of dealing with the
poems which I had selected; but there is nothing hard and
fast about this arrangement. Most of the poems would
qualify for several sections: I was hard put to it whether to
place Housman's verse about the Grizzly Bear who eats the
Infant Child under Beasts and Birds or Children; and I
suppose it might just as well have gone under Victuals and
Drink. *John Barleycorn* too might have gone there for it is
about the magic of drink. I certainly hope that nobody
will forever think of *The Great Silkie* as 'An Animal Poem'
or of *The Ancient Mariner* as 'A Poem of the Sea'.

Introduction

There are a few pages of Further Information after the poems. These are not Notes, intended to clear up all puzzles and difficulties; I have only aimed at giving particular information about the circumstances of the poem—on what occasion it was written, for example, or for what purpose—where this might add to the reader's appreciation. I have also given further information about those poems of which only a part has been printed.

One reason for having the ages of eight to fourteen in mind is that I, and many others, have found that the poetry we most enjoyed reading in those years has stuck in our minds, without any deliberate learning, in a way that poetry learnt more recently has not. So it seems reasonable to give children poems to read at this age that they will like to find in their heads twenty or thirty years later. When I try unsuccessfully to remember a good poem that I committed to memory five years ago, I find it intensely irritating to remember instead a bad poem that I learnt 35 years ago. It is like going to the attic to look for the comfortable sofa you stored there not so long ago; not only has it vanished, but in the place where it ought to be are a couple of broken-down cane chairs with holes in their seats. So, to the main purpose of this collection, which is to give you pleasure now, I would add a secondary one: to stock up the attics of your mind with enjoyment for the future.

One of the greatest pleasures of poetry is the discovery that a poem which you have always known means far more than you could realise when you first met it and liked it. This is a process that goes on as long as we read poetry at all: nobody can ever re-read *The Ancient Mariner*, or see a Shakespeare play again, without finding that his experience has now led him to find new meanings in the familiar words. So I have inclined towards poems which, though there is some strong reason why children like them now, have these reserves of meaning. I shall not be worried if anybody criticizes me for including poems which children cannot 'understand'. The poems are here for pleasure: the understanding will grow with the reader. 'That which can be made Explicit to the Idiot', said William Blake, 'is not written with any care. The wisest of the Ancients consider'd what is not too Explicit as the fittest for Instruction, because it rouses the faculties to act.' There is, too, an active pleasure in the unknown or half-known, whether it is a word or a feeling: in, as Andrew Lang put it in his Introduction to the *Blue Poetry Book*, 'the sense of a margin beyond, as in a wood full of unknown glades, and birds, and flowers unfamiliar.'

Though I began to make this collection with no purpose beyond this giving of enjoyment, this furnishing of the attics of the mind, a further purpose developed as I arranged the poems. I found myself, in making the final selection, choosing poems that showed a variety of mood and tone, that responded to the same theme in widely different ways. There is for instance Macaulay's *Armada*, a splendid piece of patriotic fireworks composed 250 years after the event; and a poem by an anonymous Elizabethan, *Some Years of Late, in Eighty-eight* which dwells on facts, like the Spaniards' ration of bacon and biscuit, rather than on feelings, and which is confident but not glorious in tone. Then there is the Waterloo of Byron, who remembers his Highland blood and imagines himself with the Highland regiments in the thick of it; and the quiet lines by Thomas Hardy who, writing nearly a century after, sees the battle as an outrage on Nature. I was anxious to show through the poems that Love is not always romantic, that God and Death need not always be talked of in a special tone of voice. So in the Love section you will find both the passionate expression of a man absorbed in love (*O my Luve is like a red, red rose*); and the feelings of a lover who can still tot up how much money and trouble his lady has cost him (*Greensleeves*). There is Robert Graves's forlorn lover whose grief has quickened all his senses; and William

Walsh's, whose commonsense comes uppermost the minute he actually looks at the precipice over which he has proposed to throw himself in his despair. There is Burd Isbel, who follows Young Bekie over the sea for love; Leezie Lindsay, who will *not* elope to the Highlands until she knows her lover's rank, and then skips off with alacrity; and the strong-minded young woman who pursues her Simple Ploughboy to his ship, buys him off his Captain and rows him to land and marriage.

Among the Dirges, Coronachs and Elegies there are straightforward poems of regret and lamentation, like *The Flowers of the Forest* and Nashe's *In Plague Time*. But *A Lyke-Wake Dirge* is more in the nature of a prayer, or spell for safe passage of the soul to Heaven; *The Bonnie Earl of Moray* is an accusation as well as a lament; *An Irish Airman foresees his Death* is the statement of a man who accepts the likeliness of death as the price he has to pay for the only kind of life he wants to live. There is nothing terrible about Milton's University Carrier who died easily at a ripe old age, a cheerful stoicism in Martial's epigram, and more hope than grief in Shelley's lines on Plato's tomb.

I have no patience with those who say that love and death are not proper subjects for children. Children can often respond to these large subjects with minds less coarsened and imaginations less infected than their print-sodden elders. It is largely in childhood, and largely through books, that we learn of attitudes to admire, which we can then try out in real life—the heroic, the quixotic, the stoical, the impossibly magnanimous. It is not that we necessarily identify ourselves with every person in the poems or stories we read: but that we learn from them a language of feeling and enlarge our own vocabularies. And the attitudes which we finally choose will, whether consciously or not, affect our behaviour all our lives. Poems can help us in this choice by showing us something of the variety of possible attitudes and moods. A child who has learnt that death can be looked at in more ways than one is better able to cope with a loss of his own than one who has only learnt the stereotyped responses of the newspaper or cinema. Stereotyped emotion—which approximates all battles to Heroism, all love to Romance, all death to Tragedy, which cannot respond to irony or wit at all—is always something coarser than any individual is capable of feeling.

Feelings have to be trained: you can learn to feel and to discriminate between feelings, as you can learn to swim or ride a bicycle or play the flute. And if you do not learn what your powers of feelings are, and how to live with your feelings and not be overwhelmed by them, then you will be easy game for those who wish to impose emotions on you for commercial or political ends. We should never despise an emotion just because we share it with a great number of other people—at, say, a party, a Coronation, a Test Match, a performance of *King Lear*. But we should be chary if someone is bullying or cajoling us to feel an emotion for some purpose of his own. This training of the feelings is part of what Blake called 'Instruction' in the words I quoted earlier: the 'rousing of the faculties to act'. And in the same letter of Blake's I find the best words to introduce a book of verse for children.

'Neither Youth nor Childhood is Folly or Incapacity. Some Children are Fools and so are some Old Men. But there is a vast Majority on the side of Imagination or Spiritual Sensation.'

JANET ADAM SMITH

ACKNOWLEDGMENTS

MY first acknowledgment is to my helpers. I cannot mention all those who by suggestion and criticism have left their imprint on this book, but I should like to thank warmly and publicly six who have helped me throughout: Andrew, Henrietta and Adam Roberts, Rose Thomson, Janet Clarke and Anna Madge: and I hope that they will all consider it as being in a special sense their book.

While making this anthology I avoided other anthologies of comparable scope as I was anxious not to be influenced, however unwittingly, by their contents or arrangement. I must, however, record having taken, at the instigation of one of my advisers, Robert Hayman's ' Of the Great and Famous Sir Francis Drake', which I had never seen printed elsewhere, from Walter de la Mare's *Come Hither;* and 'Some Years of late, in eighty-eight' and 'The Strange Visitor' from W. H. Auden's and John Garratt's *The Poet's Tongue* where I had first met them many years ago. And I must confess my gratitude and obligation to a number of specialised anthologies: in particular, Norman Ault's *Elizabethan Lyrics, Seventeenth Century Lyrics* and *A Treasury of Unfamiliar Lyrics; The Oxford Books of Sixteenth* and *Seventeenth Century Verse; The Cambridge Book of Lesser Poets;* T. F. Higham's and C. M. Bowra's *From the Greek;* Iona and Peter Opie's *Oxford Dictionary of Nursery Rhymes;* Norah and William Montgomerie's *Scottish Nursery Rhymes* and the Samson Press *Nicht at Eenie.* For permission to reproduce copyright poems I am indebted to the following: the author and Faber & Faber for 'Epilogue' by W. H. Auden from his *Collected Shorter Poems;* the author and Gerald Duckworth & Co. for the poems by Hilaire Belloc from his *Sonnets and Verse* and *Cautionary Verses;* the author and the Clarendon Press for 'A Maltese Dog' by Edmund Blunden from *From the Greek;* Miss D. E. Collins and Methuen & Co. for 'The Rolling English Road' by G. K. Chesterton from his

Collected Poems; the author and Faber & Faber for the poems
by Walter de la Mare, from his *Collected Poems;* the author
and Faber & Faber for the poems by T. S. Eliot from his
Collected Poems and *Old Possum's Book of Practical Cats;* Mrs.
Flower and Constable & Co. for 'Pangur Bán' by Robin
Flower from his *Poems and Translations;* the author and
Jonathan Cape for the poems by Robert Frost from *The
Complete Poems of Robert Frost;* the author and Constable &
Co. for 'Verse' by O. St. J. Gogarty from his *Collected Poems;*
Mr. John Graves and Longmans for the late A. P. Graves's
'Song to the Wind' from his *Welsh Poetry Old and New;* Mr.
Robert Graves for 'Wild Strawberries' (from *Poems* 1914–
1926) and for '1805', 'Lost Love' and 'Warning to Children'
(from *Collected Poems* 1914–1947, Cassell); the trustees of the
Hardy Estate and Macmillan & Co. for the poems by
Thomas Hardy from his *Collected Poems* and *The Dynasts;* the
author and the Clarendon Press for 'Country Gods' by T. F.
Higham from *From the Greek;* the author and Macmillan &
Co. for 'Reason has Moons' by Ralph Hodgson from his
Poems; the Society of Authors—as literary representatives of
the Trustees of the A. E. Housman estate—and Jonathan
Cape, for the poems by A. E. Housman; the trustees of the
James Joyce Estate and Jonathan Cape for James Joyce's
'All Day I Hear the Noise of Waters' from *Chamber Music;*
Mrs. George Bambridge and Methuen & Co. for Rudyard
Kipling's 'Song of the Banjo' and 'The Last Chantey'(from
The Seven Seas); Mrs. Bambridge and Macmillan & Co.
for 'Puck's Song' (from *Puck of Pook's Hill*, in the expanded
version printed in *Collected Poems*), 'A St. Helena Lullaby'
and 'The Way through the Woods' (from *Rewards and
Fairies*); also the Macmillan Co. of Canada; Mrs. Frieda
Lawrence and William Heinemann for 'Bavarian Gentians'
by D. H. Lawrence from his *Collected Poems*; Dr. John
Masefield, O.M. and the Society of Authors and the
Macmillan Co. of Canada for 'Trade Winds' from his

Collected Poems; Mr. Hugh MacDiarmid and William Blackwood & Sons for 'The Bonnie Broukit Bairn'; the poet's executors and Constable & Co. for the translations by Kuno Meyer from *Ancient Irish Poetry;* the author and John Lane The Bodley Head for Ewart Milne's 'Diamond Cut Diamond' from the book of that name; the author and Faber & Faber for Edwin Muir's 'Horses' from his *Collected Poems;* Mr. Ogden Nash and J. M. Dent & Sons for 'The One-l Lama' from *Family Reunion;* the poet's executors and John Murray for Sir Henry Newbolt's 'Drake's Drum' from his *Poems New and Old;* the author and Faber & Faber for two poems by Ezra Pound from *Personae;* the author and Hamish Hamilton for 'Spell of Creation' by Kathleen Raine from *The Year One;* the poet's executors and Constable & Co. for Sir Walter Raleigh's 'Wishes of an Elderly Man'; Mr. John Crowe Ransom and Alfred A. Knopf Inc. and Eyre & Spottiswoode for 'Survey of Literature' from *Selected Poems by John Crowe Ransom;* copyright 1927, 1945 by Alfred A. Knopf Inc.; Mrs. Michael Roberts and Jonathan Cape for Michael Roberts's 'Hymn to the Sun' and 'St. Gervais' from his *Poems;* Charles Scribner's Sons for 'Miniver Cheevy' from *The Town Down the River* by Edwin Arlington Robinson, copyright 1910 by Charles Scribner's Sons, 1938 by Ruth Nivison; J. M. Dent & Sons for 'Carol' by John Short from *The Oak and the Ash;* Dr. Edith Sitwell and Gerald Duckworth & Co. for 'Madam Mouse Trots' from her *Collected Poems;* Mrs. W. R. Sorley and the Cambridge University Press for the two poems by Charles Sorley from *Marlborough and Other Poems;* Mrs. Helen Thomas and Faber & Faber for the three poems by Edward Thomas from his *Collected Poems;* the author and Allen & Unwin for the translations by Arthur Waley from his *Chinese Poems;* Mr. Gwyn Williams for 'O Send to me an Apple' from *The Rent that's Due to Love;* Mrs. W. B. Yeats and Macmillan & Co. for the poems by W. B. Yeats from his *Collected Poems ;*

Acknowledgments

the Executor of Miss Nancy McIntosh for *Etiquette* and *The Yarn of the 'Nancy Bell'* by Sir William Schwenck Gilbert.

POETRY, MUSIC AND DANCING

VERSE

What should we know,
For better or worse,
Of the Long Ago,
Were it not for Verse:
What ships went down;
What walls were razed;
Who won the crown;
What lads were praised?
A fallen stone,
Or a waste of sands;
And all is known
Of Art-less lands.
But you need not delve
By the sea-side hills
Where the Muse herself
All Time fulfils,
Who cuts with his scythe
All things but hers;
All but the blithe
Hexameters.

O. ST. J. GOGARTY

WILD STRAWBERRIES

Strawberries that in gardens grow
  Are plump and juicy fine,
But sweeter far, as wise men know,
  Spring from the woodland vine.

No need for bowl or silver spoon,
    Sugar or spice or cream,
Has the wild berry plucked in June
    Beside the trickling stream.

One such, to melt at the tongue's root
    Confounding taste with scent,
Beats a full peck of garden fruit:
    Which points my argument:—

May sudden justice overtake
    And snap the froward pen,
That old and palsied poets shake
    Against the minds of men.

Blasphemers trusting to hold caught
    In far-flung webs of ink
The utmost ends of human thought
    Till nothing's left to think.

But may the gift of heavenly peace
    And glory for all time
Keep the boy Tom who tending geese
    First made the nursery rhyme.

                    ROBERT GRAVES

SONG'S ETERNITY

What is song's eternity?
    Come and see.
Can it noise and bustle be?
    Come and see.
Praises sung or praises said
    Can it be?

Wait awhile and these are dead—
    Sigh—sigh;
Be they high or lowly bred
    They die.

What is song's eternity?
    Come and see.
Melodies of earth and sky,
    Here they be.
Song once sung to Adam's ears
    Can it be?
Ballads of six thousand years
    Thrive, thrive;
Songs awaken with the spheres
    Alive.

Mighty songs that miss decay,
    What are they?
Crowds and cities pass away
    Like a day.
Books are out and books are read;
    What are they?
Years will lay them with the dead—
    Sigh, sigh;
Trifles unto nothing wed,
    They die.

Dreamers, mark the honey bee;
    Mark the tree
Where the blue cap *'tootle tee'*
    Sings a glee
Sung to Adam and to Eve—
    Here they be.
When floods covered every bough,
    Noah's ark

Heard that ballad singing now;
   Hark, hark,

'*Tootle tootle tootle tee*'—
   Can it be
Pride and fame must shadows be?
   Come and see—
Every season own her own;
   Bird and bee
Sing creation's music on;
   Nature's glee
Is in every mood and tone
   Eternity.

JOHN CLARE

Piping down the valleys wild,
Piping songs of pleasant glee,
On a cloud I saw a child,
And he laughing said to me:

'Pipe a song about a Lamb!'
So I piped with merry chear.
'Piper, pipe that song again;'
So I piped: he wept to hear.

'Drop thy pipe, thy happy pipe;
'Sing thy songs of happy chear:'
So I sung the same again,
While he wept with joy to hear.

'Piper, sit thee down and write
'In a book, that all may read.'

So he vanish'd from my sight,
And I pluck'd a hollow reed,

And I made a rural pen,
And I stain'd the water clear,
And I wrote my happy songs
Every child may joy to hear.

WILLIAM BLAKE

THE SCRIBE

What lovely things
  Thy hand hath made:
The smooth-plumed bird
  In its emerald shade,
The seed of the grass,
  The speck of stone
Which the wayfaring ant
  Stirs—and hastes on!

Though I should sit
  By some tarn in thy hills,
Using its ink
  As the spirit wills
To write of Earth's wonders,
  Its live, willed things,
Flit would the ages
  On soundless wings
Ere unto Z
  My pen drew nigh;
Leviathan told,
  And the honey-fly:
And still would remain
  My wit to try—

33

My worn reeds broken,
   The dark tarn dry,
All words forgotten—
   Thou, Lord, and I.

WALTER DE LA MARE

ON FIRST LOOKING INTO
CHAPMAN'S HOMER

Much have I travell'd in the realms of gold,
   And many goodly states and kingdoms seen;
   Round many western islands have I been
Which bards in fealty to Apollo hold.
Oft of one wide expanse had I been told
   That deep-brow'd Homer ruled as his demesne;
   Yet did I never breathe its pure serene
Till I heard Chapman speak out loud and bold:
Then felt I like some watcher of the skies
   When a new planet swims into his ken;
Or like stout Cortez when with eagle eyes
   He star'd at the Pacific—and all his men
Look'd at each other with a wild surmise—
   Silent, upon a peak in Darien.

JOHN KEATS

SURVEY OF LITERATURE

In all the good Greek of Plato
I lack my roastbeef and potato.

A better man was Aristotle,
Pulling steady on the bottle.

Poetry, Music and Dancing

I dip my hat to Chaucer,
Swilling soup from his saucer,

And to Master Shakespeare
Who wrote big on small beer.

The abstemious Wordsworth
Subsisted on a curd's-worth,

But a slick one was Tennyson,
Putting gravy on his venison.

What these men had to eat and drink
Is what we say and what we think.

The influence of Milton
Came wry out of Stilton.

Sing a song for Percy Shelley,
Drowned in pale lemon jelly,

And for precious John Keats,
Dripping blood of pickled beets.

Then there was poor Willie Blake,
He foundered on sweet cake.

God have mercy on the sinner
Who must write with no dinner,

No gravy and no grub,
No pewter and no pub,

No belly and no bowels,
Only consonants and vowels.

JOHN CROWE RANSOM

MUSIC

Orpheus with his lute made trees,
    And the mountain-tops that freeze,
Bow themselves when he did sing.
    To his music plants and flowers
Ever sprung: as sun and showers
    There had made a lasting spring.
Everything that heard him play,
    Even the billows of the sea,
Hung their heads, and then lay by.
    In sweet music is such art,
Killing care and grief of heart
    Fall asleep, or, hearing, die.

JOHN FLETCHER

FAINT MUSIC

The meteor's arc of quiet; a voiceless rain;
The mist's mute communing with a stagnant moat;
The sigh of a flower that has neglected lain;
    That bell's unuttered note:

A hidden self rebels, its slumber broken;
Love secret as crystal forms within the womb;
The heart may as faithfully beat, the vow unspoken;
    All sounds to silence come.

WALTER DE LA MARE

THE SPLENDOUR FALLS

The splendour falls on castle walls
    and snowy summits old in story:
The long light shakes across the lakes,
    And the wild cataract leaps in glory,

Blow, bugle, blow, set the wild echoes flying,
Blow, bugle; answer, echoes, dying, dying, dying.

O hark, O hear! how thin and clear,
    And thinner, clearer, farther going!
O sweet and far from cliff and scar
    The horns of Elfland faintly blowing!
Blow, let us hear the purple glens replying:
Blow, bugle; answer, echoes, dying, dying, dying.

O love, they die in yon rich sky,
    They faint on hill or field or river:
Our echoes roll from soul to soul,
    And grow for ever and for ever.
Blow, bugle, blow, set the wild echoes flying,
And answer, echoes, answer, dying, dying, dying.

LORD TENNYSON

THE SONG OF THE BANJO

You couldn't pack a Broadwood half a mile—
    You mustn't leave a fiddle in the damp—
You couldn't raft an organ up the Nile,
    And play it in an Equatorial swamp.
I travel with the cooking-pots and pails—
    I'm sandwiched 'tween the coffee and the pork—
And when the dusty column checks and tails,
    You should hear me spur the rearguard to a walk!

With my '*Pilly-willy-winky-winky-popp!*'
    (Oh, it's any tune that comes into my head!)
So I keep 'em moving forward till they drop;
    So I play 'em up to water and to bed.

37

In the silence of the camp before the fight,
    When it's good to make your will and say your
        prayer,
You can hear my *strumpty-trumpty* overnight,
    Explaining ten to one was always fair.
I'm the Prophet of the Utterly Absurd,
    Of the Patently Impossible and Vain—
And when the Thing that Couldn't has occurred,
    Give me time to change my leg and go again.

With my '*Tumpa-tumpa-tumpa-tumpa-tump!*'
    In the desert where the dung-fed camp-smoke curled.
There was never voice before us till I led our lonely
        chorus,
        I—the war-drum of the White Man round the world!

By the bitter road the Younger Son must tread,
    Ere he win to hearth and saddle of his own,—
'Mid the riot of the shearers at the shed,
    In the silence of the herder's hut alone—
In the twilight, on a bucket upside down,
    Hear me babble what the weakest won't confess—
I am Memory and Torment—I am Town!
    I am all that ever went with evening dress!

With my '*Tunka-tunka-tunka-tunka-tunk!*'
    (So the lights—the London Lights—grow near and
        plain!)
So I rowel 'em afresh towards the Devil and the Flesh
    Till I bring my broken rankers home again.

In desire of many marvels over sea,
    Where the new-raised tropic city sweats and roars,
I have sailed with Young Ulysses from the Quay
    Till the anchor rumbled down on stranger shores.

He is blooded to the open and the sky,
    He is taken in a snare that shall not fail,
He shall hear me singing strongly, till he die,
    Like the shouting of a backstay in a gale

With my '*Hya! Heeya! Heeya! Hullah! Haul!*'
    (Oh, the green that thunders aft along the deck!)
Are you sick o' towns and men? You must sign and sail
            again,
        For it's 'Johnny Bowlegs, pack your kit and trek!'

Through the gorge that gives the stars at noon-day clear—
    Up the pass that packs the scud beneath our wheel—
Round the bluff that sinks her thousand fathom sheer—
    Down the valley with our guttering brakes asqueal:
Where the trestle groans and quivers in the snow,
    Where the many-shedded levels loop and twine,
Hear me lead my reckless children from below
    Till we sing the Song of Roland to the pine!

With my '*Tinka-tinka-tinka-tinka-tink!*'
    (Oh, the axe has cleared the mountain, croup and crest!)
And we ride the iron stallions down to drink,
    Through the cañons to the waters of the West!

And the tunes that mean so much to you alone—
    Common tunes that make you choke and blow your
            nose,
Vulgar tunes that bring the laugh that brings the groan—
    I can rip your very heartstrings out with those;
With the feasting, and the folly, and the fun—
    And the lying, and the lusting, and the drink,
And the merry play that drops you, when you're done,
    To the thoughts that burn like irons if you think.

39

With my '*Plunka-lunka-lunka-lunka-lunk*'
    Here's a trifle on account of pleasure past,
Ere the wit that made you win gives you eyes to see your sin
    And—the heavier repentance at the last!

Let the organ moan her sorrow to the roof—
    I have told the naked stars the Grief of Man!
Let the trumpet snare the foeman to the proof—
    I have known Defeat, and mocked it as we ran!
My bray ye may not alter nor mistake
    When I stand to jeer the fatted Soul of Things,
But the Song of Lost Endeavour that I make,
    Is it hidden in the twanging of the strings?

With my '*Ta-ra-rara-rara-ra-ra-rrrp!*'
    (Is it naught to you that hear and pass me by?)
But the word—the word is mine, when the order moves the
        line
    And the lean, locked ranks go roaring down to die!

The grandam of my grandam was the Lyre—
    (Oh, the blue below the little fisher-huts!)
That the Stealer stooping beachward filled with fire,
    Till she bore my iron head and ringing guts!
By the wisdom of the centuries I speak—
    To the tune of yestermorn I set the truth—
I, the joy of life unquestioned—I, the Greek—
    I, the everlasting Wonder-song of Youth!

With my '*Tinka-tinka-tinka-tinka-tink!*'
    (What d'ye lack, my noble masters? What d'ye lack?)
So I draw the world together link by link:
    Yea, from Delos up to Limerick and back!

RUDYARD KIPLING

THE FIDDLER OF DOONEY

When I play on my fiddle in Dooney
Folk dance like a wave of the sea;
My cousin is priest in Kilvarnet,
My brother in Mocharabuiee.

I passed my brother and cousin:
They read in their books of prayer;
I read in my book of songs
I bought at the Sligo fair.

When we come at the end of time
To Peter sitting in state,
He will smile on the three old spirits,
But call me first through the gate;

For the good are always the merry,
Save by an evil chance,
And the merry love the fiddle,
And the merry love to dance:

And when the folk there spy me,
They will all come up to me,
With 'Here is the fiddler of Dooney!'
And dance like a wave of the sea.

W. B. Yeats

SONG FOR A DANCE

Shake off your heavy trance!
And leap into a dance
Such as no mortals use to tread:
Fit only for Apollo
To play to, for the moon to lead.
And all the stars to follow!

FRANCIS BEAUMONT

DANCE SONG

The unicorn's hoofs!
The duke's sons throng.
Alas for the unicorn!

The unicorn's brow!
The duke's kinsmen throng.
Alas for the unicorn!

The unicorn's horn!
The duke's clansmen throng.
Alas for the unicorn!

ANON: *translated from the Chinese by* ARTHUR WALEY

THE DANCE

Robin is a lovely lad,
No lass a smoother ever had.
Tommy hath a look as bright
As is the rosy morning light.

Tib is dark and brown of hue,
But like her colour firm and true.
Jinny hath a lip to kiss
Wherein a spring of nectar is.
Simkin well his mirth can place
And words to win a woman's grace.
Sib is all in all to me,
There is no queen of love but she.
Let us in a lovers' round
Circle all this hallowed ground.
Softly, softly trip and go,
The light-foot fairies jet it so.
Forward then and back again,
Here and there and everywhere,
Winding to and winding fro,
Skipping high and louting low.
And like lovers hand in hand
March around and make a stand.

THOMAS CAMPION (?)

FANCY'S KNELL

When lads were home from labour
    At Abdon under Clee,
A man would call his neighbour
    And both would send for me.
And where the light in lances
    Across the mead was laid,
There to the dances
    I fetched my flute and played.

Ours were idle pleasures,
    Yet oh, content we were,

The young to wind the measures,
  The old to heed the air;
And I to lift with playing
  From tree and tower and steep
The light delaying,
  And flute the sun to sleep.

The youth toward his fancy
  Would turn his brow of tan,
And Tom would pair with Nancy
  And Dick step off with Fan;
The girl would lift her glances
  To his, and both be mute:
Well went the dances
  At evening to the flute.

Wenlock Edge was umbered,
  And bright was Abdon Burf,
And warm between them slumbered
  The smooth green miles of turf;
Until from grass and clover
  The upshot beam would fade,
And England over
  Advanced the lofty shade.

The lofty shade advances,
  I fetch my flute and play:
Come, lads, and learn the dances
  And praise the tune to-day.
To-morrow, more's the pity,
  Away we both must hie,
To air the ditty,
  And to earth I.

A. E. HOUSMAN

TARANTELLA

Do you remember an Inn,
Miranda?
Do you remember an Inn?
And the tedding and the spreading
Of the straw for a bedding,
And the fleas that tease in the High Pyrenees,
And the wine that tasted of the tar?
And the cheers and the jeers of the young muleteers
(Under the dark of the vine verandah)?
Do you remember an Inn, Miranda,
Do you remember an Inn?
And the cheers and the jeers of the young muleteers
Who hadn't got a penny,
And who weren't paying any,
And the hammer at the doors and the Din?
And the Hip! Hop! Hap!
Of the clap
Of the hands to the twirl and the swirl
Of the girl gone chancing,
Glancing,
Dancing,
Backing and advancing,
Snapping of the clapper to the spin
Out and in—
And the Ting, Tong, Tang of the Guitar!
Do you remember an Inn,
Miranda?
Do you remember an Inn?

    Never more;
    Miranda,
    Never more.
    Only the high peaks hoar:

And Aragon a torrent at the door.
No sound
In the walls of the Halls where falls
The tread
Of the feet of the dead to the ground.
No sound:
Only the boom
Of the far Waterfall like Doom.

HILAIRE BELLOC

My Cousin German came from France
   To learn me the Polka dance.
First the heels and then the toes,
   That's the way the Polka goes.

ANON

NIGHT AND DAY,
SEASONS AND WEATHERS

Hark! Hark! the lark at heaven's gate sings,
    And Phoebus 'gins arise,
His steeds to water at those springs
    On chaliced flowers that lies;
And winking Mary-buds begin
    To ope their golden eyes;
With every thing that pretty is,
    My lady sweet, arise!
        Arise, arise!

WILLIAM SHAKESPEARE

MORNING

To find the Western path
Right thro' the Gates of Wrath
I urge my way;
Sweet Mercy leads me on:
With soft repentant moan
I see the break of day.

The war of swords & spears
Melted by dewy tears
Exhales on high;
The Sun is freed from fears
And with soft grateful tears
Ascends the sky.

WILLIAM BLAKE

THE STAR THAT BIDS THE SHEPHERD FOLD

The Star that bids the Shepherd fold,
Now the top of Heav'n doth hold,
And the gilded Car of Day,
His glowing Axle doth allay
In the steep *Atlantick* stream,
And the slope Sun his upward beam
Shoots against the dusky Pole,
Pacing toward the other goal
Of his Chamber in the East.
Meanwhile welcome Joy, and Feast,
Midnight shout, and revelry,
Tipsy dance, and Jollity.
Braid your Locks with rosy Twine
Dropping odours, dropping Wine.
Rigour now is gone to bed,
And Advice with scrupulous head,
Strict Age, and sour Severity,
With their grave Saws in slumber lie.
We that are of purer fire
Imitate the Starry Quire,
Who in their nightly watchful Spheres,
Lead in swift round the Months and Years.
The Sounds, and Seas with all their finny drove
Now to the Moon in wavering Morris move,
And on the Tawny Sands and Shelves,
Trip the pert Fairies and the dapper Elves;
By dimpled Brook, and Fountain brim,
The Wood-Nymphs decked with Daisies trim,
Their merry wakes and pastimes keep:
What hath night to do with sleep?

JOHN MILTON

SONG ON THE WATER

As mad sexton's bell, tolling
   For earth's loveliest daughter
Night's dumbness breaks rolling
     Ghostlily:
So our boat breaks the water
     Witchingly.

As her look the dream troubles
   Of her tearful-eyed lover,
So our sails in the bubbles
     Ghostlily
Are mirrored, and hover
     Moonily.

T. L. Beddoes

THE MOON

And, like a dying lady lean and pale,
Who totters forth, wrapp'd in a gauzy veil,
Out of her chamber, led by the insane
And feeble wanderings of her fading brain,
The moon arose up in the murky east
A white and shapeless mass.

   Art thou pale for weariness
Of climbing heaven and gazing on the earth,
   Wandering companionless
Among the stars that have a different birth,
And ever changing, like a joyless eye
That finds no object worth its constancy?

P. B. Shelley

SPRING

Sound the Flute!
Now it's mute.
Birds delight
Day and Night;
Nightingale
In the dale,
Lark in Sky,
Merrily,
Merrily, Merrily, to welcome in the Year.

Little Boy,
Full of joy;
Little Girl,
Sweet and small;
Cock does crow,
So do you;
Merry voice,
Infant noise,
Merrily, Merrily, to welcome in the Year.

Little Lamb,
Here I am;
Come and lick
My white neck;
Let me pull
Your soft Wool;
Let me kiss
Your soft face:
Merrily, Merrily, we welcome in the Year.

WILLIAM BLAKE

MARCH

The Sun at noon to higher air,
Unharnessing the silver Pair
That late before his chariot swam,
Rides on the gold wool of the Ram.

So braver notes the storm-cock sings
To start the rusted wheel of things,
And brutes in field and brutes in pen
Leap that the world goes round again.

The boys are up the woods with day
To fetch the daffodils away,
And home at noonday from the hills
They bring no dearth of daffodils.

Afield for palms the girls repair,
And sure enough the palms are there,
And each will find by hedge or pond
Her waving silver-tufted wand.

In farm and field through all the shire
The eye beholds the heart's desire;
Ah, let not only mine be vain,
For lovers should be loved again.

A. E. HOUSMAN

TO DAFFODILS

Fair daffodils, we weep to see
   You haste away so soon;
As yet the early-rising sun
   Has not attain'd his noon.

Stay, stay
Until the hasting day
Has run
But to the evensong;
And, having pray'd together, we
Will go with you along.

We have short time to stay, as you,
We have as short a spring;
As quick a growth to meet decay,
As you, or anything.
We die
As your hours do, and dry
Away
Like to the summer's rain;
Or as the pearls of morning's dew,
Ne'er to be found again.

ROBERT HERRICK

When daffodils begin to peer,
With heigh! the doxy, over the dale,
Why, then comes in the sweet o' the year;
For the red blood reigns in the winter's pale.

The white sheet bleaching on the hedge,
With heigh! the sweet birds, O, how they sing!
Doth set my pugging tooth on edge,
For a quart of ale is a dish for a king.

The lark, that tirra-lirra chants,
With heigh! with heigh! the thrush and the jay,
Are summer songs for me and my aunts,
While we lie tumbling in the hay.

WILLIAM SHAKESPEARE

When as the rye reach to the chin,
 And chopcherry, chopcherry ripe within,
Strawberries swimming in the cream,
And school-boys playing in the stream;
  Then O, then O, then O my true love said,
   Till that time come again,
  She could not live a maid.

GEORGE PEELE

HYMN TO THE SUN

'Voy wawm' said the dustman
one bright August morning—
But that was in Longbenton,
Under the trees.

He was Northumbrian, he'd never known
horizons shimmering in the sun,
men with swart noontide faces sleeping, thick with flies,
by roadside cherry trees.

He was Northumbrian, how should he know
mirage among blue hills,
thin streams that tinkle silence in the still
pulsating drone of summer—

How should he know
how cool the darkness in the white-washed inns
after the white road dancing, and the stones,
and quick dry lizards, round Millevaches?

'*Fait chaud*', as each old woman said,
going over the hill, in Périgord,
prim in tight bonnets, worn black dresses, and content
with the lilt of sunlight in their bones.

MICHAEL ROBERTS

BAVARIAN GENTIANS

Not every man has gentians in his house
in soft September, at slow, sad Michaelmas.

Bavarian gentians, big and dark, only dark
darkening the day-time torch-like with the smoking blueness
      of Pluto's gloom,
ribbed and torch-like, with their blaze of darkness spread
      blue
down flattening into points, flattened under the sweep of
      white day
torch-flower of the blue-smoking darkness, Pluto's dark-
      blue daze,
black lamps from the halls of Dis, burning dark blue,
giving off darkness, blue darkness, as Demeter's pale lamps
      give off light,
lead me then, lead me the way.

Reach me a gentian, give me a torch
let me guide myself with the blue, forked torch of this flower
down the darker and darker stairs, where blue is darkened on
      blueness,
even where Persephone goes, just now, from the frosted
      September
to the sightless realm where darkness is awake upon the dark
and Persephone herself is but a voice
or a darkness invisible enfolded in the deeper dark
of the arms Plutonic, and pierced with the passion of dense
      gloom,
among the splendour of torches of darkness, shedding
      darkness on the lost bride and her groom.

D. H. LAWRENCE

SUMMER IS GONE

My tidings for you: the stag bells,
Winter snows, summer is gone.

Wind high and cold, low the sun,
Short his course, sea running high.

Deep-red the bracken, its shape all gone—
The wild-goose has raised his wonted cry.

Cold has caught the wings of birds;
Season of ice—these are my tidings.

ANON: *translated from the*
Irish by KUNO MEYER

SONG

The feathers of the willow
Are half of them grown yellow
    Above the swelling stream;
And ragged are the bushes,
And rusty now the rushes,
    And wild the clouded gleam.

The thistle now is older,
His stalk begins to moulder,
    His head is white as snow;
The branches all are barer,
The linnet's song is rarer,
    The robin pipeth now.

R. W. DIXON

Fall, leaves, fall; die, flowers, away;
    Lengthen night and shorten day,
Every leaf speaks bliss to me
Fluttering from the autumn tree.
I shall smile when wreaths of snow
Blossom where the rose should grow;
I shall sing when night's decay
Ushers in a drearier day.

EMILY BRONTË

HIEMS

When icicles hang by the wall,
    And Dick the shepherd blows his nail,
And Tom bears logs into the hall,
    And milk comes frozen home in pail;
When blood is nipped, and ways be foul,
Then nightly sings the staring owl.
Tu-whit, tu-who! a merry note,
While greasy Joan doth keel the pot.

When all aloud the wind doth blow,
    And coughing drowns the parson's saw,
And birds sit brooding in the snow,
    And Marian's nose looks red and raw,
When roasted crabs hiss in the bowl,
Then nightly sings the staring owl,
Tu-whit, tu-who! a merry note,
While greasy Joan doth keel the pot.

WILLIAM SHAKESPEARE

ON THE FROZEN LAKE

And in the frosty season, when the sun
Was set, and, visible for many a mile
The cottage-windows through the twilight blaz'd
I heeded not the summons—happy time
It was, indeed, for all of us; to me
It was a time of rapture: clear and loud
The village clock toll'd six; I wheel'd about,
Proud and exulting, like an untired horse,
That cares not for his home.—All shod with steel,
We hiss'd along the polish'd ice, in games
Confederate, imitative of the chace
And woodland pleasures, the resounding horn,
The Pack loud bellowing, and the hunted hare.
So through the darkness and the cold we flew,
And not a voice was idle; with the din,
Meanwhile, the precipices rang aloud,
The leafless trees, and every icy crag
Tinkled like iron, while the distant hills
Into the tumult sent an alien sound
Of melancholy, not unnoticed, while the stars,
Eastward, were sparkling clear, and in the west
The orange sky of evening died away.
    Not seldom from the uproar I retired
Into a silent bay, or sportively
Glanced sideway, leaving the tumultuous throng,
To cut across the image of a star
That gleam'd upon the ice: and oftentimes
When we had given our bodies to the wind,
And all the shadowy banks, on either side,
Came sweeping through the darkness, spinning still
The rapid line of motion; then at once
Have I, reclining back upon my heels,
Stopp'd short; yet still the solitary Cliffs,

Wheeled by me, even as if the earth had roll'd
With visible motion her diurnal round;
Behind me did they stretch in solemn train
Feebler and feebler, and I stood and watch'd
Till all was tranquil as a dreamless sleep.

WILLIAM WORDSWORTH

STOPPING BY WOODS ON
A SNOWY EVENING

Whose woods these are I think I know.
His house is in the village though;
He will not see me stopping here
To watch his woods fill up with snow.

My little horse must think it queer
To stop without a farmhouse near
Between the woods and frozen lake
The darkest evening of the year.

He gives his harness bells a shake
To ask if there is some mistake.
The only other sound's the sweep
Of easy wind and downy flake.

The woods are lovely, dark and deep.
But I have promises to keep,
And miles to go before I sleep,
And miles to go before I sleep.

ROBERT FROST

WEATHERS

This is the weather the cuckoo likes,
    And so do I;
When showers betumble the chestnut spikes,
    And nestlings fly:
And the little brown nightingale bills his best,
And they sit outside at 'The Travellers' Rest',
And maids come forth sprig-muslin drest,
And citizens dream of the south and west,
    And so do I.

This is the weather the shepherd shuns,
    And so do I;
When beeches drip in browns and duns,
    And thresh, and ply;
And hill-hid tides throb, throe on throe,
And meadow rivulets overflow,
And drops on gate-bars hang in a row,
And rooks in families homeward go,
    And so do I.

THOMAS HARDY

A SONG TO THE WIND

Guess who is this creature
    Before us outspeeding,
    Of strength so exceeding;
Begot ere the flood,
Without flesh, without blood,
Without bones, without veins,
Without head, without foot,
Not older or younger
    Than when he drew breath

At earth's first beginning;
And no design spinning
   Of fear or of death,
Through thirst or through hunger,
   Through anger or scaith.

Great God! when he cometh,
How the sea foameth
At the breath of his nostrils,
   The blast of his mouth!
   As it smites from the south—
Foameth and spumeth
   And roars on the shores!
Now on the wold,
And now in the wood,
Without hand or foot
Escaping pursuit;
Jealous Destiny's rage
Cannot wrinkle his age,
   Though coeval was he
With all cycles of Time,
Nay, still in his prime
   Ere they were beginning to be!

All the face of the earth
   Is his mighty demesne;
He has ne'er come to birth;
   He has never been seen,
   Yet causeth, I ween,
Consternation and dearth!

On the sea, on the land,
   Unviewed and unviewing,
   Pursued and pursuing,
Yet never at hand.
On the land, on the sea,

Unviewing, unviewed,
Though in sight of the Sun;
Ne'er at command,
    Howe'er he be sued!
Indispensable,
Imcomprehensible,
    Matchless one!

Out of four regions,
Alone, yet in legions,
        He winneth!
Over the seat
    Of the great, storm-blown
    Marble stone
        His journey with joy he beginneth.
He is loud-voiced and mute
He yields no salute;
Vehement, bold,
O'er the desolate wold
        He outrunneth!

He is mute and loud-voiced;
    With bluster defying,
O'er the half of the world
His banner unfurled
    He is flying!
He is good, he is evil—
Half angel, half devil;
        Manifest never,
        Hidden for ever!

He is evil and good!
Hither and yonder
Intent upon plunder;
In repairing it mindless,

Yet, therewithal, sinless!
He is moist, he is dry,
He will fly
From the glow of the sun,
And the chill of the moon,
Who yieldeth small worth
Of heat for the earth;
To profit thereby.

The Master that made him
    Gave all things their birth
God himself, the Beginner
    And Ender of Earth.
Who praise not His power
    Still strike a false string,
Who exalt not the Father
    Shall tunelessly sing!

TALIESSIN: *translated from the
Welsh by* A. P. GRAVES

THE WIND

Arthur O'Bower has broken his bands,
And he's come roaring owre the lands;
    The King o' Scots, and a' his power
    Canna turn Arthur O'Bower.

ANON

BEASTS AND BIRDS

AUGURIES OF INNOCENCE

To see a World in a Grain of Sand
And a Heaven in a Wild Flower,
Hold Infinity in the palm of your hand
And Eternity in an hour.

A Robin Red breast in a Cage
Puts all Heaven in a Rage.
A dove house fill'd with doves & Pigeons
Shudders Hell thro' all its regions.
A dog starv'd at his Master's Gate
Predicts the ruin of the State.
A Horse misus'd upon the Road
Calls to Heaven for Human blood.
Each outcry of the hunted Hare
A fibre from the Brain does tear.
A Skylark wounded in the wing,
A Cherubim does cease to sing.
The Game Cock clip'd & arm'd for fight
Does the Rising Sun affright.
Every Wolf's & Lion's howl
Raises from Hell a Human Soul.
The wild deer, wand'ring here & there,
Keeps the Human Soul from Care.
The Lamb misus'd breeds Public strife
And yet forgives the Butcher's Knife.
The Bat that flits at close of Eve
Has left the Brain that won't Believe.
The Owl that calls upon the Night
Speaks the Unbeliever's fright.
He who shall hurt the little Wren
Shall never be belov'd by Men.

He who the Ox to wrath has mov'd
Shall never be by Woman lov'd.
The wanton Boy that kills the Fly
Shall feel the Spider's enmity.
He who torments the Chafer's sprite
Weaves a Bower in endless Night.
The Catterpiller on the Leaf
Repeats to thee thy Mother's grief.
Kill not the Moth nor Butterfly,
For the Last Judgment draweth nigh.

WILLIAM BLAKE

A LARK'S NEST

Now's the time for mirth and play,
Saturday's an holiday;
Praise to heav'n unceasing yield,
I've found a lark's nest in the field.

A lark's nest, then your play-mate begs
You'd spare herself and speckled eggs;
Soon she shall ascend and sing
Your praise to th' eternal King.

CHRISTOPHER SMART

THE TYGER

Tyger! Tyger! burning bright
In the forests of the night,
What immortal hand or eye
Could frame thy fearful symmetry?

In what distant deeps or skies
Burnt the fire of thine eyes?

On what wings dare he aspire?
What the hand dare seize the fire?

And what shoulder, & what art,
Could twist the sinews of thy heart?
And when thy heart began to beat,
What dread hand? & what dread feet?

What the hammer? what the chain?
In what furnace was thy brain?
What the anvil? what dread grasp
Dare its deadly terrors clasp?

When the stars threw down their spears,
And water'd heaven with their tears,
Did he smile his work to see?
Did he who made the Lamb make thee?

Tyger! Tyger! burning bright
In the forests of the night,
What immortal hand or eye,
Dare frame thy fearful symmetry?

WILLIAM BLAKE

AY ME, ALAS

Ay me, alas, heigh ho, heigh ho!
Thus doth Messalina go
Up and down the house a-crying,
For her monkey lies a-dying.
Death, thou art too cruel
To bereave her jewel,
Or to make a seizure

Of her only treasure.
If her monkey die,
She will sit and cry,
Fie fie fie fie fie!

THOMAS WEELKES

Well I never, did you ever,
See a monkey dressed in leather?
Leather eyes, leather nose,
Leather breeches to his toes.

ANON

A MELANCHOLY LAY

Three Turkeys fair their last have breathed,
And now this world for ever leaved,
Their Father and their Mother too,
Will sigh and weep as well as you,
Mourning for their offspring fair,
Whom they did nurse with tender care.
Indeed the rats their bones have crunch'd,
To eternity are they launch'd;
Their graceful form and pretty eyes
Their fellow fowls did not despise,
A direful death indeed they had,
That would put any parent mad,
But she was more than usual calm
She did not give a single dam.
Here ends this melancholy lay:
Farewell poor Turkeys I must say.

MARJORY FLEMING, age 8

THE NYMPH AND HER FAWN

With sweetest milk and sugar first
I it at mine own fingers nursed;
And as it grew, so every day
It wax'd more white and sweet than they—
It had so sweet a breath! and oft
I blush'd to see its foot more soft
And white, shall I say, than my hand?
Nay, any lady's of the land!
It is a wondrous thing how fleet
'Twas on those little silver feet;
With what a pretty skipping grace
It oft would challenge me the race;
And, when't had left me far away
'Twould stay, and run again, and stay;
For it was nimbler much than hinds,
And trod as if on the four winds.

I have a garden of my own,
But so with roses overgrown
And lilies, that you would it guess
To be a little wilderness;
And all the spring-time of the year
It only lovèd to be there.
Among the beds of lilies I
Have sought it oft, where it should lie;
Yet could not, till itself would rise,
Find it, although before mine eyes:
For in the flaxen lilies' shade,
It like a bank of lilies laid.
Upon the roses it would feed,
Until its lips even seem'd to bleed,
And then to me 'twould boldly trip,
And print those roses on my lip.

But all its chief delight was still
On roses thus itself to fill,
And its pure virgin limbs to fold
In whitest sheets of lilies cold,—
Had it lived long, it would have been
Lilies without, roses within.

ANDREW MARVELL

THE FAUN

Ha! sir, I have seen you sniffing and snoozling
      about among my flowers.
And what, pray, do you know about
      horticulture, you capriped?
'Come, Auster, come, Apeliota,
And see the faun in our garden.
But if you move or speak
This thing will run at you
And scare itself to spasms.'

EZRA POUND

THE GREAT SILKIE OF SULE SKERRIE

An earthly nourrice sits and sings,
    And aye she sings, 'Ba, lily wean!
Little ken I my bairn's father,
    Far less the land that he staps in.'

Then ane arose at her bed-fit,
    An' a grumly guest I'm sure was he:
'Here am I, thy bairn's father,
    Although that I be not comelie.

nourrice, nurse; *silkie, seal*

I am a man, upo' the lan',
  An' I am a silkie in the sea;
And when I'm far and far frae lan',
  My dwelling is in Sule Skerrie.'

'It was na weel,' quo' the maiden fair,
  'It was na weel, indeed,' quo' she,
'That the Great Silkie of Sule Skerrie
  Suld hae come and aught a bairn to me.'

Now he has ta'en a purse of goud,
  And he has pat it upo' her knee,
Sayin', 'Gie to me my little young son,
  An' tak thee up thy nourrice-fee.

'An' it sall pass on a simmer's day,
  When the sin shines het on evera stane,
That I will tak my little young son,
  An' teach him for to swim his lane.

'An' thu sall marry a proud gunner,
  An' a proud gunner I'm sure he'll be,
An' the very first schot that ere he schoots,
  He'll schoot baith my young son and me.'

ANON

THE CAT AND THE MOON

The cat went here and there
And the moon spun round like a top,
And the nearest kin of the moon,
The creeping cat, looked up.
Black Minnaloushe stared at the moon,

For, wander and wail as he would,
The pure cold light in the sky
Troubled his animal blood.
Minnaloushe runs in the grass
Lifting his delicate feet.
Do you dance, Minnaloushe, do you dance?
When two close kindred meet,
What better than call a dance?
Maybe the moon may learn,
Tired of that courtly fashion,
A new dance turn.
Minnaloushe creeps through the grass
From moonlit place to place,
The sacred moon overhead
Has taken a new phase.
Does Minnaloushe know that his pupils
Will pass from change to change,
And that from round to crescent,
From crescent to round they range?
Minnaloushe creeps through the grass
Alone, important and wise,
And lifts to the changing moon
His changing eyes.

W. B. YEATS

PANGUR BÁN

*Written by a student of the monastery of Carinthia
on a copy of St Paul's Epistles, in the eighth century*

I and Pangur Bán, my cat,
'Tis a like task we are at;
Hunting mice is his delight,
Hunting words I sit all night.

Beasts and Birds

Better far than praise of men
'Tis to sit with book and pen;
Pangur bears me no ill-will,
He too plies his simple skill.

'Tis a merry thing to see
At our tasks how glad are we,
When at home we sit and find
Entertainment to our mind.

Oftentimes a mouse will stray
In the hero Pangur's way;
Oftentimes my keen thought set
Takes a meaning in its net.

'Gainst the wall he sets his eye
Full and fierce and sharp and sly;
'Gainst the wall of knowledge I
All my little wisdom try.

When a mouse darts from its den,
O how glad is Pangur then!
O what gladness do I prove
When I solve the doubts I love!

So in peace our tasks we ply,
Pangur Bán, my cat, and I;
In our arts we find our bliss,
I have mine and he has his.

Practice every day has made
Pangur perfect in his trade;
I get wisdom day and night
Turning darkness into light.

ANON: translated from the
Gaelic by ROBIN FLOWER

MY CAT JEOFFRY

For I will consider my Cat Jeoffry.

For he is the servant of the Living God, duly and daily serving him.

For at the first glance of the glory of God in the East he worships in his way.

For is this done by wreathing his body seven times round with elegant quickness.

For then he leaps up to catch the musk, which is the blessing of God upon his prayer.

For he rolls upon prank to work it in.

For having done duty and received blessing he begins to consider himself.

For this he performs in ten degrees.

For first he looks upon his fore-paws to see if they are clean.

For secondly he kicks up behind to clear away there.

For thirdly he works it upon stretch with the fore-paws extended.

For fourthly he sharpens his paws by wood.

For fifthly he washes himself.

For sixthly he rolls upon wash.

For seventhly he fleas himself, that he may not be interrupted upon the beat.

For eightly he rubs himself against a post.

For ninthly he looks up for his instructions.

For tenthly he goes in quest of food.

For having consider'd God and himself he will consider his neighbour.

For if he meets another cat he will kiss her in kindness.

For when he takes his prey he plays with it to give it [a] chance.

For one mouse in seven escapes by his dallying.

For when his day's work is done his business more properly begins.

For he keeps the Lord's watch in the night against the
   adversary.

For he counteracts the powers of darkness by his electrical
   skin & glaring eyes.

For he counteracts the Devil, who is death, by brisking
   about the life.

For in his morning orisons he loves the sun and the sun
   loves him.

For he is of the tribe of Tiger.

For the Cherub Cat is a term of the Angel Tiger.

For he has the subtlety and hissing of a serpent, which in
   goodness he suppresses.

For he will not do destruction, if he is well-fed, neither will
   he spit without provocation.

For he purrs in thankfulness, when God tells him he's a
   good Cat.

For he is an instrument for the children to learn benevolence
   upon.

For every house is incompleat without him & a blessing is
   lacking in the spirit.

CHRISTOPHER SMART

Who's that ringing at my door bell?
   A little pussy cat that isn't very well.
Rub its little nose with a little mutton fat,
   For that's the best cure for a little pussy cat.

ANON

TO A CAT

Cat! who hast pass'd thy grand climacteric,
    How many mice and rats hast in thy days
    Destroy'd?—How many titbits stolen? Gaze
With those bright languid segments green, and prick
Those velvet ears—but pr'ythee do not stick
    Thy latent talons in me—and upraise
    Thy gentle mew—and tell me all thy frays
Of fish and mice, and rats and tender chick.
Nay, look not down, nor lick thy dainty wrists—
    For all the wheezy asthma,—and for all
Thy tail's tip is nick'd off—and though the fists
    Of many a maid have given thee many a maul,
Still is that fur as soft as when the lists
    In youth thou enter'dst on glass bottled wall.

JOHN KEATS

CHEETIE-POUSSIE-CATTIE, O

There was a wee bit mousikie,
That leeved in Gilberaty, O;
It couldna get a bit o cheese,
For Cheetie-Poussie-Cattie, O.

It said unto the cheesikie,
'O fain wad I be at ye, O,
If it werena for the cruel paws
O' Cheetie-Poussie-Cattie, O.'

ANON

74

THE SONG OF THE JELLICLES

Jellicle Cats come out to-night,
Jellicle Cats come one come all:
The Jellicle Moon is shining bright—
Jellicles come to the Jellicle Ball.

Jellicle Cats are black and white,
Jellicle Cats are rather small;
Jellicle Cats are merry and bright,
And pleasant to hear when they caterwaul.
Jellicle Cats have cheerful faces,
Jellicle Cats have bright black eyes;
They like to practise their airs and graces
And wait for the Jellicle Moon to rise.

Jellicle Cats develop slowly,
Jellicle Cats are not too big;
Jellicle Cats are roly-poly,
They know how to dance a gavotte and a jig.
Until the Jellicle Moon appears
They make their toilette and take their repose:
Jellicles wash behind their ears,
Jellicles dry between their toes.

Jellicle Cats are white and black,
Jellicle Cats are of moderate size;
Jellicles jump like a jumping-jack,
Jellicle Cats have moonlit eyes.
They're quiet enough in the morning hours,
They're quiet enough in the afternoon,
Reserving their terpsichorean powers
To dance by the light of the Jellicle Moon.

Jellicle Cats are black and white,
Jellicle Cats (as I said) are small;

75

If it happens to be a stormy night
They will practise a caper or two in the hall.
If it happens the sun is shining bright
You would say they had nothing to do at all:
They are resting and saving themselves to be right
For the Jellicle Moon and the Jellicle Ball.

T. S. ELIOT

DIAMOND CUT DIAMOND

Two cats
One up a tree
One under the tree
The cat up a tree is he
The cat under the tree is she
The tree is witch elm, just incidentally.
He takes no notice of she, she takes no notice of he.
He stares at the woolly clouds passing, she stares at the tree.
There's been a lot written about cats, by Old Possum, Yeats and Compa
But not Alfred de Musset or Lord Tennyson or Poe or anybody
Wrote about one cat under, and one cat up, a tree.
God knows why this should be left for me
Except I like cats as cats be
Especially one cat up
And one cat under
A witch elm
Tree.

EWART MILNE

76

Beasts and Birds

There was a Presbyterian cat
Went forth to catch her prey;
She brought a mouse intill the house,
Upon the Sabbath day.
The minister, offended
With such an act profane,
Laid down his book, the cat he took,
And bound her with a chain.

Thou vile malicious creature,
Thou murderer, said he,
Oh do you think to bring to Hell
My holy wife and me?
But be thou well assured,
That blood for blood shall pay,
For taking of the mouse's life
Upon the Sabbath Day.

Then he took doun his Bible,
And fervently he prayed,
That the great sin the cat had done
Might not on him be laid.
Then forth to exe-cu-ti-on,
Poor Baudrons she was drawn,
And on a tree they hanged her hie,
And then they sung a psalm.

ANON

The herring loves the merry moonlight,
    The mackerel loves the wind,
But the oyster loves the dredging sang,
    For they come of a gentle kind.

SIR WALTER SCOTT

MADAME MOUSE TROTS

'Dame Souris trotte gris dans le noir'—VERLAINE

> Madame Mouse trots,
> Grey in the black night!
> Madame Mouse trots:
> Furred is the light.
> The elephant-trunks
> Trumpet from the sea . . .
> Grey in the black night
> The mouse trots free.
> Hoarse as a dog's bark
> The heavy leaves are furled . . .
> The cat's in his cradle,
> All's well with the world!

EDITH SITWELL

HORSES

Those lumbering horses in the steady plough,
On the bare field—I wonder why, just now,
They seemed terrible, so wild and trange,
Like magic power on the stony grange.

Perhaps some childish hour has come again,
When I watched fearful, through the blackening rain,
Their hooves like pistons in an ancient mill
Move up and down, yet seem as standing still.

Their conquering hooves which trod the stubble down
Were ritual that turned the field to brown,
And their great hulks were seraphim of gold,
Or mute ecstatic monsters on the mould.

78

And oh the rapture, when, one furrow done,
They marched broad-breasted to the sinking sun!
The light flowed off their bossy sides in flakes;
The furrows rolled behind like struggling snakes.

But when at dusk with steaming nostrils home
They came, they seemed gigantic in the gloam,
And warm and glowing with mysterious fire
That lit their smouldering bodies in the mire.

Their eyes as brilliant and as wide as night
Gleamed with a cruel apocalyptic light.
Their manes the leaping ire of the wind
Lifted with rage invisible and blind.

Ah, now it fades! it fades! and I must pine
Again for that dread country crystalline,
Where the blank field and the still-standing tree
Were bright and fearful presences to me.

EDWIN MUIR

THE RUNAWAY

Once when the snow of the year was beginning to fall,
We stopped by a mountain pasture to say, 'Whose colt?'
A little Morgan had one forefoot on the wall,
The other curled at his breast. He dipped his head
And snorted at us. And then he had to bolt.
We heard the miniature thunder where he fled,
And we saw him, or thought we saw him, dim and grey,
Like a shadow against the curtain of falling flakes.
'I think the little fellow's afraid of the snow.
He isn't winter-broken. It isn't play

With the little fellow at all. He's running away.
I doubt if even his mother could tell him, "Sakes,
It's only weather". He'd think she didn't know!
Where is his mother? He can't be out alone.'
And now he comes again with clatter of stone,
And mounts the wall again with whited eyes
And all his tail that isn't hair up straight.
He shudders his coat as if to throw off flies.
'Whoever it is that leaves him out so late,
When other creatures have gone to stall and bin,
Ought to be told to come and take him in.'

ROBERT FROST

ON A SPANIEL CALLED BEAU
KILLING A YOUNG BIRD

A Spaniel, Beau, that fares like you,
    Well-fed, and at his ease,
Should wiser be, than to pursue
    Each trifle that he sees.

But you have kill'd a tiny bird,
    Which flew not till to-day,
Against my orders, whom you heard
    Forbidding you the prey.

Nor did you kill, that you might eat,
    And ease a doggish pain,
For him, though chas'd with furious heat,
    You left where he was slain.

Nor was he of the thievish sort,
    Or one whom blood allures,

But innocent was all his sport,
    Whom you have torn for yours.

My dog! what remedy remains,
    Since, teach you all I can,
I see you, after all my pains,
    So much resemble man!

BEAU'S REPLY

Sir! when I flew to seize the bird,
    In spite of your command,
A louder voice than yours I heard
    And harder to withstand:

You cried—Forbear!—but in my breast
    A mightier cried—Proceed!
'Twas nature, Sir, whose strong behest
    Impell'd me to the deed.

Yet much as nature I respect,
    I ventur'd once to break
(As you perhaps may recollect)
    Her precept, for your sake;

And when your linnet, on a day,
    Passing his prison-door,
Had flutter'd all his strength away,
    And panting press'd the floor,

Well knowing him a sacred thing,
    Not destin'd to my tooth,
I only kiss'd his ruffled wing,
    And lick'd the feathers smooth.

Let my obedience then excuse
   My disobedience now,
Nor some reproof yourself refuse
   From your aggriev'd Bow-wow!

If killing birds be such a crime,
   (Which I can hardly see)
What think you, Sir, of killing Time
   With verse address'd to me?

WILLIAM COWPER

ELEGY ON THE DEATH OF A
MAD DOG

Good people all, of every sort,
   Give ear unto my song;
And if you find it wondrous short,
   It cannot hold you long.

In Islington there was a man,
   Of whom the world might say,
That still a godly race he ran,
   Whene'er he went to pray.

A kind and gentle heart he had,
   To comfort friends and foes;
The naked every day he clad,
   When he put on his clothes.

And in that town a dog was found,
   As many dogs there be,
Both mongrel, puppy, whelp, and hound,
   And curs of low degree.

This dog and man at first were friends;
    But when a pique began,
The dog, to gain some private ends,
    Went mad and bit the man.

Around from all the neighbouring streets
    The wondering neighbours ran,
And swore the dog had lost his wits,
    To bite so good a man.

The wound it seem'd both sore and sad
    To every Christian eye;
And while they swore the dog was mad,
    They swore the man would die.

But soon a wonder came to light,
    That show'd the rogues they lied:
The man recover'd of the bite,
    The dog it was that died.

OLIVER GOLDSMITH

A MALTESE DOG

He came from Malta; and Eumêlus says
He had no better dog in all his days.
We called him Bull; he went into the dark.
Along those roads we cannot hear him bark.

TYMNÈS (2nd cent. B.C.): *Translated from
the Greek by* EDMUND BLUNDEN

THE SPARROW'S DIRGE

When I remember again
How my Philip was slain,
Never half the pain
Was between you twain
Pyramus and Thesbe,
As then befell to me.
I wept and I wailed,
The tearës down hailed,
But nothing it availed
To call Philip again,
Whom Gib, our cat, hath slain.

   Gib, I say, our cat
Worried her on that
Which I loved best.
It cannot be expressed,
My sorrowful heaviness,
But all without redress;
For within that stound,
Half slumbering in a sound,
I fell down to the ground. . . .

   It was so pretty a fool;
It would sit on a stool
And learned after my school
For to keep his cut,
With, 'Philip, keep your cut!'

   It had a velvet cap,
And would sit upon my lap
And seek after small worms
And sometime whit bread crumbs;
And many times and oft
Between my brestës soft
It would lie and rest;
It was proper and prest.

Sometime he would gasp
When he saw a wasp;
A fly or a gnat,
He would fly at that;
And prettily he would pant
When he saw an ant;
Lord, how he would pry
After the butterfly!
Lord, how he would hop
After the gressop!
And when I said, 'Phip! Phip!'
Then he would leap and skip,
And take me by the lip.
Alas, it will me slo
That Philip is gone me fro!
 Si iniquitates.
Alas, I was evil at ease!
De profundis clamavi,
When I saw my sparrow die!

JOHN SKELTON

CALICO PIE

Calico Pie,
The little Birds fly
Down to the calico tree,
Their wings were blue,
And they sang 'Tilly-loo!'
Till away they flew,—
And they never came back to me!
They never came back!
They never came back!
They never came back to me!

Calico Jam,
The little Fish swam,
Over the syllabub sea,
He took off his hat,
To the Sole and the Sprat,
And the Willeby-wat,—
But he never came back to me!
He never came back!
He never came back!
He never came back to me!

Calico Ban,
The little Mice ran,
To be ready in time for tea,
Flippity flup,
They drank it all up,
And danced in the cup,—
But they never came back to me!
They never came back!
They never came back!
They never came back to me!

Calico Drum,
The Grasshoppers come,
The Butterfly, Beetle, and Bee,
Over the ground,
Around and round,
With a hop and a bound,—
But they never came back!
They never came back!
They never came back!
They never came back to me!

EDWARD LEAR

THE OWL

When cats run home and light is come,
  And dew is cold upon the ground,
And the far-off stream is dumb,
  And the whirring sail goes round,
  And the whirring sail goes round;
    Alone and warming his five wits,
    The white owl in the belfry sits.

When merry milkmaids click the latch,
  And rarely smells the new-mown hay,
And the cock hath sung beneath the thatch
  Twice or thrice his roundelay,
  Twice or thrice his roundelay;
    Alone and warming his five wits,
    The white owl in the belfry sits.

LORD TENNYSON

THE OWL AND THE PUSSY CAT

The Owl and the Pussy-cat went to sea
  In a beautiful pea-green boat,
They took some honey, and plenty of money.
  Wrapped up in a five-pound note.
The Owl looked up to the stars above,
  And sang to a small guitar,
'O lovely Pussy! O Pussy, my love,
  What a beautiful Pussy you are,
      You are
      You are!
  What a beautiful Pussy you are!'

Pussy said to the Owl, 'You elegant fowl!
  How charmingly sweet you sing!

O let us be married! too long we have tarried:
　　But what shall we do for a ring?'
They sailed away, for a year and a day,
　　To the land where the Bong-tree grows
And there in a wood a Piggy-wig stood
　　With a ring at the end of his nose,
　　　　His nose,
　　　　His nose,
　　With a ring at the end of his nose.

'Dear Pig, are you willing to sell for one shilling
　　Your ring?' Said the Piggy, 'I will.'
So they took it away, and were married next day
　　By the Turkey who lives on the hill.
They dined on mince, and slices of quince,
　　Which they ate with a runcible spoon;
And hand in hand, on the edge of the sand,
　　They danced by the light of the moon,
　　　　The moon,
　　　　The moon,
　　They danced by the light of the moon.

EDWARD LEAR

THE COMMON CORMORANT

The common cormorant or shag
Lays eggs inside a paper bag
The reason you will see no doubt
It is to keep the lightning out.
But what these unobservant birds
Have never noticed is that herds
Of wandering bears may come with buns
And steal the bags to hold the crumbs.

ANON

THE EAGLE

He clasps the crag with crooked hands;
Close to the sun in lonely lands,
Ring'd with the azure world, he stands.

The wrinkled sea beneath him crawls;
He watches from his mountain walls,
And like a thunderbolt he falls.

LORD TENNYSON

THE SILVER SWAN

The silver swan, who living had no note,
When death approached, unlocked her silent throat,
Leaning her breast against the reedy shore,
Thus sung her first and last, and sung no more:
Farewell all joys! O death, come close mine eyes;
More geese than swans now live, more fools than wise.

ANON

HOW DOTH THE LITTLE CROCODILE

How doth the little crocodile
    Improve his shining tail;
And pour the waters of the Nile
    On every golden scale!

How cheerfully he seems to grin,
    How neatly spreads his claws,
And welcomes little fishes in,
    With gently smiling jaws!

LEWIS CARROLL

THE LLAMA

The Llama is a woolly sort of fleecy hairy goat,
With an indolent expression and an undulating throat
   Like an unsuccessful literary man.
And I know the place he lives in (or at least—I think I do)
It is Ecuador, Brazil or Chili—possibly Peru;
   You must find it in the Atlas if you can.
The Llama of the Pampasses you never should confound
(In spite of a deceptive similarity of sound)
   With the Lhama who is Lord of Turkestan.
For the former is a beautiful and valuable beast
But the latter is not lovable nor useful in the least;
And the Ruminant is preferable surely to the Priest
Who battens on the woeful superstititions of the East
   The Mongol of the Monastery of Shan.

HILAIRE BELLOC

The one-l lama,
He's a priest.
The two-l llama,
He's a beast.
And I will bet
A silk pyjama
There isn't any
Three-l lllama.

OGDEN NASH

THE POBBLE WHO HAS NO TOES

The Pobble who has no toes
   Had once as many as we;
When they said, 'Some day you may lose them all;'—
   He replied,—'Fish fiddle de-dee!'
And his Aunt Jobiska made him drink,
Lavender water tinged with pink,
For she said, 'The World in general knows
There's nothing so good for a Pobble's toes!'

The Pobble who has no toes,
   Swam across the Bristol Channel;
But before he set out he wrapped his nose
   In a piece of scarlet flannel.
For his Aunt Jobiska said, 'No harm
'Can come to his toes if his nose is warm;
'And it's perfectly known that a Pobble's toes
'Are safe,—provided he minds his nose.'

The Pobble swam fast and well
   And when boats or ships came near him
He tinkledy-binkledy-winkled a bell
   So that all the world could hear him.
And all the Sailors and Admirals cried,
When they saw him nearing the further side,—
'He has gone to fish, for his Aunt Jobiska's
'Runcible Cat with crimson whiskers!'

But before he touched the shore,
   The shore of the Bristol Channel,
A sea-green Porpoise carried away
   His wrapper of scarlet flannel.
And when he came to observe his feet
Formerly garnished with toes so neat
His face at once became forlorn
On perceiving that all his toes were gone!

And nobody ever knew
    From that dark day to the present,
Whoso had taken the Pobble's toes,
    In a manner so far from pleasant.
Whether the shrimps or crawfish gray,
Or crafty Mermaids stole them away—
Nobody knew; and nobody knows
How the Pobble was robbed of his twice five toes!

The Pobble who has no toes
    Was placed in a friendly Bark,
And they rowed him back, and carried him up,
    To his Aunt Jobiska's Park.
And she made him a feast at his earnest wish
Of eggs and buttercups fried with fish;—
And she said,—'It's a fact the whole world knows,
'That Pobbles are happier without their toes.'

EDWARD LEAR

The horny-goloch is an awesome beast,
Soople an scaly;
It has twa horns, an a hantle o feet,
An a forkie tailie.

ANON

CHILDREN

Monday's child is fair of face
Tuesday's child is full of grace,
Wednesday's child is full of woe,
Thursday's child has far to go,
Friday's child is loving and giving,
Saturday's child works hard for his living,
And the child that is born on the Sabbath day
Is bonny and blithe, and good and gay.

ANON

CAN YE SEW CUSHIONS?

O can ye sew cushions?
  Or can ye sew sheets?
An' can ye sing ba-la-loo
  When the bairnie greets?
An' hee an' ba, birdie,
  An' hee an' ba, lamb,
An' hee an' ba, birdie,
  My bonnie wee man.

  Hee O, wee O, what' ll I dae wi' ye?
  Black is the life that I lead wi' ye,
  Mony o' ye, little to gie ye,
  Hee O, wee O, what' ll I dae wi' ye?

Now hush-a-ba, lammie,
  An' hush-a-ba, dear,
Now hush-a-ba, lammie,
  Thy minnie is here.

Children

The wild wind is ravin',
　Thy minnie's heart's sair;
The wild wind is ravin',
　An' ye dinna care.

Sing ba-la-loo, lammie,
　Sing ba-la-loo, dear,
Does wee lammie ken
　That his daddie's no here?
Ye're rockin' fu' sweetly
　Upon my warm knee,
But your daddie's a-rockin'
　Upon the saut sea.

ANON

GOOD AND BAD CHILDREN

Children, you are very little,
And your bones are very brittle;
If you would grow great and stately,
You must try to walk sedately.

You must still be bright and quiet,
And content with simple diet;
And remain, through all bewild'ring,
Innocent and honest children.

Happy hearts and happy faces,
Happy play in grassy places—
That was how, in ancient ages,
Children grew to kings and sages.

But the unkind and the unruly,
And the sort who eat unduly,
They must never hope for glory—
Theirs is quite a different story!

Cruel children, crying babies,
All grow up as geese and gabies,
Hated, as their age increases,
By their nephews and their nieces.

R. L. STEVENSON

JEMIMA

There was a little girl, and she wore a little curl
  Right down the middle of her forehead
When she was good, she was very, very, good,
  But when she was bad, she was horrid!

One day she went upstairs, while her parents, unawares,
  In the kitchen down below were occupied with meals,
And she stood upon her head, on her little truckle bed,
  And she then began hurraying with her heels.

Her mother heard the noise, and thought it was the boys
  A-playing at a combat in the attic,
But when she climbed the stair and saw Jemima there,
  She took and she did whip her most emphatic.

ANON

MATILDA

Who told Lies, and was Burned to Death

Matilda told such Dreadful Lies,
It made one Gasp and Stretch one's Eyes;
Her Aunt, who, from her Earliest Youth,
Had kept a Strict Regard for Truth,
Attempted to Believe Matilda:
The effort very nearly killed her,
And would have done so, had not She
Discovered this Infirmity.
For once, towards the Close of Day,
Matilda, growing tired of play,
And finding she was left alone,
Went tiptoe to the Telephone
And summoned the Immediate Aid
Of London's Noble Fire-Brigade.
Within an hour the Gallant Band
Were pouring in on every hand,
From Putney, Hackney Downs and Bow,
With Courage high and Hearts a-glow
They galloped, roaring through the Town,
'Matilda's House is Burning Down!'
Inspired by British Cheers and Loud
Proceeding from the Frenzied Crowd,
They ran their ladders through a score
Of windows on the Ball Room Floor;
And took Peculiar Pains to Souse
The Pictures up and down the House,
Until Matilda's Aunt succeeded
In showing them they were not needed
And even then she had to pay
To get the Men to go away!
  . . . .

It happened that a few Weeks later

Her Aunt was off to the Theatre
To see that Interesting Play
The Second Mrs. Tanqueray.
She had refused to take her Niece
To hear this Entertaining Piece:
A Deprivation Just and Wise
To Punish her for Telling Lies.
That Night a Fire *did* break out—
You should have heard Matilda Shout!
You should have heard her Scream and Bawl,
And throw the window up and call
To People passing in the Street—
(The rapidly increasing Heat
Encouraging her to obtain
Their confidence)—but all in vain!
For every time She shouted 'Fire!'
They only answered 'Little Liar!'
And therefore when her Aunt returned,
Matilda, and the House, were Burned.

HILAIRE BELLOC

SPEAK ROUGHLY TO YOUR LITTLE BOY

Speak roughly to your little boy,
    And beat him when he sneezes;
He only does it to annoy,
    Because he knows it teases.
       Wow! Wow! Wow!

I speak severely to my boy,
    I beat him when he sneezes;
For he can thoroughly enjoy
    The pepper when he pleases!
       Wow! Wow! Wow!

LEWIS CARROLL

INFANT INNOCENCE

The Grizzly Bear is huge and wild;
He has devoured the infant child.
The infant child is not aware
He has been eaten by the bear.

A. E. HOUSMAN

WARNING TO CHILDREN

Children, if you dare to think
Of the greatness, rareness, muchness,
Fewness of this precious only
Endless world in which you say
You live, you think of things like this:
Blocks of slate enclosing dappled
Red and green, enclosing tawny
Yellow nets, enclosing white
And black acres of dominoes,
Where a neat brown paper parcel
Temps you to untie the string.
In the parcel a small island,
On the island a large tree,
On the tree a husky fruit.
Strip the husk and cut the rind off:
In the centre you will see
Blocks of slate enclosed by dappled
Red and green, enclosed by tawny
Yellow nets, enclosed by white
And black acres of dominoes,
Where the same brown paper parcel—
Children, leave the string untied!
For who dares undo the parcel
Finds himself at once inside it,

On the island, in the fruit,
Blocks of slate about his head,
Finds himself enclosed by dappled
Green and red, enclosed by yellow
Tawny nets, enclosed by black
And white acres of dominoes,
But the same brown paper parcel
Still untied upon his knee.
And, if he then should dare to think
Of the fewness, muchness, rareness,
Greatness of this endless only
Precious world in which he says
He lives—he then unties the string.

ROBERT GRAVES

THE CHILD AT PLAY

1. WHERE GO THE BOATS?

Dark brown is the river,
   Golden is the sand.
It flows along for ever,
   With trees on either hand.

Green leaves a-floating,
   Castles of the foam,
Boats of mine a-boating—
   Where will all come home?

On goes the river
   And out past the mill,
Away down the valley,
   Away down the hill.

Away down the river,
   A hundred miles or more,
Other little children
   Shall bring my boats ashore.

II. TRAVEL

I should like to rise and go
Where the golden apples grow;
Where below another sky
Parrot islands anchored lie,
And, watched by cockatoos and goats,
Lonely Crusoes building boats;
Where in sunshine reaching out
Eastern cities, miles about,
Are with mosque and minaret
Among sandy gardens set,
And the rich goods from near and far
Hang for sale in the bazaar;
Where the Great Wall round China goes,
And on one side the desert blows,
And with bell and voice and drum,
Cities on the other hum;
Where are forests, hot as fire,
Wide as England, tall as a spire,
Full of apes and cocoa-nuts
And the negro hunters' huts;
Where the knotty crocodile
Lies and blinks in the Nile,
And the red flamingo flies
Hunting fish before his eyes;
Where in jungles, near and far,
Man-devouring tigers are,
Lying close and giving ear
Lest the hunt be drawing near,
Or a comer-by be seen

Swinging in a palanquin;
Where among the desert sands
Some deserted city stands,
All its children, sweep and prince,
Grown to manhood ages since,
Not a foot in street or house,
Not a stir of child or mouse,
And when kindly falls the night,
In all the town no spark of light.
There I'll come when I'm a man
With a camel caravan;
Light a fire in the gloom
Of some dusty dining-room;
See the pictures on the walls,
Heroes, fights and festivals;
And in a corner find the toys
Of the old Egyptian boys.

R. L. STEVENSON

NEW HAMPSHIRE

Children's voices in the orchard
Between the blossom- and the fruit-time:
Golden head, crimson head,
Between the green tip and the root.
Black wing, brown wing, hover over;
Twenty years and the spring is over;
To-day grieves, to-morrow grieves,
Cover me over, light-in-leaves;
Golden head, black wing,
Cling, swing,
Spring, sing,
Swing up into the apple-tree.

T. S. ELIOT

THE SCHOOLBOY

I love to rise in a summer morn
When the birds sing on every tree;
The distant huntsman winds his horn,
And the sky-lark sings with me.
O! what sweet company.

But to go to school in a summer morn,
O! it drives all joy away;
Under a cruel eye outworn,
The little ones spend the day
In sighing and dismay.

Ah! then at times I drooping sit,
And spend many an anxious hour,
Nor in my book can I take delight,
Nor sit in learning's bower,
Worn thro' with the dreary shower.

How can the bird that is born for joy
Sit in a cage and sing?
How can a child, when fears annoy,
But droop his tender wing,
And forget his youthful spring?

O! father & mother, if buds are nip'd
And blossoms blown away,
And if the tender plants are strip'd
Of their joy in the springing day,
By sorrow and care's dismay,

How shall the summer arise in joy,
Or the summer fruits appear?
Or how shall we gather what griefs destroy,
Or bless the mellowing year,
When the blasts of winter appear?

WILLIAM BLAKE

THERE WAS A BOY

There was a Boy; ye knew him well, ye cliffs
And islands of Winander!—many a time,
At evening, when the earliest stars began
To move along the edges of the hills,
Rising or setting, would he stand alone,
Beneath the trees, or by the glimmering lake;
And there, with fingers interwoven, both hands
Pressed closely palm to palm and to his mouth
Uplifted, he, as through an instrument,
Blew mimic hootings to the silent owls,
That they might answer him.—And they would shout
Across the watery vale, and shout again,
Responsive to his call,—with quivering peals,
And long halloos, and screams, and echoes loud
Redoubled and redoubled; concourse wild
Of jocund din! And, when there came a pause
Of silence such as baffled his best skill:
Then, sometimes, in that silence, while he hung
Listening, a gentle shock of mild surprise
Has carried far into his heart the voice
Of mountain-torrents; or the visible scene
Would enter unawares into his mind
With all its solemn imagery, its rocks,
Its woods, and that uncertain heaven received
Into the bosom of the steady lake.

WILLIAM WORDSWORTH

IN A MOONLIGHT WILDERNESS

Encintured with a twine of leaves,
That leafy twine his only dress!
A lovely Boy was plucking fruits,
By moonlight, in a wilderness.
The moon was bright, the air was free,
And fruits and flowers together grew
On many a shrub and many a tree:
And all put on a gentle hue,
Hanging in the shadowy air
Like a picture rich and rare.
It was a climate where, they say,
The night is more belov'd than day.
But who that beauteous Boy beguil'd,
That beauteous Boy, to linger here?
Alone, by night, a little child,
In place so silent and so wild—
Has he no friend, no loving mother near?

S. T. COLERIDGE

UPON PAGGET

Pagget, a School-boy, got a Sword, and then
He vow'd Destruction both to Birch, and Men:
Who wo'd not think this Yonker fierce to fight?
Yet coming home, but somewhat late, (last night)
Untruss, his Master bade him; and that word
Made him take up his shirt, lay down his sword.

ROBERT HERRICK

My Mother said that I never should
Play with the gypsies in the wood,
The wood was dark; the grass was green;
In came Sally with a tambourine.

I went to the sea—no ship to get across;
I paid ten shillings for a blind white horse;
I up on his back and was off in a crack,
Sally tell my Mother I shall never come back.

ANON

THE FALSE KNIGHT AND THE WEE BOY

'O whare are ye gaun?'
   Quo' the fause knicht upon the road:
'I'm gaun to the scule,'
   Quo' the wee boy, and still he stude.

'What is that upon your back?'
   Quo' the fause knicht upon the road:
'Atweel it is my bukes,'
   Quo' the wee boy, and still he stude.

'What's that ye've got in your arm?'
   Quo' the fause knicht upon the road:
'Atweel it is my peit,'
   Quo' the wee boy, and still he stude.

'Wha's aucht thae sheep?'
   Quo' the fause knicht upon the road:
'They are mine and my mither's,'
   Quo' the wee boy, and still he stude.

'How mony o' them are mine?'
  Quo' the fause knicht upon the road:
'A' they that hae blue tails,'
  Quo' the wee boy, and still he stude.

'I wiss ye were on yon tree,'
  Quo' the fause knicht upon the road:
'And a gude ladder under me,'
  Quo' the wee boy, and still he stude.

'And the ladder for to break,'
  Quo' the fause knicht upon the road:
'And for you to fa' down,'
  Quo' the wee boy, and still he stude.

'I wiss ye were in yon sie,'
  Quo' the fause knicht upon the road:
'And a gude bottom under me,'
  Quo' the wee boy, and still he stude.

'And the bottom for to break,'
  Quo' the fause knicht upon the road:
'*And ye to be drowned,*'
  Quo' the wee boy, and still he stude.

ANON

TO HIS SON, VINCENT CORBET

on his Birth-Day, November 10, 1630, being then three years old

What I shall leave thee none can tell,
But all shall say I wish thee well;
I wish thee, Vin, before all wealth,
Both bodily and ghostly health:

Nor too much wealth, nor wit, come to thee;
So much of either may undo thee.
I wish thee learning, not for show,
Enough for to instruct, and know;
Not such as gentlemen require,
To prate at table or at fire.
I wish thee all thy mother's graces,
Thy father's fortunes and his places.
I wish thee friends, and one at court,
Not to build on, but support;
To keep thee, not in doing many
Oppressions, but from suffering any.
I wish thee peace in all thy ways,
Nor lazy nor contentious days;
And when thy soul and body part,
As innocent as now thou art.

BISHOP RICHARD CORBET

IF I SHOULD EVER BY CHANCE

If I should ever by chance grow rich
I'll buy Codham, Cockridden, and Childerditch,
Roses, Pyrgo, and Lapwater,
And let them all to my elder daughter.
The rent I shall ask of her will be only
Each year's first violets, white and lonely,
The first primroses and orchises—
She must find them before I do, that is.
But if she finds a blossom on furze
Without rent they shall all for ever be hers,
Whenever I am sufficiently rich:
Codham, Cockridden, and Childerditch,
Roses, Pyrgo and Lapwater—
I shall give them all to my elder daughter.

EDWARD THOMAS

WHAT SHALL I GIVE?

What shall I give my daughter the younger
More than will keep her from cold and hunger?
I shall not give her anything.
If she shared South Weald and Havering,
Their acres, the two brooks running between,
Paine's Brook and Weald Brook,
With peewit, woodpecker, swan, and rook,
She would be no richer than the queen
Who once on a time sat in Havering Bower
Alone, with the shadows, pleasure and power.
She could do no more with Samarcand,
Or the mountains of a mountain land
And its far white house above cottages
Like Venus above the Pleiades.
Her small hands I would not cumber
With so many acres and their lumber,
But leave her Steep and her own world
And her spectacled self with hair uncurled,
Wanting a thousand little things
That time without contentment brings.

EDWARD THOMAS

VICTUALS AND DRINK

A CHILD'S GRACE

Here a little child I stand
Heaving up my either hand;
Cold as paddocks though they be,
Here I lift them up to Thee,
For a benison to fall
On our meat and on us all. Amen.

ROBERT HERRICK

HOMELY MEATS

*The author loving these homely meats specially, viz.: cream,
pancakes, buttered pippin-pies (laugh, good people) and tobacco;
writ to that worthy and virtuous gentlewoman, whom he
calleth Mistress, as followeth*

If there were, oh! an Hellespont of cream
Between us, milk-white mistress, I would swim
To you, to show to both my love's extreme,
Leander-like,—yea! dive from brim to brim.
But met I with a buttered pippin-pie
Floating upon 't, that would I make my boat
To waft me to you without jeopardy,
Though sea-sick I might be while it did float.
Yet if a storm should rise, by night or day,
Of sugar-snows and hail of caraways,
Then, if I found a pancake in my way,
It like a plank should bring me to your kays;
    Which having found, if they tobacco kept,
    The smoke should dry me well before I slept.

JOHN DAVIES

There was an old woman, and what do you think,
She lived upon nothing but victuals and drink.
Victuals and drink were the whole of her diet,
Yet this plaguey old woman would never keep quiet.

ANON

THE LYCHEE

Fruit white and lustrous as a pearl . . .
Lambent as the jewel of Ho, more strange
Than the saffron-stone of Hsia.
Now sigh we at the beauty of its show,
Now triumph in its taste.
Sweet juices lie in the mouth,
Soft scents invade the mind.
All flavours here are joined, yet none is master;
A hundred diverse tastes
Blend in such harmony no man can say
That one outstrips the rest. Sovereign of sweets,
Peerless, pre-eminent fruit, who dwellest apart
In noble solitude!

WANG I: Translated from the
Chinese by ARTHUR WALEY

A TERNARIE OF LITTLES, UPON A PIPKIN OF JELLY SENT TO A LADY

A little Saint best fits a little Shrine,
A little Prop best fits a little Vine,
As my small Cruse best fits my little Wine.

A little Seed best fits a little Soil,
A little Trade best fits a little Toil:
As my small Jar best fits my little Oil.

A little Bin best fits a little Bread,
A little Garland fits a little Head:
As my small stuff best fits my little Shed.

A little Hearth best fits a little Fire,
A little Chapel fits a little Quire,
As my small Bell best fits my little Spire.

A little stream best fits a little Boat;
A little lead best fits a little Float;
As my small Pipe best fits my little note.

A little meat best fits a little belly,
As sweetly Lady, give me leave to tell ye,
This little Pipkin fits this little Jelly.

ROBERT HERRICK

A TABLE RICHLY SPREAD

A Table richly spread, in regal mode,
With dishes piled, and meats of noblest sort
And savour, Beasts of chase, or Fowl of game,
In pastry built, or from the spit, or boiled,
Gris-amber-steamed; all Fish from Sea or Shore,
Freshet, or purling Brook, of shell or fin,
And exquisitest name, for which was drained
Pontus and *Lucrine* Bay, and *Afric* Coast.
Alas how simple, to these Cates compared,
Was that crude Apple that diverted *Eve*!
And at a stately side-board by the wine

That fragrant smell diffused, in order stood
Tall stripling youths rich clad, of fairer hue
Then *Ganymede* or *Hylas*, distant more
Under the Trees now tripped, now solemn stood
Nymphs of *Diana's* train, and *Naiades*
With fruits and flowers from *Amalthea's* horn,
And Ladies of th' *Hesperides*, that seemed
Fairer then feigned of old, or fabled since
Of Fairy Damsels met in Forest wide
By Knights of *Logres*, or of *Lyonesse*,
Lancelot or *Pelleas*, or *Pellenore*,
And all the while Harmonious Airs were heard
Of chiming strings, or charming pipes and winds
Of gentlest gale *Arabian* odors fanned
From their soft wings, and *Flora's* earliest smells.

JOHN MILTON

Nose, nose, jolly red nose,
And who gave thee this jolly red nose?
Nutmegs and ginger, cinnamon and cloves,
And they gave me this jolly red nose.

BEAUMONT AND FLETCHER

AIKEN DRUM

There was a man lived in the moon,
    and his name was Aiken Drum.
And he played upon a ladle,
    and his name was Aiken Drum.

And his hat was made of good cream cheese,
    and his name was Aiken Drum.
And he played upon a ladle, etc.

And his coat was made of good roast beef,
    and his name was Aiken Drum.

And his buttons were made of penny loaves,
    and his name was Aiken Drum.

His waistcoat was made of crust of pies,
    and his name was Aiken Drum.

His breeches were made of haggis bags,
    and his name was Aiken Drum.

There was a man in another town,
    and his name was Willy Wood;
And he played upon a razor,
    and his name was Willy Wood.

And he ate up all the good cream cheese,
    and his name was Willy Wood.
And he played upon a razor, etc.

And he ate up all the good roast beef,
    and his name was Willy Wood.

And he ate up all the penny loaves,
    and his name was Willy Wood.

And he ate up all the good pie crust,
    and his name was Willy Wood.

But he choked upon the haggis bags,
    and there was an end of Willy Wood.
And he played upon a razor,
    and his name was Willy Wood.

ANON

IN PRAISE OF ALE

When that the chill Charocco blows
  And winter tells a heavy tale,
When pies and daws and rooks and crows
Do sit and curse in frost and snows,
    Then give me ale.

Ale in a Saxon rumkin then,
  Such as will make grimalkin prate,
Bids valour burgeon in tall men,
Quickens the poet's wit and pen,
    Despises fate.

Ale, that the absent battle fights,
  And scorns the march of Swedish drum;
Disputes of princes, laws and rights;
What's done and past tells mortal wights,
    And what's to come.

Ale, that the ploughman's heart up keeps
  And equals it to tyrants' thrones;
That wipes the eye that fain would weep,
And lulls in sweet and dainty sleep
    The o'erwearied bones.

Grandchild of Ceres, barley's daughter,
  Wine's emulous neighbour if but stale,
Ennobling all the nymphs of water
And filling each man's mouth with laughter—
    Oh, give me ale!

THOMAS BONHAM

114

TWO GRACES

Some hae meat, and canna eat,
   And some wad eat that want it;
But we hae meat and we can eat,
   And sae the Lord be thankit!

ROBERT BURNS

Hurly, hurly, roon the table,
Eat as muckle as you're able.
Eat muckle, pooch nane,
Hurly, hurly, AMEN.

ANON

SIR GEOFFREY CHAUCER

His stature was not very tall,
Lean he was, his legs were small,
Hosed within a stock of red,
A buttoned bonnet on his head,
From under which did hang, I ween,
Silver hairs both bright and sheen.
His beard was white, trimmed round,
His countenance blithe and merry found.
A sleeveless jacket large and wide,
With many plights and skirts side,
Of water camlet did he wear;
A whittle by his belt he bare,
His shoes were corned, broad before,
His inkhorn at his side he wore,
And in his hand he bore a book.
Thus did this ancient poet look.

ROBERT GREENE

side, long   *whittle*, knife   *corned*, peaked   *camlet*, material made of hair

MISTRESS MARGARET HUSSEY

Merry Margaret, as midsummer flower,
Gentle as falcon or hawk of the tower,
With solace and gladness,
Much mirth and no madness,
All good and no badness;
So joyously,
So maidenly,
So womanly,

Her demeaning;
In every thing
Far far passing
That I can indite
Or suffice to write
Of merry Margaret, as midsummer flower,
Gentle as falcon or hawk of the tower.
As patient and as still,
And as full of good will,
As the fair Isyphill,
Coliander,
Sweet pomander,
Good Cassander;
Steadfast of thought,
Well made, well wrought.
Far may be sought
Erst than ye can find
So courteous, so kind,
As merry Margaret, the midsummer flower,
Gentle as falcon or hawk of the tower.

JOHN SKELTON

MEG MERRILIES

Old Meg she was a Gipsy
   And liv'd upon the Moors:
Her bed it was the brown heath turf,
   And her house was out of doors.

Her apples were swart blackberries,
   Her currants pods o' broom;
Her wine was dew o' the wild white rose
   Her book a churchyard tomb.

Some People

Her Brothers were the craggy hills,
  Her Sisters larchen trees—
Alone with her great family
  She liv'd as she did please.

No breakfast had she many a morn,
  No dinner many a noon,
And 'stead of supper she would stare
  Full hard against the Moon.

But every morn of woodbine fresh
  She made her garlanding,
And every night the dark glen Yew
  She wove, and she would sing.

And with her fingers old and brown
  She plaited Mats o' Rushes,
And gave them to the Cottagers
  She met among the Bushes.

Old Meg was brave as Margaret Queen
  And tall as Amazon:
An old red blanket cloak she wore;
  A chip hat had she on.
God rest her aged bones somewhere—
  She died full long agone!

                                        JOHN KEATS

AN OLD MAN

       The little hedgerow birds,
That peck along the roads, regard him not.
He travels on, and in his face, his step,
His gait, is one expression: every limb,

His look and bending figure, all bespeak
A man who does not move with pain, but moves
With thought.—He is insensibly subdued
To settled quiet: he is one by whom
All effort seems forgotten; one to whom
Long patience hath such mild composure given,
That patience now doth seem a thing of which
He hath no need. He is by nature led
To peace so perfect that the young behold
With envy, what the Old Man hardly feels.

WILLIAM WORDSWORTH

THE SOLITARY REAPER

Behold her, single in the field,
Yon solitary Highland Lass!
Reaping and singing by herself;
Stop here, or gently pass!
Alone she cuts and binds the grain,
And sings a melancholy strain;
O listen! for the Vale profound
Is overflowing with the sound.

No Nightingale did ever chaunt
More welcome notes to weary bands
Of travellers in some shady haunt,
Among Arabian sands:
A voice so thrilling ne'er was heard
In spring-time from the Cuckoo-bird.
Breaking the silence of the seas
Among the farthest Hebrides.

Will no one tell me what she sings?—
Perhaps the plaintive numbers flow

For old, unhappy, far-off things,
And battles long ago:
Or is it some more humble lay,
Familiar matter of to-day?
Some natural sorrow, loss, or pain,
That has been, and may be again?

Whate'er the theme, the Maiden sang
As if her song could have no ending;
I saw her singing at her work,
And o'er the sickle bending;—
I listened, motionless and still;
And, as I mounted up the hill,
The music in my heart I bore,
Long after it was heard no more.

WILLIAM WORDSWORTH

MINIVER CHEEVY

Miniver Cheevy, child of scorn,
  Grew lean while he assailed the seasons;
He wept that he was ever born,
  And he had reasons.

Miniver loved the days of old
  When swords were bright and steeds were prancing;
The vision of a warrior bold
  Would set him dancing.

Miniver sighed for what was not,
  And dreamed, and rested from his labours;
He dreamed of Thebes and Camelot,
  And Priam's neighbours.

Some People

Miniver mourned the ripe renown
    That made so many a name so fragrant;
He mourned Romance, now on the town;
    And Art, a vagrant.

Miniver loved the Medici,
    Albeit he had never seen one;
He would have sinned incessantly
    Could he have been one.

Miniver cursed the commonplace
    And eyed a khaki suit with loathing;
He missed the mediaeval grace
    Of iron clothing.

Miniver scorned the gold he sought,
    But sore annoyed was he without it;
Miniver thought, and thought, and thought,
    And thought about it.

Miniver Cheevy, born too late,
    Scratched his head and kept on thinking;
Miniver coughed, and called it fate,
    And kept on drinking.

EDWIN ARLINGTON ROBINSON

THE AKOND OF SWAT

Who or why, or which, or *what*,
                Is the Akond of SWAT?

Is he tall or short, or dark or fair?
Does he sit on a stool or a sofa or chair, or SQUAT,
                The Akond of Swat?

Some People

Is he wise or foolish, young or old?
Does he drink his soup and his coffee cold, or HOT,
                The Akond of Swat?

Does he sing or whistle, jabber or talk,
And when riding abroad does he gallop or walk, or TROT,
                The Akond of Swat?

Does he wear a turban, a fez, or a hat?
Does he sleep on a mattress, a bed, or a mat, or a COT,
                The Akond of Swat?

When he writes a copy in round-hand size,
Does he cross his T's and finish his I's with a DOT,
                The Akond of Swat?

Can he write a letter concisely clear
Without a speck or a smudge or smear or BLOT,
                The Akond of Swat?

Do his people like him extremely well?
Or do they, whenever they can, rebel, or PLOT,
                At the Akond of Swat?

If he catches them then, either old or young,
Does he have them chopped in pieces or hung, or SHOT,
                The Akond of Swat?

Do his people prig in the lanes or park?
Or even at times, when days are dark, GAROTTE?
                O the Akond of Swat!

Does he study the wants of his own dominion?
Or doesn't he care for public opinion a JOT,
                The Akond of Swat?

Some People

To amuse his mind do his people show him
Pictures, or any one's last new poem, or WHAT,
                              For the Akond of Swat?

At night if he suddenly screams and wakes,
Do they bring him only a few small cakes, or a LOT,
                              For the Akond of Swat?

Does he live on turnips, tea, or tripe?
Does he like his shawl to be marked with a stripe, or a DOT,
                              The Akond of Swat?

Does he like to lie on his back in a boat
Like the lady who lived in that isle remote, SHALLOTT
                              The Akond of Swat?

Is he quiet, or always making a fuss?
Is his steward a Swiss or a Swede or a Russ, or a SCOT,
                              The Akond of Swat?

Does he like to sit by the calm blue wave?
Or to sleep and snore in a dark green cave, or a GROTT,
                              The Akond of Swat?

Does he drink small beer from a silver jug?
Or a bowl? or a glass? or a cup? or a mug? or a POT,
                              The Akond of Swat?

Does he beat his wife with a gold-topped pipe,
When she lets the gooseberries grow too ripe, or ROT,
                              The Akond of Swat?

Does he wear a white tie when he dines with friends,
And tie it neat in a bow with ends, or a KNOT,
                              The Akond of Swat?

Does he like new cream, and hate mince-pies?
When he looks at the sun does he wink his eyes, or NOT,
                              The Akond of Swat?

Does he teach his subjects to roast and bake?
Does he sail about on an inland lake, in a YACHT,
                              The Akond of Swat?

Some one, or nobody, knows I wot
Who or which or why or what
                              Is the Akond of Swat!
                                    EDWARD LEAR

SELF-PORTRAIT OF
THE LAUREATE OF NONSENSE

How pleasant to know Mr. Lear!
    Who has written such volumes of stuff!
Some think him ill-tempered and queer,
    But a few think him pleasant enough.

His mind is concrete and fastidious,
    His nose is remarkably big;
His visage is more or less hideous,
    His beard it resembles a wig.

He has ears, and two eyes, and ten fingers,
    Leastways, if you reckon two thumbs;
Long ago he was one of the singers,
    But now he is one of the dumbs.

He sits in a beautiful parlour,
    With hundreds of books on the wall;
He drinks a great deal of Marsala,
    But never gets tipsy at all.

Some People

He has many friends, laymen and clerical;
    Old Foss is the name of his cat;
His body is perfectly spherical,
    He weareth a runcible hat.

When he walks in a waterproof white,
    The children run after him so!
Calling out, 'He's come out in his night-
    Gown, that crazy old Englishman, oh!'

He weeps by the side of the ocean,
    He weeps on the top of the hill;
He purchases pancakes and lotion,
    And chocolate shrimps from the mill.

He reads but he cannot speak Spanish,
    He cannot abide ginger-beer:
Ere the days of his pilgrimage vanish,
    How pleasant to know Mr. Lear!

EDWARD LEAR

FOUR COUNTRIES

And did those feet in ancient time
Walk upon England's mountains green?
And was the holy Lamb of God
On England's pleasant pastures seen?

And did the Countenance Divine
Shine forth upon our clouded hills?
And was Jerusalem builded here
Among these dark Satanic Mills?

Bring me my Bow of burning gold:
Bring me my Arrows of desire:
Bring me my Spear: O clouds unfold!
Bring me my Chariot of fire.

I will not cease from Mental Fight,
Nor shall my Sword sleep in my hand
Till we have built Jerusalem
In England's green & pleasant Land.

WILLIAM BLAKE

THE NEW LONDON

Methinks already, from this Chymick flame,
    I see a City of more precious mould,
Rich as the Town which gives the *Indies* name,
    With Silver paved, and all divine with Gold.

Already, Labouring with a mighty fate,
    She shakes the rubbish from her mounting brow,
And seems to have renewed her Charter's date,
    Which Heaven will to the death of time allow.

Four Countries

More great than humane, now, and more *August*,
  New deified she from her fires does rise:
Her widening streets on new foundations trust,
  And, opening, into larger parts she flies.

Before, she like some Shepherdess did show,
  Who sate to bathe her by a River's side:
Not answering to her fame, but rude and low,
  Nor taught the beauteous Arts of Modern pride.

Now, like a Maiden Queen, she will behold,
  From her high Turrets, hourly Suitors come:
The East with Incense, and the West with Gold,
  Will stand, like Suppliants, to receive her doom.

The silver *Thames*, her own domestick Flood,
  Shall bear her vessels, like a sweeping Train;
And often wind (as of his Mistress proud)
  With longing eyes to meet her face again.

The wealthy *Tagus*, and the wealthier *Rhine*,
  The glory of their Towns no more shall boast:
And *Seine*, That would with *Belgian* River joyn,
  Shall find her lustre stain'd, and Traffick lost.

The venturous Merchant, who designed more far,
  And touches on our hospitable shore:
Charmed with the splendour of this Northern Star,
  Shall here unlade him, and depart no more.

Our powerful Navy shall no longer meet,
  The wealth of *France* or *Holland* to invade:
The beauty of this Town, without a Fleet,
  From all the world shall vindicate her Trade.

And, while this famed Emporium we prepare,
  The *British* Ocean shall such triumphs boast,
That those who now disdain our Trade to share,
  Shall rob like Pirates on our wealthy Coast.

Already we have conquered half the War,
  And the less dangerous part is left behind:
Our trouble now is but to make them dare,
  And not so great to vanquish as to find.

Thus to the Eastern wealth through storms we go;
  But now, the Cape once doubled, fear no more:
A constant Trade-wind will securely blow,
  And gently lay us on the Spicy shore.

JOHN DRYDEN

COMPOSED UPON WESTMINSTER BRIDGE
SEPT. 3, 1802

Earth has not anything to show more fair:
Dull would he be of soul who could pass by
A sight so touching in its majesty:
This City now doth, like a garment, wear
The beauty of the morning; silent, bare,
Ships, towers, domes, theatres, and temples lie
Open unto the fields, and to the sky;
All bright and glittering in the smokeless air.
Never did sun more beautifully steep
In his first splendour, valley, rock, or hill;
Ne'er saw I, never felt, a calm so deep!
The river glideth at his own sweet will:
Dear God! the very houses seem asleep;
And all that mighty heart is lying still!

WILLIAM WORDSWORTH

RIVERS

Fair Danubie is praised for being wide;
   Nilus commended for the sevenfold head
Euphrates for the swiftness of the tide,
   And for the garden whence his course is led
   The banks of Rhine with vines are overspread:
Take Loire and Po, yet all may not compare
With English Thamesis for buildings rare.

THOMAS STORER

PUCK'S SONG

See you the ferny ride that steals
Into the oak-woods far?
O that was whence they hewed the keels
That rolled to Trafalgar.

And mark you where the ivy clings
To Bayham's mouldering walls?
O there we cast the stout railings
That stand around St. Paul's.

See you the dimpled track that runs
All hollow through the wheat?
O that was where they hauled the guns
That smote King Philip's fleet

(Out of the Weald, the secret Weald,
Men sent in ancient years
The horse-shoes red at Flodden Field,
The arrows at Poitiers!)

See you our little mill that clacks,
So busy by the brook?
She has ground her corn and paid her tax
Ever since Domesday Book.

See you our stilly woods of oak,
And the dread ditch beside?
O that was where the Saxons broke
On the day that Harold died.

See you the windy levels spread
About the gates of Rye?
O that was where the Northmen fled,
When Alfred's ships came by.

See you our pastures wide and lone,
Where the red oxen browse?
O there was a City thronged and known,
Ere London boasted a house.

And see you, after rain, the trace
Of mound and ditch and wall?
O that was a Legion's camping-place,
When Caesar sailed from Gaul.

And see you marks that show and fade,
Like shadows on the Downs?
O they are the lines the Flint Men made,
To guard their wondrous towns.

Trackway and Camp and City lost,
Salt Marsh where now is corn—
Old Wars, old Peace, old Arts that cease,
And so was England born!

Fair these broad meads—these hoary woods are grand
But we are exiles from our fathers' land.

From the lone shieling of the misty island
   Mountains divide us, and the waste of seas,
Yet still the blood is strong, the heart is Highland,
   And we in dreams behold the Hebrides.

We ne'er shall tread the fancy-haunted valley,
   Where 'tween the dark hills creeps the small clear stream
In arms around the patriarch banner rally,
   Nor see the moon on royal tombstones gleam.

When the bold kindred in the time long vanished,
   Conquered the soil and fortified the keep—
No seer foretold the children would be banished,
   That a degenerate lord might boast his sheep.

Come foreign rage—let Discord burst in slaughter!
   O then for clansmen true, and stern claymore,
The hearts that would have given their blood like water,
   Beat heavily beyond the Atlantic roar.
     Fair these broad meads—these hoary woods are grand:
     But we are exiles from our fathers' land.

                         ANON

ARRAN

Arran of the many stags,
The sea strikes against its shoulder,
Isle in which companies are fed,
Ridge on which blue spears are reddened.

Skittish deer are on her peaks,
Delicious berries on her manes,

Cool water in her rivers,
Mast upon her dun oaks.

Greyhounds are in it and beagles,
Blackberries and sloes of the dark blackthorn,
Her dwellings close against the woods,
Deer scattered about her oak-woods.

Gleaning of purple upon her rocks,
Faultless grass upon her slopes,
Over her fair shapely crags
Noise of dappled fawns a-skipping.

Smooth is her level land, fat are her swine,
Bright are her fields,
Her nuts upon the tops of her hazel-wood,
Long galleys sailing past her.

Delightful it is when the fair season comes,
Trout under the brinks of her rivers,
Seagulls answer each other round her white cliff,
Delightful at all times is Arran!

*ANON: translated from
the Irish by* KUNO MEYER

THE IRISH DANCER

I am of Ireland,
And of the holy land
    Of Ireland.
Good sir, pray I thee,
For of saint charity,
Come and dance with me
    In Ireland.

ANON

RED HANRAHAN'S SONG ABOUT IRELAND

The old brown thorn-trees break in two high over Cummen
　　　Strand,
Under a bitter black wind that blows from the left hand;
Our courage breaks like an old tree in a black wind and dies,
But we have hidden in our hearts the flame out of the eyes
Of Cathleen, the daughter of Houlihan.

The wind has bundled up the clouds high over Knocknarea,
And thrown the thunder on the stones for all that Maeve can
　　　say.
Angers that are like noisy clouds have set our hearts abeat;
But we have all bent low and low and kissed the quiet feet
Of Cathleen, the daughter of Houlihan.

The yellow pool has overflowed high up on Clooth-na-Bare,
For the wet winds are blowing out of the clinging air;
Like heavy flooded waters our bodies and our blood;
But purer than a tall candle before the Holy Rood
Is Cathleen, the daughter of Houlihan.　　　W. B. YEATS

USK

Do not suddenly break the branch, or
Hope to find
The white hart behind the white well.
Glance aside, not for lance, do not spell
Old enchantments. Let them sleep.
'Gently dip, but not too deep',
Lift your eyes
Where the roads dip and where the roads rise
Seek only there
Where the grey light meets the green air
The hermit's chapel, the pilgrim's prayer.
　　　　　　　　　　　　T. S. ELIOT

KINGS, QUEENS AND HEROES

OZYMANDIAS

I met a traveller from an antique land
Who said: Two vast and trunkless legs of stone
Stand in the desert. . . . Near them, on the sand,
Half sunk, a shattered visage lies, whose frown,
And wrinkled lip, and sneer of cold command,
Tell that its sculptor well those passions read
Which yet survive, stamped on these lifeless things,
The hand that mocked them, and the heart that fed:
And on the pedestal these words appear:
'My name is Ozymandias, king of kings:
Look on my works, ye Mighty, and despair!'
Nothing beside remains. Round the decay
Of that colossal wreck, boundless and bare
The lone and level sands stretch far away.

P. B. SHELLEY

WHEN ALYSANDYR OUR KING WAS DEDE

When Alysandyr our King was dede
   That Scotland led in luve and le,
Away was sons of ale and brede,
   Of wine and wax, of gamyn and gle;
Our gold was changyd into lede.
   Christ born into Virginitie
Succour Scotland and remede
   That stad is in perplexytie.

ANON

le, law   *sons*, plenty   *gamyn*, sport   *stad*, stayed

A DITTY

In praise of Eliza, Queen of the Shepherds

See where she sits upon the grassy green,
    (O seemly sight!)
Yclad in Scarlet, like a maiden Queen,
    And ermines white:
Upon her head a Cremosin coronet
With Damask roses and Daffadillies set:
    Bay leaves between,
    And primroses green,
Embellish the sweet Violet.

Tell me, have ye seen her angelic face
    Like Phoebe fair?
Her heavenly haviour, her princely grace,
    Can you well compare?
The Red rose meddled with the White yfere,
In either cheek depeincten lively cheer:
    Her modest eye,
    Her Majesty,
Where have you seen the like but there?

I see Calliope speed her to the place,
    Where my Goddess shines;
And after her the other Muses trace
    With their Violins.
Be they not Bay branches which they do bear,
All for Eliza in her hand to wear?
    So sweetly they play,
    And sing all the way,
That it a heaven is to hear.

Lo, how finely the Graces can it foot,
    To the Instrument:

They dauncen deftly, and singen soot,
    In their merriment.
Wants not a fourth Grace to make the dance even?
Let that room to my Lady be given.
    She shall be a Grace,
    To fill the fourth place,
And reign with the rest in heaven.

Bring hither the Pink and purple Columbine,
    With Gilliflowers;
Bring Coronations, and Sops-in-wine
    Worn of Paramours:
Strow me the ground with Daffadowndillies,
And Cowslips, and Kingcups, and lovèd Lilies:
    The pretty Pawnce,
    And the Chevisaunce,
Shall match with the fair flower Delice.

Now rise up, Eliza, deckèd as thou art
    In royal array;
And now ye dainty Damsels may depart
    Each one her way.
I fear I have troubled your troops too long:
Let dame Eliza thank you for her song:
    And if you come hither
    When Damsons I gather,
I will part them all you among.

                              EDMUND SPENSER

ELIZABETH OF BOHEMIA

You meaner beauties of the night,
   That poorly satisfy our eyes
More by your number than your light,
   You common people of the skies;
   What are you when the moon shall rise?

You curious chanters of the wood,
   That warble forth Dame Nature's lays,
Thinking your passions understood
   By your weak accents; what's your praise
   When Philomel her voice shall raise?

You violets that first appear,
   By your pure purple mantles known
Like the proud virgins of the year,
   As if the spring were all your own;
   What are you when the rose is blown?

So, when my mistress shall be seen
   In form and beauty of her mind,
By virtue first, then choice, a Queen,
   Tell me, if she were not design'd
   Th' eclipse and glory of her kind.

                     SIR HENRY WOTTON

As I was going by Charing Cross,
I saw a black man upon a black horse;
They told me it was King Charles the First—
Oh dear, my heart was ready to burst!

                       ANON

WHEN THE KING ENJOYS HIS OWN AGAIN

What Booker can prognosticate,
    Concerning king's or kingdom's fate?
I think myself to be as wise
    As he that gazeth on the skies:
        My skill goes beyond
        The depth of a Pond,
    Or Rivers in the greatest rain;
        Whereby I can tell,
        All things will be well,
When the king enjoys his own again.

There's neither Swallow, Dove nor Dade,
    Can soar more high, nor deeper wade;
Nor show a reason from the stars,
    What causeth peace or civil wars:
        The man in the moon
        May wear out his shoon,
    By running after Charles his wain;
        But all's to no end,
        For the times will not mend,
Till the king enjoys his own again.

Though for a time we see Whitehall
    With cobwebs hanging on the wall,
Instead of silk and silver brave,
    Which formerly it used to have;
        With rich perfume
        In every room,
    Delightful to that princely train,
        Which again you shall see,
        When the time it shall be,
That the king enjoys his own again.

Full forty years the royal crown
   Hath been his father's and his own;
And is there any one but he
   That in the same should sharer be?
      For who better may
      The sceptre sway,
   Than he that hath such right to reign?
      Then let's hope for a peace,
      For the wars will not cease,
Till the king enjoys his own again.

Till then upon Ararat's hill
   My Hope shall cast her anchor still,
Until I see some peaceful dove
   Bring home the branch she dearly love:
      Then will I wait,
      Till the waters abate,
   Which now disturb my troubled brain,
      Else never rejoice,
      Till I hear the voice,
That the king enjoys his own again.

MARTIN PARKER

O'ER THE WATER TO CHARLIE

   We'll o'er the water and o'er the sea,
      We'll o'er the water to Charlie;
   Come weal, come woe, we'll gather and go,
      And live and die wi' Charlie.

Come boat me o'er, come row me o'er,
   Come boat me o'er to Charlie;
I'll gie John Ross another bawbee,
   To boat me o'er to Charlie.

I lo'e weel my Charlie's name,
   Tho' some there be abhor him;
But O, to see auld Nick gaun hame,
   And Charlie's faes before him!

I swear and vow by moon and stars,
   And sun that shines so early,
If I had twenty thousand lives,
   I'd die as aft for Charlie.

     We'll o'er the water and o'er the sea,
      We'll o'er the water to Charlie;
     Come weal, come woe, we'll gather and go,
      And live and die wi' Charlie.

ROBERT BURNS

ROBERT THE BRUCE TO HIS ARMY

I. FREEDOM

Ah! Freedom is a noble thing!
Freedom makes man to have liking:
Freedom all solace to man gives:
He lives at ease that freely lives!
A noble heart may have none ease,
Nor nothing else that may him please,
If freedom fail; for free liking
Is yearned over all other thing.
Nor he, that aye has lived free,
May not know well the property,
The anger, nor the wretched doom,
That is coupled to foul thraldom.
But if he had assayed it,
Then all perquer he should it wit;
And should think freedom more to prize
Than all the gold in world that is.

JOHN BARBOUR

perquer, by heart

II. BEFORE BANNOCKBURN

Scots, wha hae wi' Wallace bled,
Scots, wham Bruce has aften led,
Welcome to your gory bed,
    Or to victorie.

Now's the day, and now's the hour;
See the front o' battle lour!
See approach proud Edward's power—
    Chains and slaverie!

Wha will be a traitor knave?
Wha can fill a coward's grave?
Wha sae base as be a slave?
    Let him turn and flee!

Wha for Scotland's King and law
Freedom's sword will strongly draw,
Freeman stand, or freeman fa'?
    Let him follow me!

By oppressions woes and pains!
By your sons in servile chains!
We will drain our dearest veins,
    But they shall be free!

Lay the proud usurpers low!
Tyrants fall in every foe!
Liberty's in every blow!
    Let us do or die!

ROBERT BURNS

HOME-THOUGHTS, FROM THE SEA

Nobly, nobly Cape Saint Vincent to the North-west died
    away;
Sunset ran, one glorious blood-red, reeking into Cadiz Bay;
Bluish 'mid the burning water, full in face Trafalgar lay;
In the dimmest North-east distance dawned Gibraltar grand
    and gray;
'Here and here did England help me: how can I help Eng-
    land?'—say,
Whoso turns as I, this evening, turn to God to praise and
    pray,
While Jove's planet rises yonder, silent over Africa.

ROBERT BROWNING

UPON SIR FRANCIS DRAKE'S RETURN

from his Voyage about the World, and the Queen's meeting him

Sir Francis, Sir Francis, Sir Francis is come;
Sir Robert, and eke Sir William his son,
And eke the good Earl of Huntington
Marched gallantly on the road.

Then came the Lord Chamberlain with his white staff,
And all the people began to laugh;
And then the Queen began to speak,
'You're welcome home, Sir Francis Drake.'

You gallants all o' the British blood,
Why don't you sail o' the ocean flood?
I protest you're not all worth a filbert
If once compared to Sir Humphry Gilbert.

For he went out on a rainy day,
And to the new-found land found out his way,
With many a gallant both fresh and green,
And he ne'er came home again. God bless the Queen!

ANON

OF THE GREAT AND FAMOUS

Ever to be honoured Knight, Sir Francis Drake,
and of my little-little selfe

The Dragon that our Seas did raise his Crest
And brought back heapes of gold unto his nest,
Unto his Foes more terrible than Thunder,
Glory of his age, After-ages' wonder,
Excelling all those that excelled before;
It's feared we shall have none such any more;
Effecting all he sole did undertake,
Valiant, just, wise, milde, honest, Godly *Drake*.
This man when I was little I did meete
As he was walking up Totnes' long street.
He asked me whose I was? I answered him.
He asked me if his good friend were within?
A faire red Orange in his hand he had,
He gave it me whereof I was right glad,
Takes and kist me, and prayes *God blesse my boy*:
Which I record *with comfort* to this day.
Could he on me have breathèd with his breath,
His gifts, Elias-like, after his death,
Then had I beene enabled for to doe
Many brave things I have a heart unto.
I have as great desire as e'er had *hee*
To joy, annoy, friends, foes; but 'twill not be.

ROBERT HAYMAN

1805

At Viscount Nelson's lavish funeral,
 While the mob milled and yelled about the Abbey
A General chatted with an Admiral:

'One of your Colleagues, Sir, remarked today
 That Nelson's *exit*, though to be lamented,
Falls not inopportunely, in its way.'

'He was a thorn in our flesh,' came the reply—
 'The most bird-witted, unaccountable,
Odd little runt that ever I did spy.

'One arm, one peeper, vain as Pretty Poll,
 A meddler, too, in foreign politics
And gave his heart in pawn to a plain moll.

'He would dare lecture us Sea Lords, and then
 Would treat his ratings as though men of honour
And play at leap-frog with his midshipmen!

'We tried to box him down, but up he popped,
 And when he'd banged Napoleon at the Nile
Became too much the hero to be dropped.

'You've heard that Copenhagen "blind eye" story?
 We'd tied him to Nurse Parker's apron-strings—
By G–d, he snipped them through and snatched the glory!'

'Yet,' cried the General, 'six-and-twenty sail
 Captured or sunk by him off Tráfalgár—
That writes a handsome *finis* to the tale.'

'Handsome enough. The seas are England's now.
 That fellow's foibles need no longer plague us.
He died most creditably, I'll allow.'

'And, Sir, the secret of his victories?'
  'By his unServicelike, familiar ways, Sir,
He made the whole Fleet love him, damn his eyes!'

ROBERT GRAVES

NAPOLEON

'What is the world, O soldiers?
          It is I:
I, this incessant snow,
      This northern sky;
Soldiers, this solitude
      Through which we go
          Is I.'

WALTER DE LA MARE

A ST. HELENA LULLABY

'How far is St. Helena from a little child at play?'
What makes you want to wander there with all the world be-
          tween?
Oh, Mother, call your son again or else he'll run away.
(*No one thinks of winter when the grass is green!*)

'How far is St. Helena from a fight in Paris Street?'
I haven't time to answer now—the men are falling fast.
The guns begin to thunder, and the drums begin to beat.
(*If you take the first step, you will take the last!*)

'How far is St. Helena from the field of Austerlitz?'
You couldn't hear me if I told—so loud the cannons roar.
But not so far for people who are living by their wits.
(*'Gay go up' means 'Gay go down' the wide world o'er!*)

147

'How far is St. Helena from an Emperor of France?'
I cannot see—I cannot tell—the Crowns they dazzle so.
The Kings sit down to dinner, and the Queens stand up to
    dance.
(*After open weather you may look for snow!*)

'How far is St. Helena from the Cape of Trafalgar?'
A longish way—a longish way—with ten year more to run.
It's South across the water underneath a falling star.
(*What you cannot finish you must leave undone!*)

'How far is St. Helena from the Beresina ice?'
An ill way—a chill way—the ice begins to crack.
But not so far for gentlemen who never took advice.
(*When you can't go forward you must e'en come back!*)

'How far is St. Helena from the field of Waterloo?'
A near way—a clear way—the ship will take you soon.
A pleasant place for gentlemen with little left to do.
(*Morning never tries you till the afternoon!*)

'How far from St. Helena to the Gate of Heaven's Grace?'
That no one knows—that no one knows—and no one ever
    will.
But fold your hands across your heart and cover up your
    face,
And after all your trapesings, child, lie still!

RUDYARD KIPLING

O CAPTAIN! MY CAPTAIN!

O Captain! my Captain! our fearful trip is done,
The ship has weather'd every rack, the prize we sought is
      won,
The port is near, the bells I hear, the people all exulting,
While follow eyes the steady keel, the vessel grim and daring;
    But O heart! heart! heart!
      O the bleeding drops of red,
        Where on the deck my Captain lies,
        Fallen cold and dead.

O Captain! my Captain! rise up and hear the bells;
Rise up—for you the flag is flung—for you the bugle trills,
For you bouquets and ribbon'd wreaths—for you the shores
      a-crowding,
For you they call, the swaying mass, their eager faces turning;
    Here Captain! dear father!
      This arm beneath your head!
        It is some dream that on the deck,
        You've fallen cold and dead.

My Captain does not answer, his lips are pale and still,
My father does not feel my arm, he has no pulse nor will,
The ship is anchor'd safe and sound, its voyage closed and
      done,
From fearful trip the victor ship comes in with object won;
    Exult O shores, and ring O bells!
      But I with mournful tread,
        Walk the deck my Captain lies,
        Fallen cold and dead.

WALT WHITMAN

HORATIUS

Lars Porsena of Clusium
  By the Nine Gods he swore
That the great house of Tarquin
  Should suffer wrong no more.
By the Nine Gods he swore it,
  And named a trysting day,
And bade his messengers ride forth,
East and west and south and north,
  To summon his array.

East and west and south and north,
  The messengers ride fast,
And tower and town and cottage
  Have heard the trumpet's blast.
Shame on the false Etruscan
  Who lingers in his home,
When Porsena of Clusium
  Is on the march for Rome.

The horsemen and the footmen
  Are pouring in amain
From many a stately market-place;
  From many a fruitful plain;
From many a lonely hamlet,
  Which, hid by beech and pine,
Like an eagle's nest hangs on the crest
  Of purple Apennine;

From lordly Volaterrae,
  Where scowls the far-famed hold
Piled by the hands of giants
  For godlike kings of old;

From sea-girt Populonia,
　　Whose sentinels descry
Sardinia's snowy mountain-tops
　　Fringing the southern sky.

And now hath every city
　　Sent up her tale of men;
The foot are fourscore thousand,
　　The horse are thousands ten.
Before the gates of Sutrium
　　Is met the great array.
A proud man was Lars Porsena
　　Upon the trysting day.

But by the yellow Tiber
　　Was tumult and affright:
From all the spacious champaign
　　To Rome men took their flight.
A mile around the city,
　　The throng stopped up the ways;
A fearful sight it was to see
　　Through two long nights and days.

Now, from the rock Tarpeian,
　　Could the wan burghers spy
The line of blazing villages
　　Red in the midnight sky.
The Fathers of the City,
　　They sat all night and day,
For every hour some horsemen came
　　With tidings of dismay.

To eastward and to westward
　　Have spread the Tuscan bands;
Nor house, nor fence, nor dovecote
　　In Crustumerium stands.

Verbenna down to Ostia
   Hath wasted all the plain;
Astur hath stormed Janiculum,
   And the stout guards are slain.

I wis, in all the Senate,
   There was no heart so bold,
But sore it ached, and fast it beat,
   When that ill news was told.
Forthwith up rose the Consul,
   Up rose the Fathers all;
In haste they girded up their gowns,
   And hied them to the wall.

They held a council standing
   Before the River-Gate;
Short time was there, ye well may guess,
   For musing or debate.
Out spake the Consul roundly:
   'The bridge must straight go down;
For, since Janiculum is lost,
   Nought else can save the town.'

Just then a scout came flying,
   All wild with haste and fear:
'To arms! to arms! Sir Consul:
   Lars Porsena is here.'
On the low hills to westward
   The Consul fixed his eye,
And saw the swarthy storm of dust
   Rise fast along the sky.

And nearer fast and nearer
   Doth the red whirlwind come;
And louder still and still more loud,
From underneath that rolling cloud,

Is heard the trumpet's war-note proud
    The trampling and the hum.
And plainly and more plainly
    Now through the gloom appears,
Far to left and far to right,
In broken gleams of dark-blue light,
The long array of helmets bright,
    The long array of spears.

Fast by the royal standard,
    O'erlooking all the war,
Lars Porsena of Clusium
    Sat in his ivory car.
By the right wheel rode Mamilius,
    Prince of the Latian name;
And by the left false Sextus,
    That wrought the deed of shame.

But the Consul's brow was sad,
    And the Consul's speech was low,
And darkly looked he at the wall,
    And darkly at the foe.
'Their van will be upon us
    Before the bridge goes down;
And if they once may win the bridge,
    What hope to save the town?'

Then out spake brave Horatius,
    The Captain of the Gate:
'To every man upon this earth
    Death cometh soon or late.
And how can man die better
    Than facing fearful odds,
For the ashes of his fathers,
    And the temples of his Gods.

Hew down the bridge, Sir Consul,
　With all the speed ye may;
I, with two more to help me,
　Will hold the foe in play.
In yon strait path a thousand
　May well be stopped by three.
Now who will stand on either hand,
　And keep the bridge with me?'

Then out spake Spurius Lartius,
　A Ramnian proud was he:
'Lo, I will stand at thy right hand,
　And keep the bridge with thee.'
And out spake strong Herminius,
　Of Titian blood was he:
'I will abide on thy left side,
　And keep the bridge with thee.'

'Horatius,' quoth the Consul,
　'As thou sayest, so let it be.'
And straight against that great array
　Forth went the dauntless Three.
For Romans in Rome's quarrel
　Spared neither land nor gold,
Nor son nor wife, nor limb nor life,
　In the brave days of old.

Then none was for a party;
　Then all were for the state;
Then the great man helped the poor,
　And the poor man loved the great:
Then lands were fairly portioned;
　Then spoils were fairly sold;
The Romans were like brothers
　In the brave days of old.

Now while the Three were tightening
    Their harness on their backs,
The Consul was the foremost man
    To take in hand an axe:
And Fathers mixed with Commons
    Seized hatchet, bar, and crow,
And smote upon the planks above,
    And loosed the props below.

Meanwhile the Tuscan army,
    Right glorious to behold,
Came flashing back the noonday light,
Rank behind rank, like surges bright
    Of a broad sea of gold.
Four hundred trumpets sounded
    A peal of warlike glee,
As that great host, with measured tread,
And spears advanced, and ensigns spread,
Rolled slowly towards the bridge's head,
    Where stood the dauntless Three.

The Three stood calm and silent,
    And looked upon the foes,
And a great shout of laughter
    From all the vanguard rose:
And forth three chiefs came spurring
    Before that deep array;
To earth they sprang, their swords they drew,
And lifted high their shields, and flew
    To win the narrow way;

Aunus from green Tifernum,
    Lord of the Hill of Vines;
And Seius, whose eight hundred slaves
    Sicken in Ilva's mines;

And Picus, long to Clusium
   Vassal in peace and war,
Who led to fight his Umbrian powers
From that grey crag where, girt with towers,
The fortress of Nequinum lowers
   O'er the pale waves of Nar.

Stout Lartius hurled down Aunus
   Into the stream beneath:
Herminius struck at Seius,
   And clove him to the teeth:
At Picus brave Horatius
   Darted one fiery thrust;
And the proud Umbrian's gilded arms
   Clashed in the bloody dust.

(Several Etruscan heroes challenge the Three, but in their turn are laid low. Their fellow-warriors grow apprehensive.)

But all Etruria's noblest
   Felt their hearts sink to see
On the earth the bloody corpses,
   In the path the dauntless Three:
And, from the ghastly entrance
   Where those bold Romans stood,
All shrank, like boys who unaware,
Ranging the woods to start a hare,
Come to the mouth of the dark lair
Where, growling low, a fierce old bear
   Lies amidst bones and blood.

Was none who would be foremost
   To lead such dire attack:
But those behind cried 'Forward!'
   And those before cried 'Back!'

And backward now and forward
    Wavers the deep array;
And on the tossing sea of steel,
To and fro the standards reel;
And the victorious trumpet-peal
    Dies fitfully away.

But meanwhile axe and lever
    Have manfully been plied;
And now the bridge hangs tottering
    Above the boiling tide.
'Come back, come back, Horatius!'
    Loud cried the Fathers all.
'Back, Lartius! back, Herminius!
    Back, ere the ruin fall!'

Back darted Spurius Lartius;
    Herminius darted back:
And, as they passed, beneath their feet
    They felt the timbers crack.
But, when they turned their faces,
    And on the farther shore
Saw brave Horatius stand alone,
    They would have crossed once more.

But with a crash like thunder
    Fell every loosened beam,
And, like a dam, the mighty wreck
    Lay right athwart the stream:
And a long shout of triumph
    Rose from the walls of Rome,
As to the highest turret-tops
    Was splashed the yellow foam.

And, like a horse unbroken
　　When first he feels the rein,
The furious river struggled hard,
　　And tossed his tawny mane,
And burst the curb, and bounded,
　　Rejoicing to be free,
And whirling down, in fierce career,
Battlement, and plank, and pier,
　　Rushed headlong to the sea.

Alone stood brave Horatius,
　　But constant still in mind;
Thrice thirty thousand foes before,
　　And the broad flood behind.
'Down with him!' cried false Sextus,
　　With a smile on his pale face.
'Now yield thee,' cried Lars Porsena,
　　'Now yield thee to our grace.'

Round turned he, as not deigning
　　Those craven ranks to see;
Nought spake he to Lars Porsena,
　　To Sextus nought spake he;
But he saw on Palatinus
　　The white porch of his home;
And he spake to the noble river
　　That rolls by the towers of Rome.

'O Tiber! father Tiber!
　　To whom the Romans pray,
A Roman's life, a Roman's arms,
　　Take thou in charge this day!'
So he spake, and speaking sheathed
　　The good sword by his side,
And with his harness on his back,
　　Plunged headlong in the tide.

No sound of joy or sorrow
    Was heard from either bank;
But friends and foes in dumb surprise,
With parted lips and straining eyes,
    Stood gazing where he sank;
And when above the surges
    They saw his crest appear,
All Rome sent forth a rapturous cry,
And even the ranks of Tuscany
    Could scarce forbear to cheer.

But fiercely ran the current,
    Swollen high by months of rain:
And fast his blood was flowing;
    And he was sore in pain,
And heavy with his armour,
    And spent with changing blows:
And oft they thought him sinking,
    But still again he rose.

'Curse on him!' quoth false Sextus;
    'Will not the villain drown?
But for this stay, ere close of day
    We should have sacked the town!'
'Heaven help him!' quoth Lars Porsena,
    'And bring him safe to shore;
For such a gallant feat of arms
    Was never seen before.'

And now he feels the bottom;
    Now on dry earth he stands;
Now round him throng the Fathers
    To press his gory hands;

And now with shouts and clapping,
    And noise of weeping loud,
He enters through the River-Gate,
    Borne by the joyous crowd.

They gave him of the corn-land,
    That was of public right,
As much as two strong oxen
    Could plough from morn till night;
And they made a molten image,
    And set it up on high,
And there it stands unto this day
    To witness if I lie.

And still his name sounds stirring
    Unto the men of Rome,
As the trumpet-blast that cries to them
    To charge the Volscian home;
And wives still pray to Juno
    For boys with hearts as bold
As his who kept the bridge so well
    In the brave days of old.

LORD MACAULAY

THE PIED PIPER OF HAMELIN

I

Hamelin Town's in Brunswick,
    By famous Hanover city;
The river Weser, deep and wide,
Washes its wall on the southern side;
A pleasanter spot you never spied;

But, when begins my ditty,
Almost five hundred years ago,
To see the townsfolk suffer so
From vermin, was a pity.

II

Rats!
They fought the dogs and killed the cats,
    And bit the babies in the cradles,
And ate the cheeses out of the vats,
    And licked the soup from the cooks' own ladles,
Split open the kegs of salted sprats,
Made nests inside men's Sunday hats,
And even spoiled the women's chats
        By drowning their speaking
        With shrieking and squeaking
In fifty different sharps and flats.

III

At last the people in a body
    To the Town Hall came flocking:
' 'Tis clear,' cried they, 'our Mayor's a noddy;
    And as for our Corporation—shocking
To think we buy gowns lined with ermine
For dolts that can't or won't determine
What's best to rid us of our vermin!
You hope, because you're old and obese,
To find in the furry civic robe ease?
Rouse up, Sirs! Give your brains a racking
To find the remedy we're lacking,
Or, sure as fate, we'll send you packing!'
At this the Mayor and Corporation
Quaked with a mighty consternation.

IV

An hour they sat in council,
    At length the Mayor broke silence:
'For a guilder I'd my ermine gown sell,
    I wish I were a mile hence!
It's easy to bid one rack one's brain—
I'm sure my poor head aches again
I've scratched it so, and all in vain.
Oh for a trap, a trap, a trap!'
Just as he said this, what should hap
At the chamber door but a gentle tap?
'Bless us,' cried the Mayor, 'what's that?'
(With the Corporation as he sat,
Looking little though wondrous fat;
Nor brighter was his eye, nor moister
Than a too-long-opened oyster,
Save when at noon his paunch grew mutinous
For a plate of turtle green and glutinous)
'Only a scraping of shoes on the mat?
Anything like the sound of a rat
Makes my heart go pit-a-pat!'

V

'Come in!'—the Mayor cried, looking bigger:
And in did come the strangest figure!
His queer long coat from heel to head
Was half of yellow and half of red,
And he himself was tall and thin,
With sharp blue eyes, each like a pin,
And light loose hair, yet swarthy skin,
No tuft on cheek nor beard on chin,
But lips where smiles went out and in;
There was no guessing his kith and kin:
And nobody could enough admire

The tall man and his quaint attire.
Quoth one: 'It's as my great-grandsire,
Starting up at the Trump of Doom's tone,
Had walked this way from his painted tombstone!'

VI

He advanced to the council-table:
And, 'Please your honours,' said he, 'I'm able,
By means of a secret charm, to draw
    All creatures living beneath the sun,
    That creep or swim or fly or run,
After me so as you never saw!
And I chiefly use my charm
On creatures that do people harm,
The mole and toad and newt and viper;
And people call me the Pied Piper.'
(And here they noticed round his neck
    A scarf of red and yellow stripe,
To match with his coat of the self-same cheque;
    And at the scarf's end hung a pipe;
And his fingers, they noticed, were ever straying
As if impatient to be playing
Upon this pipe, as low it dangled
Over his vesture so old-fangled.)
'Yet,' said he, 'poor piper as I am,
In Tartary I freed the Cham,
    Last June, from his huge swarms of gnats;
I eased in Asia the Nizam
    Of a monstrous brood of vampyre-bats:
And as for what your brain bewilders,
    If I can rid your town of rats
Will you give me a thousand guilders?'
'One? fifty thousand!'—was the exclamation
Of the astonished Mayor and Corporation.

VII

Into the street the Piper stept,
    Smiling first a little smile,
As if he knew what magic slept
    In his quiet pipe the while;
Then, like a musical adept,
To blow the pipe his lips he wrinkled,
And green and blue his sharp eyes twinkled
Like a candle-flame where salt is sprinkled;
And ere three shrill notes the pipe uttered,
You heard as if an army muttered;
And the muttering grew to a grumbling;
And the grumbling grew to a mighty rumbling;
And out of the houses the rats came tumbling.
Great rats, small rats, lean rats, brawny rats,
Brown rats, black rats, grey rats, tawny rats,
Grave old plodders, gay young friskers,
    Fathers, mothers, uncles, cousins,
Cocking tails and pricking whiskers,
    Families by ten and dozens,
Brothers, sisters, husbands, wives—
Followed the Piper for their lives.
From street to street he piped advancing,
And step for step they followed dancing,
Until they came to the river Weser
    Wherein all plunged and perished!
—Save one who, stout as Julius Caesar,
Swam across and lived to carry
    (As he, the manuscript he cherished)
To Rat-land home his commentary:
Which was, 'At the first shrill notes of the pipe,
I heard a sound as of scraping tripe,
And putting apples, wondrous ripe,
Into a cider-press's gripe:

And a moving away of pickle-tub-boards,
And a leaving ajar of conserve-cupboards,
And a drawing the corks of train-oil-flasks,
And a breaking the hoops of butter-casks:
And it seemed as if a voice
  (Sweeter far than by harp or by psaltery
Is breathed) called out, "Oh rats, rejoice!
  The world is grown to one vast drysaltery!
So munch on, crunch on, take your nuncheon,
Breakfast, supper, dinner, luncheon!"
And just as a bulky sugar-puncheon,
All ready staved, like a great sun shone
Glorious scarce an inch before me,
Just as methought it said, "Come, bore me!"
—I found the Weser rolling o'er me.'

VIII

You should have heard the Hamelin people
Ringing the bells till they rocked the steeple.
'Go,' cried the Mayor, 'and get long poles!
Poke out the nests and block up the holes!
Consult with carpenters and builders,
And leave in our town not even a trace
Of the rats!'—when suddenly, up the face
Of the Piper perked in the market-place,
With a, 'First, if you please, my thousand guilders!'

IX

A thousand guilders! The Mayor looked blue;
So did the Corporation too.
For council dinners made rare havoc
With Claret, Moselle, Vin-de-Grave, Hock;
And half the money would replenish
Their cellar's biggest butt with Rhenish.

To pay this sum to a wandering fellow
With a gipsy coat of red and yellow!
'Beside,' quoth the Mayor with a knowing wink,
'Our business was done at the river's brink;
We saw with our eyes the vermin sink,
And what's dead can't come to life, I think.
So, friend, we're not the folks to shrink
From the duty of giving you something for drink,
And a matter of money to put in your poke;
But as for the guilders, what we spoke
Of them, as you very well know, was in joke.
Beside, our losses have made us thrifty.
A thousand guilders! Come, take fifty!'

X

The Piper's face fell, and he cried
'No trifling! I can't wait, beside!
I've promise to visit by dinner time
Bagdat, and accept the prime
Of the Head-Cook's pottage, all he's rich in,
For having left, in the Caliph's kitchen,
Of a nest of scorpions no survivor:
With him I proved no bargain-driver,
With you, don't think I'll bate a stiver!
And folks who put me in a passion
May find me pipe after another fashion.'

XI

'How?' cried the Mayor, 'd'ye think I brook
Being worse treated than a Cook?
Insulted by a lazy ribald
With idle pipe and vesture piebald?
You threaten us, fellow? Do your worst,
Blow you pipe there till you burst!'

XII

Once more he stept into the street;
   And to his lips again
   Laid his long pipe of smooth straight cane;
And ere he blew three notes (such sweet
Soft notes as yet musician's cunning
   Never gave the enraptured air)
There was a rustling that seemed like a bustling
Of merry crowds justling at pitching and hustling,
Small feet were pattering, wooden shoes clattering,
Little hands clapping and little tongues chattering,
And, like fowls in a farm-yard when barley is scattering,
Out came the children running.
All the little boys and girls,
With rosy cheeks and flaxen curls,
And sparkling eyes and teeth like pearls,
Tripping and skipping, ran merrily after
The wonderful music with shouting and laughter.

XIII

The Mayor was dumb, and the Council stood
As if they were changed into blocks of wood,
Unable to move a step, or cry
To the children merrily skipping by,
—Could only follow with the eye
That joyous crowd at the Piper's back.
But how the Mayor was on the rack,
And the wretched Council's bosoms beat,
As the Piper turned from the High Street
To where the Weser rolled its waters
Right in the way of their sons and daughters!
However, he turned from South to West,
And to Koppelberg Hill his steps addressed,
And after him the children pressed;

Great was the joy in every breast.
'He never can cross that mighty top!
He's forced to let the piping drop,
And we shall see our children stop!'
When, lo, as they reached the mountain-side,
A wondrous portal opened wide,
As if a cavern was suddenly hollowed;
And the Piper advanced and the children followed,
And when all were in to the very last,
The door in the mountain-side shut fast.
Did I say, all? No! One was lame,
   And could not dance the whole of the way;
And in after years, if you would blame
   His sadness, he was used to say,—
'It's dull in our town since my playmates left!
I can't forget that I'm bereft
Of all the pleasant sights they see,
Which the Piper also promised me.
For he led us, he said, to a joyous land,
Joining the town and just at hand,
Where waters gushed and fruit-trees grew,
And flowers put forth a fairer hue,
And everything was bright and new;
The sparrows were brighter than peacocks here,
And their dogs outran our fallow deer,
And honey-bees had lost their stings,
And horses were born with eagles' wings:
And just as I became assured
My lame foot would be speedily cured,
The music stopped and I stood still,
And found myself outside the hill,
Left alone against my will,
To go now limping as before,
And never hear of that country more!'

XIV

Alas, alas for Hamelin!
  There came into many a burgher's pate
  A text which says, that heaven's gate
  Opes to the rich at as easy rate
As the needle's eye takes a camel in!
The Mayor sent East, West, North and South,
To offer the Piper, by word of mouth,
  Wherever it was men's lot to find him,
Silver and gold to his heart's content,
If he'd only return the way he went,
  And bring the children behind him.
But when they saw 'twas a lost endeavour,
And Piper and dancers were gone for ever,
They made a decree that lawyers never
  Should think their records dated duly
If, after the day of the month and year,
These words did not as well appear,
'And so long after what happened here
  On the Twenty-second of July,
Thirteen hundred and seventy-six:'
And the better in memory to fix
The place of the children's last retreat,
They called it, the Pied Piper's Street—
Where anyone playing on pipe or tabor
Was sure for the future to lose his labour.
Nor suffered they hostelry or tavern
  To shock with mirth a street so solemn;
But opposite the place of the cavern
  They wrote the story on a column,
And on the great church-window painted
The same, to make the world acquainted
How their children were stolen away,
And there it stands to this very day.

And I must not omit to say
That in Transylvania there's a tribe
Of alien people who ascribe
The outlandish ways and dress
On which their neighbours lay such stress,
To their fathers and mothers having risen
Out of some subterraneous prison
Into which they were trepanned
Long time ago in a mighty band
Out of Hamelin town in Brunswick land,
But how or why, they don't understand.

XV

So, Willy, let me and you be wipers
Of scores out with all men—especially pipers!
And, whether they pipe us free frôm rats or frôm mice,
If we've promised them aught, let us keep our promise!

ROBERT BROWNING

SIR EGLAMOUR

Sir Eglamour, that worthy knight,
He took his sword and went to fight:
And as he rode both hill and dale,
Armèd upon his shirt of mail,
A dragon came out of his den,
Had slain, God knows how many men!

When he espied Sir Eglamour,
Oh, if you had but heard him roar,
And seen how all the trees did shake,
The knight did tremble, horse did quake,
The birds betake them all to peeping—
It would have made you fall a weeping!

But now it is in vain to fear,
Being come unto, 'fight dog! fight bear!'
To it they go and fiercely fight
A live-long day from morn till night.
The dragon had a plaguy hide,
And could the sharpest steel abide.

No sword will enter him with cuts,
Which vexed the knight unto the guts:
But, as in choler he did burn,
He watched the dragon a good turn;
And, as a yawning he did fall,
He thrust his sword in, hilts and all.

Then, like a coward, he to fly
Unto his den that was hard by;
And there he lay all night and roared.
The knight was sorry for his sword,
But, riding thence, said, 'I forsake it,
He that will fetch it, let him take it!'

SAMUEL ROWLANDS

THE *GOLDEN VANITY*

A ship I have got in the North Country
   And she goes by the name of the *Golden Vanity*,
O I fear she'll be taken by a Spanish Ga-la-lee,
   As she sails by the Low-lands low.

To the Captain then upspake the little Cabin-boy,
He said, 'What is my fee, if the galley I destroy?
The Spanish Ga-la-lee if no more it shall annoy,
   As you sail by the Low-lands low.'

'Of silver and of gold I will give to you a store;
And my pretty little daughter that dwelleth on the shore,
Of treasure and of fee as well, I'll give to thee galore,
   As we sail by the Lowlands low'.

Then they row'd him up tight in a black bull's skin,
And he held all in his hand an augur sharp and thin,
And he swam until he came to the Spanish Gal-a-lin,
   As she lay by the Low-lands low.

He bored with his augur, he bored once and twice,
And some were playing cards, and some were playing dice,
When the water flowèd in it dazzled their eyes,
   And she sank by the Low-lands low.

So the Cabin-boy did swim all to the larboard side,
Saying 'Captain! take me in, I am drifting with the tide!'
'I will shoot you! I will kill you!' the cruel Captain cried,
   'You may sink by the Low-lands low.'

Then the Cabin-boy did swim all to the starboard side,
Saying, 'Messmates, take me in, I am drifting with the tide!'
Then they laid him on the deck, and he closed his eyes and died,
   As they sailed by the Lowlands low.

They sew'd his body tight in an old cow's hide,
And they cast the gallant cabin-boy out over the ship side,
And left him without more ado to drift with the tide,
   And to sink by the Low-lands low.

ANON

THE GIPSY LADDIE

It was late in the night when the Squire came home
Enquiring for his lady.
His servant made a sure reply:
She's gone with the gipsum Davy.
   Rattle tum a gipsum gipsum
   Rattle tum a gipsum Davy.

O go catch up my milk-white steed,
The black one's not so speedy,
I'll ride all night till broad daylight,
Or overtake my lady.

He rode and he rode till he came to the town,
He rode till he came to Barley.
The tears came rolling down his cheeks,
And then he spied his lady.

It's come go back, my dearest dear,
Come go back, my honey;
It's come go back, my dearest dear,
And you never shall lack for money.

I won't go back, my dearest dear,
I won't go back, my honey;
For I wouldn't give a kiss from gipsum's lips
For you and all your money.

It's go pull off those snow-white gloves,
A-made of Spanish leather,
And give to me your lily-white hand,
And bid farewell for ever.

It's she pulled off those snow-white gloves,
A-made of Spanish leather,
And gave to him her lily-white hand,
And bade farewell for ever.

She soon ran through her gay clothing,
Her velvet shoes and stockings;
Her gold ring off her finger's gone,
And the gold plate off her bosom.

O once I had a house and land,
Feather-bed and money;
But now I've come to an old straw pad
With the gipsies dancing round me.

ANON

LITTLE BILLEE

There were three sailors of Bristol city
Who took a boat and went to sea.
But first with beef and captain's biscuits
And pickled pork they loaded she.

There was gorging Jack and guzzling Jimmy,
And the youngest he was little Billee.
Now when they got as far as the Equator
They'd nothing left but one split pea.

Says gorging Jack to guzzling Jimmy,
'I am extremely hungaree.'
To gorging Jack says guzzling Jimmy,
'We've nothing left, us must eat we.'

Says gorging Jack to guzzling Jimmy,
'With one another we shouldn't agree!
There's little Bill, he's young and tender,
We're old and tough, so let's eat he'.

'Oh! Billy, we're going to kill and eat you,
So undo the button of your chemie.'
When Bill received this information
He used his pocket handkerchie.

'First let me say my catechism,
Which my poor mammy taught to me.'
'Make haste, make haste,' says guzzling Jimmy,
While Jack pulled out his snickersnee.

So Billy went up to the main-top gallant mast,
And down he fell on his bended knee.
He scarce had come to the twelfth commandment
When up he jumps, 'There's land I see:

'Jerusalem and Madagascar,
And North and South Amerikee:
There's the British flag a-riding at anchor,
With Admiral Napier, K.C.B.'

So when they got aboard of the Admiral's,
He hanged fat Jack and flogged Jimmee;
But as for little Bill he made him
The Captain of a Seventy-three.

W. M. THACKERAY

ETIQUETTE

The *Ballyshannon* foundered off the coast of Cariboo,
And down in fathoms many went the captain and the crew;
Down went the owners—greedy men whom hope of gain
    allured:
Oh, dry the starting tear, for they were heavily insured.

Besides the captain and the mate, the owners and the crew,
The passengers were also drowned excepting only two:
Young Peter Gray, who tasted teas for Baker, Croop, and
      Co.,
And Somers, who from Eastern shores imported indigo.

These passengers, by reason of their clinging to a mast,
Upon a desert island were eventually cast.
They hunted for their meals, as Alexander Selkirk used,
But they could not chat together—they had not been intro-
      duced.

For Peter Gray, and Somers too, though certainly in trade,
Were properly particular about the friends they made;
And somehow thus they settled it without a word of
      mouth—
That Gray should take the northern half, while Somers took
      the south.

On Peter's portion oysters grew—a delicacy rare,
But oysters were a delicacy Peter couldn't bear.
On Somers' side was turtle, on the shingle lying thick,
Which Somers couldn't eat, because it always made him sick.

Gray gnashed his teeth with envy as he saw a mighty store
Of turtle unmolested on his fellow-creature's shore,
The oysters at his feet aside impatiently he shoved,
For turtle and his mother were the only things he loved.

And Somers sighed in sorrow as he settled in the south,
For the thought of Peter's oysters brought the water to his
      mouth.
He longed to lay him down upon the shelly bed, and stuff:
He had often eaten oysters, but had never had enough.

How they wished an introduction to each other they had had
When on board the *Ballyshannon*! And it drove them nearly
    mad
To think how very friendly with each other they might get,
If it wasn't for the arbitrary rule of etiquette!

One day, when out a-hunting for the *mus ridiculus*,
Gray overheard his fellow-man soliloquizing thus:
'I wonder how the playmates of my youth are getting on,
'M'Connell, S. B. Walters, Paddy Byles, and Robinson?'

These simple words made Peter as delighted as could be,
Old Chummies at the Charterhouse were Robinson and he!
He walked straight up to Somers, then he turned extremely
    red,
Hesitated, hummed and hawed a bit, then cleared his throat
    and said:

'I beg your pardon—pray forgive me if I seem too bold,
But you have breathed a name I knew familiarly of old.
You spoke aloud of Robinson—I happened to be by—
You know him?' 'Yes, extremely well.' 'Allow me—so do I.

It was enough: they felt they could more sociably get on.
For (ah, the magic of the fact!) they each knew Robinson!
And Mr. Somers' turtle was at Peter's service quite,
And Mr. Somers punished Peter's oyster-beds all night.

They soon became like brothers from community of wrongs;
They wrote each other little odes and sang each other songs;
They told each other anecdotes disparaging their wives;
On several occasions, too, they saved each other's lives.

They felt quite melancholy when they parted for the night,
And got up in the morning soon as ever it was light:
Each other's pleasant company they so relied upon,
And all because it happened that they both knew Robinson!

They lived for many years on that inhospitable shore,
And day by day they learned to love each other more and
     more.
At last, to their astonishment, on getting up one day,
They saw a vessel anchored in the offing of the bay!

To Peter an idea occurred. 'Suppose we cross the main?
So good an opportunity may not occur again.'
And Somers thought a minute, then ejaculated, 'Done!
I wonder how my business in the City's getting on?'

'But stay,' said Mr. Peters: 'when in England, as you know,
I earned a living tasting teas for Baker, Croop, and Co.
I may be superseded, my employers think me dead!'
'Then come with me,' said Somers, 'and taste indigo instead.'

But all their plans were scattered in a moment when they
     found
The vessel was a convict ship from Portland, outward
     bound!
When a boat came off to fetch them, though they felt it very
     kind,
To go on board they firmly but respectfully declined.

As both the happy settlers roared with laughter at the joke,
They recognized an unattractive fellow pulling stroke;
'Twas Robinson—a convict, in an unbecoming frock!
Condemned to seven years for misappropriating stock!!!

They laughed no more, for Somers thought he had been
     rather rash
In knowing one whose friend had misappropriated cash;
And Peter thought a foolish tack he must have gone upon,
In making the acquaintance of a friend of Robinson.

At first they didn't quarrel very openly, I've heard;
They nodded when they met, and now and then exchanged a
      word:
The word grew rare, and rarer still the nodding of the head,
And when they meet each other now, they cut each other dead.

To allocate the island they agreed by word of mouth,
And Peter takes the north again, and Somers takes the south:
And Peter has the oysters, which he loathes with horror grim,
And Somers has the turtle—turtle disagrees with him.

Sir W. S. Gilbert

THE YARN OF THE *NANCY BELL*

'Twas on the shores that round our coast
    From Deal to Ramsgate span,
That I found alone on a piece of stone
    An elderly naval man.

His hair was weedy, his beard was long,
    And weedy and long was he,
And I heard this wight on the shore recite,
    In a singular minor key:

'Oh, I am a cook and a captain bold,
    And the mate of the *Nancy* brig,
And a bo'sun tight, and a midshipmite,
    And the crew of the captain's gig.'

And he shook his fists and he tore his hair,
    Till I really felt afraid,
For I couldn't help thinking the man had been drinking,
    And so I simply said:

'Oh, elderly man, it's little I know
   Of the duties of men of the sea,
And I'll eat my hand if I understand
   How you can possibly be

'At once a cook, and a captain bold,
   And the mate of the *Nancy* brig,
And a bo'sun tight, and a midshipmite,
   And the crew of the captain's gig.'

Then he gave a hitch to his trousers, which
   Is a trick all seamen larn,
And having got rid of a thumping quid,
   He spun this painful yarn:

' 'Twas in the good ship *Nancy Bell*
   That we sailed to the Indian sea
And there on a reef we come to grief,
   Which has often occurred to me.

'And pretty nigh all o' the crew was drowned
   (There was seventy-seven o' soul),
And only ten of the *Nancy's* men
   Said "Here!" to the muster-roll.

'There was me and the cook and the captain bold,
   And the mate of the *Nancy* brig,
And the bo'sun tight, and a midshipmite,
   And the crew of the captain's gig.

'For a month we'd neither wittles nor drink,
   Till a-hungry we did feel,
So we drawed a lot, and accordin' shot
   The captain for our meal.

'The next lot fell to the *Nancy's* mate,
   And a delicate dish he made;
Then our appetite with the midshipmite
   We seven survivors stayed.

'And then we murdered the bo'sun tight,
   And he much resembled pig;
Then we wittled free, did the cook and me,
   On the crew of the captain's gig.

'Then only the cook and me was left,
   And the delicate question, 'Which
Of us two goes to the kettle?' arose,
   And we argued it out as sich.

'For I loved that cook as a brother, I did,
   And the cook he worshipped me;
But we'd both be blowed if we'd either be stowed
   In the other chap's hold, you see.

' "I'll be eat if you dines off me," says Tom,
   "Yes, that," says I, "you'll be,"—
"I'm boiled if I die, my friend," quoth I,
   And "Exactly so," quoth he.

'Says he, "Dear James, to murder me
   Were a foolish thing to do,
For don't you see that you can't cook *me*,
   While I can—and will—cook *you*!"

'So he boils the water, and takes the salt
   And the pepper in portions true
(Which he never forgot), and some chopped shalot,
   And some sage and parsley too.

' "Come here," says he, with a proper pride,
  Which his smiling features tell,
" 'Twill soothing be if I let you see
  How extremely nice you'll smell."

'And he stirred it round and round and round,
  And he sniffed at the foaming froth;
When I ups with his heels, and smothers his squeals
  In the scum of the boiling broth.

'And I eat that cook in a week or less,
  And—as I eating be
The last of his chops, why, I almost drops,
  For a wessel in sight I see!

        *   *   *   *

'And I never larf, and I never smile,
  And I never lark nor play,
But I sit and croak, and a single joke
  I have—which is to say:

'Oh, I am a cook and a captain bold,
  And the mate of the *Nancy* brig,
And a bosun tight, *and* a midshipmite,
  And the crew of the captain's gig!'

Sir W. S. Gilbert

GROWLTIGER'S LAST STAND

Growltiger was a Bravo Cat, who lived upon a barge:
In fact he was the roughest cat that ever roamed at large.
From Gravesend up to Oxford he pursued his evil aims,
Rejoicing in his title of 'The Terror of the Thames'.

His manners and appearance did not calculate to please;
His coat was torn and seedy, he was baggy at the knees;
One ear was somewhat missing, no need to tell you why,
And he scowled upon a hostile world from one forbidding
      eye.

The cottagers of Rotherhithe knew something of his fame,
At Hammersmith and Putney people shuddered at his name.
They would fortify the hen-house, lock up the silly goose,
When the rumour ran along the shore: GROWLTIGER'S ON
      THE LOOSE!

Woe to the weak canary, that fluttered from its cage;
Woe to the pampered Pekinese, that faced Growltiger's rage.
Woe to the bristly Bandicoot, that lurks on foreign ships,
And woe to any Cat with whom Growltiger came to grips!

But most to Cats of foreign race his hatred had been vowed;
To Cats of foreign name and race no quarter was allowed.
The Persian and the Siamese regarded him with fear—
Because it was a Siamese had mauled his missing ear.

Now on a peaceful summer night, all nature seemed at play,
The tender moon was shining bright, the barge at Molesey
      lay.
All in the balmy moonlight it lay rocking on the tide—
And Growltiger was disposed to show his sentimental side.

His bucko mate, GRUMBUSKIN, long since had disappeared,
For to the Bell at Hampton he had gone to wet his beard;
And his bosun, TUMBLEBRUTUS, he too had stol'n away—
In the yard behind the Lion he was prowling for his prey.

In the forepeak of the vessel Growltiger sate alone,
Concentrating his attention on the Lady GRIDDLEBONE.

And his raffish crew were sleeping in their barrels and their
       bunks—
As the Siamese came creeping in their sampans and their
       junks.

Growltiger had no eye or ear for aught but Griddlebone,
And the Lady seemed enraptured by his manly baritone,
Disposed to relaxation, and awaiting no surprise—
But the moonlight shone reflected from a thousand bright
       blue eyes.

And closer still and closer the sampans circled round,
And yet from all the enemy there was not heard a sound.
The lovers sang their last duet, in danger of their lives—
For the foe was armed with toasting forks and cruel carving
       knives.

Then GILBERT gave the signal to his fierce Mongolian horde;
With a frightful burst of fireworks the Chinks they swarmed
       aboard.
Abandoning their sampans and their pullaways and junks,
They battened down the hatches on the crew within their
       bunks.

Then Griddlebone she gave a screech, for she was badly
       skeered;
I am sorry to admit it, but she quickly disappeared.
She probably escaped with ease, I'm sure she was not
       drowned—
But a serried ring of flashing steel Growltiger did surround.

The ruthless foe pressed forward, in stubborn rank on rank;
Growltiger to his vast surprise was forced to walk the plank.
He who a hundred victims had driven to that drop,
At the end of all his crimes was forced to go ker-flip, ker-flop.

Oh there was joy in Wapping when the news flew through
      the land;
At Maidenhead and Henley there was dancing on the strand.
Rats were roasted whole at Brentford, and at Victoria Dock,
And a day of celebration was commanded in Bangkok.

T. S. ELIOT

MAGIC

Reason has moons, but moons not hers,
  Lie mirror'd on her sea,
Confounding her astronomers,
  But, O! delighting me.

RALPH HODGSON

TOM O' BEDLAM

The moon's my constant mistress,
  And the lovely owl my marrow;
    The flaming drake,
    And the night-crow, make
  Me music to my sorrow.

I know more than Apollo;
  For oft, when he lies sleeping,
    I behold the stars
    At mortal wars,
  And the rounded welkin weeping.

The moon embraces her shepherd,
  And the Queen of Love her warrior;
    While the first does horn
    The stars of the morn,
  And the next the heavenly farrier.

With a heart of furious fancies,
  Whereof I am commander:
    With a burning spear,
    And a horse of air,
  To the wilderness I wander;

Magic

With a knight of ghosts and shadows,
　I summoned am to Tourney:
　　Ten leagues beyond
　　The wide world's end;
　Methinks it is no journey.

ANON

ELDORADO

　　Gaily bedight,
　　A gallant knight,
In sunshine and in shadow,
　　Had journeyed long,
　　Singing a song,
In search of Eldorado.

　　But he grew old—
　　This knight so bold—
And o'er his heart a shadow
　　Fell, as he found
　　No spot of ground
That looked like Eldorado.

　　And, as his strength
　　Failed him at length,
He met a pilgrim shadow—
　　'Shadow,' said he,
　　'Where can it be—
This land of Eldorado?'

　　'Over the Mountains
　　Of the Moon,
Down the Valley of the Shadow,
　　Ride, boldly ride,'
　　The shade replied,
'If you seek for Eldorado!'

EDGAR ALLAN POE

I'LL SAIL UPON THE DOG-STAR

I'll sail upon the Dog-star,
And then pursue the morning;
I'll chase the Moon till it be noon,
But I'll make her leave her horning.

I'll climb the frosty mountain,
And there I'll coin the weather;
I'll tear the rainbow from the sky
And tie both ends together.

The stars pluck from their orbs too,
And crowd them in my budget;
And whether I'm a roaring boy,
Let all the nation judge it.

THOMAS DURFEY

THREE MEN OF GOTHAM

Seamen three! What men be ye?
Gotham's three wise men we be.
Whither in your bowl so free?
To rake the moon from out the sea.
The bowl goes trim. The moon doth shine.
And our ballast is old wine.—
And your ballast is old wine.

Who art thou, so fast adrift?
I am he they call Old Care.
Here on board we will thee lift.
No: I may not enter there.
Wherefore so? 'Tis Jove's decree,
In a bowl Care may not be.—
In a bowl Care may not be.

Fear ye not the waves that roll?
No: in charmèd bowl we swim.
What the charm that floats the bowl?
Water may not pass the brim.
The bowl goes trim. The moon doth shine
And our ballast is old wine.—
And your ballast is old wine.

THOMAS LOVE PEACOCK

O BLEST UNFABLED INCENSE TREE

O blest unfabled Incense Tree,
That burns in glorious Araby,
With red scent chalicing the air,
Till earth-life grow Elysian there!

Half buried to her flaming breast
In this bright tree, she makes her nest,
Hundred-sunned Phoenix! when she must
Crumble at length to hoary dust!

Her gorgeous death-bed! her rich pyre
Burnt up with aromatic fire!
Her urn, sight-high from spoiler men!
Her birthplace when self-born again!

The mountainless green wilds among,
Here ends she her unechoing song!
With amber tears and odorous sighs
Mourned by the desert where she dies!

GEORGE DARLEY

THE RAVEN

Once upon a midnight dreary, while I pondered, weak and
      weary,
Over many a quaint and curious volume of forgotten lore—
While I nodded, nearly napping, suddenly there came a
      tapping,
As of some one gently rapping, rapping at my chamber door.
  'Tis some visitor,' I muttered, 'tapping at my chamber
     door—
      Only this and nothing more.'

Ah, distinctly I remember it was in the bleak December;
And each separate dying ember wrought its ghost upon the
      floor.
Eagerly I wished the morrow;—vainly I had sought to bor-
      row
From my books surcease of sorrow—sorrow for the lost
      Lenore—
For the rare and radiant maiden whom the angels name
      Lenore—
      Nameless *here* for evermore.

And the silken, sad, uncertain rustling of each purple curtain
Thrilled me—filled me with fantastic terrors never felt before;
So that now, to still the beating of my heart, I stood repeat-
      ing
' 'Tis some visitor entreating entrance at my chamber door—
Some late visitor entreating entrance at my chamber door;—
      This it is and nothing more.'

Presently my soul grew stronger; hesitating then no longer,
'Sir,' said I, 'or Madam, truly your forgiveness I implore;
But the fact is I was napping, and so gently you came rap-
      ping,

Magic

And so faintly you came tapping, tapping at my chamber
      door,
That I scarce was sure I heard you'—here I opened wide the
      door;
Darkness there and nothing more.

Deep into that darkness peering, long I stood there wonder-
      ing, fearing,
Doubting, dreaming dreams no mortal ever dared to dream
      before;
But the silence was unbroken, and the stillness gave no token,
And the only word there spoken was the whispered word,
      'Lenore!'
This I whispered, and an echo murmured back the word
      'Lenore!'
      Merely this and nothing more.

Back into the chamber turning, all my soul within me burn-
      ing,
Soon again I heard a tapping somewhat louder than before.
'Surely,' said I, 'surely that is something at my window
      lattice;
Let me see, then, what thereat is, and this mystery explore—
Let my heart be still a moment and this mystery explore;—
      'Tis the wind and nothing more!'

Open here I flung the shutter, when, with many a flirt and
      flutter
In there stepped a stately Raven of the saintly days of yore.
Not the least obeisance made he; not a minute stopped or
      stayed he;
But, with mien of lord or lady, perched above my chamber
      door—
Perched upon a bust of Pallas just above my chamber door—
      Perched, and sat, and nothing more.

Then this ebony bird beguiling my sad fancy into smiling,
By the grave and stern decorum of the countenance it wore,
'Though thy crest be shorn and shaven, thou,' I said, 'art
      sure no craven,
Ghastly grim and ancient Raven wandering from the Nightly
      shore—
Tell me what thy lordly name is on the Night's Plutonian
      shore!'
      Quoth the Raven, 'Nevermore.'

Much I marvelled this ungainly fowl to hear discourse so
      plainly,
Though its answer little meaning—little relevancy bore;
For we cannot help agreeing that no living human being
Ever yet was blessed with seeing bird above his chamber
      door—
Bird or beast upon the sculptured bust above his chamber
      door,
      With such name as 'Nevermore.'

But the Raven, sitting lonely on the placid bust, spoke only
That one word, as if his soul in that one word he did outpour.
Nothing farther then he uttered—not a feather then he
      fluttered—
Till I scarcely more than muttered 'Other friends have flown
      before—
On the morrow *he* will leave me, as my hopes have flown be-
      fore.'
      Then the bird said 'Nevermore.'

Startled at the stillness broken by reply so aptly spoken,
'Doubtless,' said I, 'what it utters is its only stock and
      store
Caught from some unhappy master whom unmerciful Disas-
      ter

Followed fast and followed faster till his songs one burden
       bore—
Till the dirges of his Hope that melancholy burden bore
       Of "Never—nevermore".'

But the Raven still beguiling all my fancy into smiling,
Straight I wheeled a cushioned seat in front of bird, and bust
       and door;
Then, upon the velvet sinking, I betook myself to linking
Fancy unto fancy, thinking what this ominous bird of yore—
What this grim, ungainly, ghastly, gaunt and ominous bird
       of yore
       Meant in croaking 'Nevermore'.

This I sat engaged in guessing, but no syllable expressing
To the fowl whose fiery eyes now burned into my bosom's
       core;
This and more I sat divining, with my head at ease reclining
On the cushion's velvet lining that the lamp-light gloated
       o'er,
But whose velvet violet lining with the lamp-light gloating
       o'er,
       She shall press, ah, nevermore!

Then, methought, the air grew denser, perfumed from an
       unseen censer
Swung by Seraphim whose foot-falls tinkled on the tufted
       floor.
'Wretch,' I cried, 'thy God hath lent thee—by these angels
       he hath sent thee
Respite—respite and nepenthe from thy memories of
       Lenore;
Quaff, oh quaff this kind nepenthe and forget this lost
       Lenore!'
       Quoth the Raven 'Nevermore.'

'Prophet!' said I, 'thing of evil! prophet still, if bird or
      devil!—
Whether Tempter sent, or whether tempest tossed thee here
      ashore,
Desolate yet all undaunted, on this desert land enchanted—
On this home by Horror haunted—tell me truly, I implore—
Is there—*is* there balm in Gilead?—tell me—tell me, I im-
      plore!'
      Quoth the Raven 'Nevermore',

'Prophet!' said I, 'thing of evil!—prophet still, if bird or
      devil!
By that Heaven that bends above us—by that God we both
      adore—
Tell this soul with sorrow laden if, within the distant Aidenn,
It shall clasp a sainted maiden whom the angels name
         Lenore—
Clasp a rare and radiant maiden whom the angels name
         Lenore.'
      Quoth the Raven 'Nevermore'.

'Be that word our sign of parting, bird or fiend!' I shrieked,
      up-starting—
'Get thee back into the tempest and the Night's Plutonian
      shore!
Leave no black plume as a token of that lie thy soul hath
      spoken!
Leave my loneliness unbroken!—quit the bust above my
      door!
Take thy beak from out my heart, and take thy form from off
      my door!'
      Quoth the Raven 'Nevermore'.

And the Raven, never flitting, still is sitting, *still* is sitting
On the pallid bust of Pallas just above my chamber door;

And his eyes have all the seeming of a demon's that is dream-
ing,
And the lamp-light o'er him streaming throws his shadow on
the floor;
And my soul from out that shadow that lies floating on the
floor
Shall be lifted—nevermore!

EDGAR ALLAN POE

THE STRANGE VISITOR

A wife was sitting at her reel ae night;
And aye she sat, and aye she reeled, and aye she wished for
company.

In came a pair o' braid braid soles, and sat down at the fire-
side;
And aye she sat, and aye she reeled, and aye she wished for
company.

In came a pair o' sma' legs, and sat down on the braid braid
soles;
And aye she sat, and aye she reeled, and aye she wished for
company.

In came a pair o' muckle muckle knees, and sat down on the
sma' sma' legs;
And aye she sat, and aye she reeled, and aye she wished for
company.

In came a pair o' sma' sma' thees, and sat down on the
muckle muckle knees;
And aye she sat, and aye she reeled, and aye she wished for
company.

In came a pair o' muckle muckle hips, and sat down on the
sma' sma' thees;
    And aye she sat, and aye she reeled, and aye she wished for
company.

In came a sma' sma' waist, and sat down on the muckle
muckle hips;
    And aye she sat, and aye she reeled, and aye she wished for
company.

In came a pair o' braid braid shouthers, and sat down on the
sma' sma' waist;
    And aye she sat, and aye she reeled, and aye she wished for
company.

In came a pair o' sma' sma' arms, and sat down on the braid
braid shouthers;
    And aye she sat, and aye she reeled, and aye she wished for
company.

In came a pair o' muckle muckle hands, and sat down on the
sma' sma' arms;
    And aye she sat, and aye she reeled, and aye she wished for
company.

In came a sma' sma' neck, and sat down on the braid braid
shouthers;
    And aye she sat, and aye she reeled, and aye she wished for
company.

In came a great big head, and sat down on the sma' sma'
neck;
    And aye she sat, and aye she reeled, and aye she wished for
company.

'What way hae ye sic braid braid feet?' quo' the wife.
'Muckle ganging, muckle ganging.'
'What way hae ye sic sma' sma' legs?'
'*Aih–h–h!*—late—and *wee–e–e* moul.'
'What way hae ye sic muckle muckle knees?'
'Muckle praying, muckle praying.'
'What way hae ye sic sma' sma' thees?'
'*Aih–h–h!*—late—and *wee–e–e* moul.'
'What way hae ye sic big big hips?'
'Muckle sitting, muckle sitting.'
'What way hae ye sic a sma' sma' waist?'
'*Aih–h–h!*—late—and *wee–e–e* moul.'
'What way hae ye sic braid braid shouthers?'
'Wi' carrying broom, wi' carrying broom.'
'What way hae ye sic sma' sma' arms?'
'*Aih–h–h!*—late—and *wee–e–e* moul.'
'What way hae ye sic muckle muckle hands?'
'Threshing wi' an iron flail, threshing wi' an iron flail.'
'What way hae ye sic a sma' sma' neck?'
'*Aih–h–h!*—late—and *wee–e–e* moul.'
'What way hae ye sic a muckle muckle head?'
'Muckle wit, muckle wit.'
'What do you come for?'
'For YOU!'

ANON

JOHN BARLEYCORN

There was three Kings into the east,
    Three Kings both great and high,
And they hae sworn a solemn oath
    John Barleycorn should die.

Magic

They took a plough and plough'd him down,
    Put clods upon his head,
And they hae sworn a solemn oath
    John Barleycorn was dead.

But the cheerfu' Spring came kindly on,
    And show'rs began to fall;
John Barleycorn got up again,
    And sore surpris'd them all.

The sultry suns of Summer came,
    And he grew thick and strong,
His head weel arm'd wi' pointed spears,
    That no one should him wrong.

The sober Autumn enter'd mild,
    When he grew wan and pale;
His bending joints and drooping head
    Show'd he began to fail.

His colour sicken'd more and more,
    He faded into age;
And then his enemies began
    To shew their deadly rage.

They've ta'en a weapon, long and sharp,
    And cut him by the knee;
Then tied him fast upon a cart,
    Like a rogue for forgerie.

They laid him down upon his back,
    And cudgell'd him full-sore;
They hung him up before the storm,
    And turn'd him o'er and o'er.

They fillèd up a darksome pit
    With water to the brim,
They heavèd in John Barleycorn,
    There let him sink or swim.

They laid him out upon the floor,
    To work him farther woe,
And still, as signs of life appear'd,
    They toss'd him to and fro.

They wasted, o'er a scorching flame,
    The marrow of his bones;
But a miller us'd him worst of all,
    For he crush'd him between two stones.

And they hae ta'en his very heart's blood,
    And drank it round and round;
And still the more and more they drank,
    Their joy did more abound.

John Barleycorn was a hero bold,
    Of noble enterprise,
For if you do but taste his blood,
    'Twill make your courage rise;

'Twill make a man forget his woe;
    'Twill heighten all his joy:
'Twill make the widow's heart to sing,
    Tho' the tear were in her eye.

Then let us toast John Barleycorn,
    Each man a glass in hand;
And may his great posterity
    Ne'er fail in old Scotland!

ROBERT BURNS

THE CRYSTAL CABINET

The Maiden caught me in the Wild,
Where I was dancing merrily;
She put me into her Cabinet
And Lock'd me up with a golden Key.

This Cabinet is form'd of Gold
And Pearl & Crystal shining bright,
And within it opens into a World
And a little lovely Moony Night.

Another England there I saw,
Another London with its Tower,
Another Thames & other Hills,
And another pleasant Surrey Bower,

Another Maiden like herself,
Translucent, lovely, shining clear,
Threefold each in the other clos'd—
O, what a pleasant trembling fear!

O, what a smile! a threefold Smile
Fill'd me, that like a flame I burn'd;
I bent to Kiss the lovely Maid,
And found a Threefold Kiss return'd.

I strove to seize the inmost Form
With ardor fierce & hands of flame,
But burst the Crystal Cabinet,
And like a Weeping Babe became—

A weeping Babe upon the wild,
And Weeping Woman pale reclin'd,
And in the outward air again
I fill'd with woes the passing Wind.

WILLIAM BLAKE

KUBLA KHAN

In Xanadu did Kubla Khan
A stately pleasure-dome decree:
Where Alph, the sacred river, ran
Through caverns measureless to man
   Down to a sunless sea.
So twice five miles of fertile ground
With walls and towers were girdled round:
And there were gardens bright with sinuous rills,
Where blossomed many an incense-bearing tree;
And here were forests ancient as the hills,
Enfolding sunny spots of greenery.

But oh! that deep romantic chasm which slanted
Down the green hill athwart a cedarn cover!
A savage place! as holy and enchanted
As e'er beneath a waning moon was haunted
By woman wailing for her demon-lover!
And from this chasm, with ceaseless turmoil seething,
As if this earth in fast thick pants were breathing,
A mighty fountain momently was forced:
Amid whose swift half-intermitted burst
Huge fragments vaulted like rebounding hail,
Or chaffy grain beneath the thresher's flail:
And 'mid these dancing rocks at once and ever
It flung up momently the sacred river.
Five miles meandering with a mazy motion
Through wood and dale the sacred river ran,
Then reached the caverns measureless to man,
And sank in tumult to a lifeless ocean:
And 'mid this tumult Kubla heard from far
Ancestral voices prophesying war!

  The shadow of the dome of pleasure
  Floated midway on the waves;

Where was heard the mingled measure
From the fountain and the caves.
It was a miracle of rare device,
A sunny pleasure-dome with caves of ice!

A damsel with a dulcimer
In a vision once I saw:
It was an Abyssinian maid,
And on her dulcimer she played,
Singing of Mount Abora.
Could I revive within me
Her symphony and song,
To such a deep delight 'twould win me,
That with music loud and long,
I would build that dome in air,
That sunny dome! those caves of ice!
And all who heard should see them there,
And all should cry, Beware! Beware!
His flashing eyes, his floating hair!
Weave a circle round him thrice,
And close your eyes with holy dread,
For he on honey-dew hath fed,
And drunk the milk of Paradise.

S. T. COLERIDGE

LA BELLE DAME SANS MERCI

O, what can ail thee, Knight-at-arms,
Alone and palely loitering;
The sedge is wither'd from the lake,
And no birds sing.

O, what can ail thee, Knight-at-arms,
So haggard and so woe-begone?

Magic

The squirrel's granary is full,
    And the harvest's done.

I see a lily on thy brow
    With anguish moist and fever dew;
And on thy cheek a fading rose
    Fast withereth too.

I met a lady in the meads
    Full beautiful, a faery's child;
Her hair was long, her foot was light,
    And her eyes were wild.

I made a garland for her head,
    And bracelets too, and fragrant zone;
She look'd at me as she did love,
    And made sweet moan.

I set her on my pacing steed,
    And nothing else saw all day long,
For sidelong would she bend, and sing
    A faery's song.

She found me roots of relish sweet,
    And honey wild, and manna dew;
And sure in language strange she said,
    I love thee true.

She took me to her elfin grot,
    And there she wept, and sigh'd full sore,
And there I shut her wild, wild eyes—
    With kisses four.

And there she lullèd me asleep,
    And there I dream'd, ah woe betide,

The latest dream I ever dream'd
   On the cold hill's side.

I saw pale kings, and princes too,
   Pale warriors, death-pale were they all;
Who cry'd—'La belle Dame sans Merci
   Hath thee in thrall!'

I saw their starv'd lips in the gloam
   With horrid warning gapèd wide,
And I awoke, and found me here
   On the cold hill's side.

And this is why I sojourn here
   Alone and palely loitering,
Though the sedge is wither'd from the lake,
   And no birds sing.

JOHN KEATS

WHO GOES WITH FERGUS?

Who will go drive with Fergus now,
And pierce the deep wood's woven shade,
And dance upon the level shore?
Young man, lift up your russet brow,
And lift your tender eyelids, maid,
And brood on hopes and fear no more.

And no more turn aside and brood
Upon love's bitter mystery;
For Fergus rules the brazen cars,
And rules the shadows of the wood,
And the white breast of the dim sea
And all dishevelled wandering stars.

W. B. YEATS

FAIRIES, NYMPHS AND GODS

THE FAIRIES' FAREWELL

Farewell rewards and Fairies,
    Good housewives now may say,
For now foul sluts in Dairies
    Do fare as well as they.
And though they sweep their hearths no less
    Than maids were wont to do,
Yet who of late for cleanliness,
    Finds Sixpence in her shoe?

Lament, lament, old Abbeys,
    The Fairies lost command;
They did but change Priest's babies,
    But some have chang'd your land:
And all your children stol'n from thence
    Are now grown puritans;
Who live as changelings ever since
    For love of your demains.

At morning and at evening both
    You merry were and glad,
So little care of sleep and sloth
    These pretty Ladies had;
When Tom cam home from labour,
    Or Ciss to milking rose,
Then merrily merrily went their Tabor,
    And nimbly went their Toes.

Witness those rings and roundelayes
    Of theirs, which yet remain,

Were footed in Queen Mary's days
    On many a grassy plain;
But since of late, Elizabeth
    And later James came in,
They never danced on any heath
    As when the time hath been.

BISHOP RICHARD CORBET

ROBIN GOOD-FELLOW

From Oberon in fairyland,
    The king of ghosts and shadows there,
Mad Robin I, at his command,
    Am sent to view the night sports here.
        What revel rout
        Is kept about,
    In every corner where I go,
        I will o'ersee
        And merry be
    And make good sport, with ho, ho, ho!

More swift than lightning can I fly
    About the airy welkin soon,
And in a minute's space descry
    Each thing that's done below the moon.
        There's not a hag
        Or ghost shall wag,
    Cry, ware goblins, where I go;
        But Robin I
        Their seats will spy,
    And send them home, with ho, ho, ho!

Where'er such wanderers I meet,
    As from their night sports they trudge home

With counterfeiting voice I greet
   And call them on with me to roam
      Through woods, through brakes,
      Through bogs, through lakes,
   Or else unseen with them I go,
      And in the nick
      To play some trick,
   And frolic it, with ho, ho, ho!

Sometimes I meet them like a man;
   Sometimes an ox, sometimes a hound;
And to a horse I turn me can,
   To trip and trot about them round.
      But if to ride,
      My back they stride,
   More swift than wind away I go,
      O'er hedge and lands,
      Through pools and ponds
   I whirry, laughing, ho, ho, ho!

When lazy queans have nought to do;
   But study how to cog and lie;
To make debate and mischief too
   'Twixt one another secretly:
      I mark their glose
      And it disclose
To them whom they have wronged so;
      When I have done
      I get me gone,
   And leave them scolding, ho, ho, ho!

When men do traps and engines set
   In loop-holes where the vermin creep,
Who from their folds and houses get
   Their ducks and geese and lambs asleep:

    I spy the gin,
    And enter in,
And seem a vermin taken so.
    But when they there
    Approach me near,
I leap out laughing, ho, ho, ho!

By wells and rills in meadows green,
    We nightly dance our heydeguise,
And to our fairy king and queen
    We chant our moonlight harmonies.
    When larks gin sing,
    Away we fling,
And babes new-born steal as we go;
    An elf in bed
    We leave instead,
And wend us laughing, ho, ho, ho!

From hag-bred Merlin's time have I
    Thus nightly revelled to and fro,
And for my pranks men call me by
    The name of Robin Good-fellow.
    Fiends, ghosts and sprites,
    Who haunt the nights,
The hags and goblins do me know;
    And beldames old
    My feats have told,
So *vale, vale*; ho, ho, ho!

ANON

THE FAIRIES

Up the airy mountain,
　Down the rushy glen,
We daren't go a-hunting
　For fear of little men;
Wee folk, good folk,
　Trooping all together;
Green jacket, red cap,
　And white owl's feather.

Down along the rocky shore
　Some make their home,
They live on crispy pancakes
　Of yellow tide-foam;
Some in the reeds
　Of the black mountain lake,
With frogs for their watch-dogs,
　All night awake.

High on the hill-top
　The old King sits;
He is now so old and gray
　He's nigh lost his wits.
With a bridge of white mist
　Columbkill he crosses,
On his stately journeys
　From Slieveleague to Rosses;
Or going up with music
　On cold starry nights,
To sup with the Queen
　Of the gay Northern Lights.

They stole little Bridget
　For seven years long;

When she came down again
    Her friends were all gone.
They took her lightly back,
    Between the night and morrow,
They thought that she was fast asleep,
    But she was dead with sorrow.
They have kept her ever since
    Deep within the lake,
On a bed of flag-leaves,
    Watching till she wake.

By the craggy hill-side,
    Through the mosses bare,
They have planted thorn-trees
    For pleasure here and there.
Is any man so daring
    As dig them up in spite,
He shall find their sharpest thorns
    In his bed at night.

Up the airy mountain,
    Down the rushy glen,
We daren't go a-hunting
    For fear of little men;
Wee folk, good folk,
    Trooping all together;
Green jacket, red cap,
    And white owl's feather!

WILLIAM ALLINGHAM

THE SONG OF WANDERING AENGUS

I went out to the hazel wood,
Because a fire was in my head,
And cut and peeled a hazel wand,
And hooked a berry to a thread;
And when white moths were on the wing,
And moth-like stars were flickering out,
I dropped the berry in a stream
And caught a little silver trout.

When I had laid it on the floor
I went to blow the fire aflame,
But something rustled on the floor,
And some one called me by my name:
It had become a glimmering girl
With apple blossom in her hair
Who called me by my name and ran
And faded through the brightening air.

Though I am old with wandering
Through hollow lands and hilly lands,
I will find out where she has gone,
And kiss her lips and take her hands;
And walk among long dappled grass,
And pluck till time and times are done
The silver apples of the moon,
The golden apples of the sun.

W. B. YEATS

THE WEE WEE MAN

As I was walking mine alane
    Atween a water and a wa',
There I spied a wee wee man,
    And he was the least that ere I saw.

His legs were scant a shathmont's length,
    And thick and thimber was his thie;
Atween his brows there was a span,
    And atween his shoulders there was three.

He's ta'en and flung a meikle stane,
    And he flang 't as far as I could see;
Though I had been a Wallace wight
    I couldna liften 't to my knee.

'O wee wee man, but ye be strang!
    O tell me where your dwelling be?'
'My dwelling's down by yon bonny bower;
    Fair lady, come wi' me and see.'

On we lap, and awa' we rade,
    Till we came to yon bonny green;
We lighted down to bait our steed,
    And out there came a lady sheen;

Wi' four and twenty at her back
    A' comely clad in glisterin' green;
Tho' the King of Scotland had been there,
    The warst o' them might ha' been his queen.

shathmont, measure from the point of the extended thumb to the extremity
of the palm, six inches
    thimber, stout   *thie,* thigh   *lap,* leapt   *sheen,* shining, beautiful

On we lap, and awa' we rade,
    Till we came to a bonny ha';
The roof was o' the beaten gowd,
    And the floor was o' the cristal a'.

When we came to the stair-foot,
    Ladies were dancing jimp and sma',
But in the twinkling of an eie
    My wee wee man was clean awa'.

Out gat the lights, on came the mist,
    Ladies nor mannie mair cou'd I see:
I turn'd about, and gae a look
    Just at the foot o' Benachie.

ANON

jimp, slim, slender

THOMAS THE RHYMER

True Thomas lay on Huntlie bank,
    A ferlie he spied wi' his e'e,
And there he saw a lady bright
    Come riding down by the Eildon Tree.

Her skirt was o' the grass-green silk,
    Her mantle o' the velvet fine,
At ilka tett of her horse's mane
    Hang fifty siller bells and nine.

True Thomas, he pulled aff his cap,
    And louted low down to his knee:
'All hail, thou mighty Queen of Heaven!
    For thy peer on earth I never did see.'

'O no, O no, Thomas,' she said,
   'That name does not belang to me;
I am but the queen of fair Elfland,
   That am hither come to visit thee.

'Harp and carp, Thomas,' she said,
   'Harp and carp along wi' me,
And if ye dare to kiss my lips,
   Sure of your bodie I will be.'

'Betide me weal, betide me woe,
   That weird shall never daunton me;'
Syne he has kissed her rosy lips,
   All underneath the Eildon Tree.

'Now, ye maun go wi' me,' she said,
   'True Thomas, ye maun go wi' me,
And ye maun serve me seven years,
   Thro' weal or woe, as may chance to be.'

She mounted on her milk-white steed,
   She's ta'en True Thomas up behind,
And aye whene'er her bridle rung
   The steed gaed swifter than the wind.

O they rade on, and farther on—
   The steed gaed swifter than the wind—
Until they reached a desert wide,
   And living land was left behind.

'Light down, light down, now, True Thomas,
   And lean your head upon my knee;
Abide ye there a little space,
   And I will show you ferlies three.

'O see ye not yon narrow road,
    So thick beset with thorns and briers?
That is the Path of Righteousness,
    Tho' after it but few inquires.

And see ye not that braid braid road,
    That lies across that lily leven?
That is the Path of Wickedness,
    Tho' some call it the Road to Heaven.

And see ye not that bonnie road
    That winds about the fernie brae?
That is the road to fair Elfland,
    Where thou and I this night maun gae.

'But, Thomas, ye maun hold your tongue,
    Whatever ye may hear or see,
For, if you speak word in Elfyn land,
    Ye'll ne'er get back to your ain countrie.'

O they rade on, and farther on,
    And they waded thro' rivers aboon the knee,
And they saw neither sun nor moon,
    But they heard the roaring of the sea.

It was mirk mirk night, and there was nae star light,
    And they waded thro' red blude to the knee;
For a' the blude that's shed on earth
    Rins thro' the springs o' that countrie.

Syne they came on to a garden green,
    And she pu'd an apple frae a tree;
'Take this for thy wages, True Thomas,
    It will give thee tongue that can never lie.'

'My tongue is mine ain,' True Thomas said;
  'A gudely gift ye wad gie to me!
I neither could to buy nor sell,
  At fair or tryst where I may be.

'I could neither speak to prince or peer,
  Nor ask of grace from fair ladie:'
'Now hold thy peace,' the lady said,
  'For as I say, so must it be.'

He has gotten a coat of the even cloth,
  And a pair o' shoon of the velvet green,
And till seven years were gane and past
  True Thomas on earth was never seen.

ANON

ARIEL'S SONG

Come unto these yellow sands,
  And then take hands;
Curtsied when you have, and kissed
  The wild waves whist,
Foot it featly here and there;
And, sweet sprites, the burden bear.
  Hark, hark!
    Bow, wow
  The watch-dogs bark,
    Bow, wow,
  Hark, hark! I hear
The strain of strutting Chanticleer
Cry, Cock-a-diddle-dow.

WILLIAM SHAKESPEARE

SABRINA FAIR

Sabrina fair
   Listen where thou art sitting
Under the glassy, cool, translucent wave,
   In twisted braids of Lillies knitting
The loose train of thy amber-dropping hair,
   Listen for dear honour's sake,
   Goddess of the silver lake,
               Listen and save.

Sabrina rises

   By the rushy-fringed bank,
Where grows the Willow and the Osier dank,
   My sliding Chariot stays,
Thick set with Agate, and the azurn sheen
Of Turquoise blue, and Emerald green
   That in the channel strays,
Whilst from off the waters fleet
Thus I set my printless feet
O'er the Cowslips Velvet head,
   That bends not as I tread,
Gentle swain at thy request
   I am here.

                    JOHN MILTON

THE GOD OF SHEEP

All ye woods, and trees, and bowers,
All ye virtues and ye powers
That inhabit in the lakes,
In the pleasant springs or brakes,
   Move your feet
     To our sound,

Whilst we greet
All this ground
With his honour and his name
That defends our flocks from blame.

He is great, and he is just,
He is ever good, and must
Thus be honoured. Daffadillies,
Roses, pinks and lovèd lilies
Let us fling,
Whilst we sing,
Ever holy,
Ever holy,
Ever honoured, ever young!
Thus great Pan is ever sung.

JOHN FLETCHER

HYMN OF PAN

From the forests and highlands
We come, we come:
From the river-girt islands,
Where loud waves are dumb
Listening to my sweet pipings.
The wind in the reeds and the rushes,
The bees on the bells of thyme,
The birds on the myrtle bushes,
The cicale above in the lime,
And the lizards below in the grass,
Were as silent as ever old Tmolus was,
Listening to my sweet pipings.

Liquid Peneus was flowing,
   And all dark Tempe lay
In Pelion's shadow, outgrowing
   The light of the dying day,
     Speeded by my sweet pipings.
The Sileni, and Sylvans, and Fauns,
   And the Nymphs of the woods and the waves,
To the edge of the moist river-lawns,
   And the brink of the dewy caves,
And all that did then attend and follow,
Were silent with love, as you now, Apollo,
     With envy of my sweet pipings.

I sang of the dancing stars,
   I sang of the daedal Earth,
And of Heaven—and the giant wars,
   And Love, and Death, and Birth—
     And then I changed my pipings,—
Singing how down the vale of Maenalus
   I pursued a maiden and clasped a reed.
Gods and men, we are all deluded thus!
   It breaks in our bosom and then we bleed:
All wept, as I think both ye now would,
If envy or age had not frozen your blood,
     At the sorrow of my sweet pipings.

P. B. SHELLEY

COUNTRY GODS

A. Tell me, shepherd, tell me, pray,
   Whose the trees set all a-row?
B. Olives,—Pallas' care are they;
   Vines around for Bromios grow.
A. Whose the corn? the flowers whose?
   Name a God to each demesne.
B. This Dêmêter loves: and those
   Hêra, with the Paphian Queen,
   Aphrodîtê, called The Rose.
A. Pan, dear Pan, with me remain;
   Touch the pipes and run them over;
   Somewhere in this sunny plain
   Echo waits upon her lover.

> COMÊTAS (A.D. 950), *translated
> by* T. F. HIGHAM

WITCHES, CHARMS AND SPELLS

THE NATIVITY CHANT

Sung by Meg Merrilies

Canny moment, lucky fit;
Is the lady lighter yet?
Be it lad, or be it lass,
Sign wi' cross, and sain wi' mass.

Trefoil, vervain, John's-wort, dill,
Hinders witches of their will;
Weel is them, that weel may
Fast upon Saint Andrew's day.

Saint Bride and her brat,
Saint Colme and his cat,
Saint Michael and his spear,
Keep the house frae reif and wear.

SIR WALTER SCOTT

THE HAG

The Hag is astride,
This night for to ride;
The Devil and she together:
Through thick, and through thin,
Now out, and then in,
Though ne'er so foul be the weather.

221

A Thorn or a Burr
   She takes for a Spur:
With a lash of a Bramble she rides now,
     Through Brakes and through Briars,
     O'er Ditchès, and Mires,
She follows the Spirit that guides now.

No Beast, for his food,
   Dares now range the wood;
But hush't in his lair he lies lurking:
     While mischiefs, by these,
     On Land and on Seas,
At noon of Night are a working.

The storm will arise,
   And trouble the skies;
This night, and more for the wonder,
     The ghost from the Tomb
     Affrighted shall come,
Called out by the clap of the Thunder.

ROBERT HERRICK

ALISON GROSS

O Alison Gross, that lives in yon tow'r,
   The ugliest witch i' the north countrie,
Has trysted me ae day up till her bow'r
   And mony fair speeches she made to me.

She straik'd my head an' she kaim'd my hair,
   An' she set me down saftly on her knee;
Says, 'Gin ye will be my lemman sae true,
   Sae mony braw things as I would you gie!'

trysted, invited   *lemman*, sweetheart

She show'd me a mantle o' red scarlét,
    Wi' gouden flowers an' fringes fine;
Says, 'Gin ye will be my lemman sae true,
    This gudely gift it sall be thine'—

'Awa', awa', ye ugly witch,
    Haud far awa', an' lat me be!
I never will be your lemman sae true,
    An' I wish I were out o' your company.'

She neist brought a sark o' the saftest silk,
    Well wrought wi' pearls about the band,
Says, 'Gin ye will be my lemman sae true,
    This gudely gift ye sall command.'

She show'd me a cup o' the good red gowd,
    Well set wi' jewels sae fair to see;
Says, 'Gin ye will be my lemman sae true,
    This gudely gift I will you gie.'—

'Awa', awa', ye ugly witch,
    Haud far awa', an' lat me be!
For I wouldna once kiss your ugly mouth
    For a' the gifts that ye could gie.'

She's turn'd her right an' roun' about,
    An' thrice she blaw on a grass-green horn;
An' she sware by the moon an' the stars abune
    That she'd gar me rue the day I was born.

Then out has she ta'en a silver wand,
    An' she's turn'd her three times roun' and roun';
She mutter'd sic words till my strength it fail'd,
    An' I fell down senseless upon the groun'.

She's turn'd me into an ugly worm,
    And gar'd me toddle about the tree;
An' ay, on ilka Saturday's night,
    My sister Maisry came to me.

Wi' silver bason an' silver kaim
    To kaim my headie upon her knee;
But or I had kiss'd wi' Alison Gross
    I'd sooner ha' toddled about the tree.

But as it fell out, on last Hallowe'en,
    When the Seely Court was ridin' by,
The Queen lighted down on a gowany bank
    Nae far frae the tree where I wont to lye.

She took me up in her milk-white han',
    An' she's straik'd me three times o'er her knee;
She changed me again to my ain proper shape,
    An' nae mair I toddle about the tree.

ANON

Seely Court, the Happy Court (of the Fairies)   *gowany*, daisied

Hey-How for Hallowe'en!
A the witches tae be seen,
Some black, an some green,
Hey-how for Hallowe'en!

ANON

WITCHES' CHARM

The owl is abroad, the bat and the toad,
    And so is the cat-a-mountain;
The ant and the mole sit both in a hole,
    And frog peeps out o' the fountain.

The dogs they do bay, and the timbrels play
    The spindle is now a-turning;
The moon it is red, and the stars are fled,
    But all the sky is a-burning:
The ditch is made, and our nails the spade:
With pictures full, of wax and of wool,
Their livers I stick with needles quick;
There lacks but the blood to make up the flood.
Quickly, dame, then bring your part in!
Spur, spur upon little Martin!
Merrily, merrily, make him sail,
A worm in his mouth and a thorn in's tail,
Fire above, and fire below,
With a whip i' your hand to make him go!

BEN JONSON

A man of words and not of deeds
Is like a garden full of weeds.
When the weeds begin to grow,
It's like a garden full of snow;
When the snow begins to fall,
It's like a bird upon the wall;
When the bird begins to fly,
It's like an eagle in the sky;
When the sky begins to roar,
It's like a lion at the door;
When the door begins to crack,
It's like a whip across your back;
When your back begins to smart,
It's like a penknife in your heart;
And when your heart begins to bleed,
You're dead, you're dead, you're dead indeed.

ANON

A CHARM, OR AN ALLAY FOR LOVE

If so be a Toad be laid
In a Sheeps-skin newly flayed,
And that tied to man 'twill sever
Him and his affections ever.

ROBERT HERRICK

Thrice toss these oaken ashes in the air;
Thrice sit thou mute in this enchanted chair;
Then thrice three times tie up this true love's knot,
And murmur soft: 'She will, or she will not.'

Go burn these poisonous weeds in yon blue fire,
These screech-owl's feathers and this prickling briar,
This cypress gathered at a dead man's grave,
That all thy fears and cares an end may have.

Then come, you fairies, dance with me a round;
Melt her hard heart with your melodious sound.
In vain are all the charms I can devise;
She hath an art to break them with her eyes.

THOMAS CAMPION

GIPSY SONG

The faery beam upon you,
The stars to glister on you;
A moon of light
In the noon of night,
Till the fire-drake hath o'ergone you!
The wheel of fortune guide you,

226

The boy with the bow beside you;
    Run aye in the way
    Till the bird of day,
And the luckier lot betide you!

BEN JONSON

A VOICE SPEAKS FROM THE WELL

Fair maiden, white and red,
Comb me smooth, and stroke my head;
And thou shalt have some cockle bread.
Gently dip, but not too deep,
For fear thou make the golden beard to weep.
Fair maid, white and red,
Comb me smooth, and stroke my head;
And every hair a sheave shall be,
And every sheave a golden tree.

GEORGE PEELE

THIS IS THE KEY

This is the key of the kingdom:
In that kingdom there is a city.
In that city there is a town.
In that town there is a street.
In that street there is a lane.
In that lane there is a yard.
In that yard there is a house.
In that house there is a room.
In that room there is a bed.
On that bed there is a basket.
In that basket there are some flowers

Flowers in a basket.
Basket in the bed.
Bed in the room.
Room in the house.
House in the yard.
Yard in the lane.
Lane in the street.
Street in the town.
Town in the city.
City in the kingdom.
Of the kingdom this is the key.

ANON

THE GHOST'S SONG

Wae's me! wae's me!
The acorn's not yet
Fallen from the tree
That's to grow the wood,
That's to make the cradle,
That's to rock the bairn,
That's to grow a man,
That's to lay me.

ANON

SPELL OF CREATION

Within the flower there lies a seed,
Within the seed there springs a tree,
Within the tree there spreads a wood.

In the wood there burns a fire,
And in the fire there melts a stone,
Within the stone a ring of iron.

Within the ring there lies an O
Within the O there looks an eye,
In the eye there swims a sea,

And in the sea reflected sky,
And in the sky there shines the sun,
Within the sun a bird of gold.

Within the bird there beats a heart,
And from the heart there flows a song,
And in the song there sings a word.

In the word there speaks a world,
A word of joy, a world of grief,
From joy and grief there springs my love.

Oh love, my love, there springs a world,
And on the world there shines a sun
And in the sun there burns a fire,

Within the fire consumes my heart
And in my heart there beats a bird,
And in the bird there wakes an eye,

Within the eye, earth, sea and sky,
Earth, sky and sea within an O
Lie like the seed within the flower.

KATHLEEN RAINE

GOOD WISH

Power of raven be thine,
Power of eagle be thine,
Power of the Fiann.

Power of storm be thine,
Power of moon be thine,
    Power of sun.

Power of sea be thine,
Power of land be thine,
    Power of heaven.

Goodness of sea be thine,
Goodness of earth be thine,
    Goodness of heaven.

Each day be joyous to thee,
No day be grievous to thee,
    Honour and compassion.

Love of each face be thine,
Death on the pillow be thine,
    Thy Saviour's presence.

      ANON: *translated from the*
    Gaelic by ALEXANDER CARMICHAEL

Some say the deil's deid,
The deil's deid, the deil's deid,
Some say the deil's deid,
An buried in Kirkcaldy.

Some say he'll rise again,
Rise again, rise again,
Some say he'll rise again,
An dance the Hielan Laddie.

                  ANON

MARCH AND BATTLE

PIBROCH OF DONUIL DHU

Pibroch of Donuil Dhu,
   Pibroch of Donuil,
Wake thy wild voice anew,
   Summon Clan-Conuil.
Come away, come away,
   Hark to the summons!
Come in your war array,
   Gentles and commons.

Come from deep glen, and
   From mountain so rocky,
The war-pipe and pennon
   Are at Inverlochy.
Come every hill-plaid, and
   True heart that wears one,
Come every steel blade, and
   Strong hand that bears one.

Leave untended the herd,
   The flock without shelter;
Leave the corpse uninterr'd.
   The bride at the altar;
Leave the deer, leave the steer,
   Leave nets and barges:
Come with your fighting gear,
   Broadswords and targes.

Come as the winds come, when
   Forests are rended,
Come as the waves come, when
   Navies are stranded:

Faster come, faster come,
    Faster and faster,
Chief, vassal, page and groom,
    Tenant and master.

Fast they come, fast they come;
    See how they gather!
Wide waves the eagle plume,
    Blended with heather.
Cast your plaids, draw your blades,
    Forward, each man, set!
Pibroch of Donuil Dhu,
    Knell for the onset!

SIR WALTER SCOTT

THE BATTLE OF OTTERBOURNE

It fell upon the Lammas tide,
    When the muir-men win their hay,
The doughty Douglas bound him to ride
    Into England, to drive a prey.

He chose the Gordons and the Graemes,
    With them the Lindsays, light and gay;
But the Jardines wald not with him ride,
    And they rue it to this day.

And he has burned the dales of Tyne,
    And part of Bambrough-shire;
And three good towers on Reidswire fells,
    He left them all on fire.

And he marched up to Newcastle,
    And rode it round about;

'O wha's the lord of this castle,
    Or wha's the lady o't?'

But up spake proud Lord Percy then,
    And O but he spake hie!
'I am the lord of this castle,
    My wife's the lady gay.'

'If thou'rt the lord of this castle,
    Sae weel it pleases me!
For ere I cross the Border fells,
    The tane o' us shall die.'

He took a lang spear in his hand,
    Shod with the metal free,
And for to meet the Douglas there
    He rode right furiouslie.

'Had we twa been upon the green,
    And never an eye to see,
I wad hae had you, flesh and fell;
    But your sword sall gae wi' me.'

'But gae ye up to Otterbourne,
    And wait there dayis three;
And if I come not ere three dayis end,
    A fause knight ca' ye me.'

'The Otterbourne's a bonnie burn,
    'Tis pleasant there to be;
But there is nought at Otterbourne,
    To feed my men and me.

The deer rins wild on hill and dale,
    The birds fly wild from tree to tree;

But there is neither bread nor kail
    To fend my men and me.

Yet I will stay at Otterbourne,
    Where you shall welcome be;
And if you come not at three dayis end,
    A fause lord I'll ca' thee.'

'Thither will I come,' proud Percy said,
    'By the might of Our Ladie!'
'There will I bide thee,' said the Douglas,
    'My troth I plight to thee.'

They lighted high on Otterbourne,
    Upon the bent sae brown;
They lighted high on Otterbourne,
    And threw their pallions down.

And he that had a bonnie boy,
    Sent out his horse to grass;
And he that had not a bonnie boy,
    His ain servant he was.

But up then spake a little page,
    Before the peep of dawn—
'O waken ye, waken ye, my good lord,
    For Percy's hard at hand.'

'Ye lie, ye lie, ye liar loud!
    Sae loud I hear ye lie;
For Percy had not men yestreen
    To dight my men and me.

But I hae dreamed a dreary dream,
    Beyond the Isle of Skye:

pallions, tents   *dight*, fight
234

I saw a dead man win a fight,
    And I think that man was I.'

He belted on his gude braid sword,
    And to the field he ran;
But he forgot the helmet good,
    That should have kept his brain.

When Percy wi' the Douglas met,
    I wat he was fu' fain!
They swakked their swords, till sair they swat,
    And the blood ran down like rain.

But Percy, with his good broadsword,
    That could so sharply wound,
Has wounded Douglas on the brow,
    Till he fell to the ground.

Then he called on his little foot-page,
    And said, 'Run speedilie,
And fetch my ain dear sister's son,
    Sir Hugh Montgomery.'

'My nephew good,' the Douglas said,
    'What recks the death of ane!
Last night I dreamed a dreary dream,
    And I ken the day's thy ain.

My wound is deep; I fain would sleep;
    Take thou the vanguard of the three,
And hide me by the braken bush,
    That grows on yonder lily lea.

O bury me by the braken bush,
    Beneath the blooming brier,

Let never living mortal ken
  That a kindly Scot lies here.'

He lifted up that noble lord,
  Wi' the saut tear in his e'e;
He hid him in the braken bush,
  That his merry men might not see.

The moon was clear, the day drew near,
  The spears in flinders flew,
But mony a gallant Englishman
  Ere day the Scotsmen slew.

The Gordons good, in English blood
  They steep'd their hose and shoon;
The Lindsays flew like fire about,
  Till all the fray was done.

The Percy and Montgomery met,
  That either of other were fain;
They swakked swords, and they twa swat,
  And aye the blood ran down between.

'Yield thee, O yield thee, Percy,' he said,
  'Or else I vow I'll lay thee low!'
'To whom must I yield,' quoth Earl Percy,
  'Now that I see it must be so?'

'Thou shalt not yield to lord nor loun,
  Nor yet shalt thou yield to me;
But yield thee to the braken bush,
  That grows upon yon lily lea!'

'I will not yield to a braken bush,
  Nor yet will I yield to a brier;

But I would yield to Earl Douglas,
  Or Sir Hugh Montgomery, if he were here.'

As soon as he knew it was Montgomery,
  He struck his sword's point in the ground;
The Montgomery was a courteous knight,
  And quickly took him by the hand.

This deed was done at Otterbourne
  About the breaking of the day;
Earl Douglas was buried at the braken bush,
  And the Percy led captive away.

ANON

AGINCOURT

Fair stood the wind for France
  When we our sails advance,
Nor now to prove our chance
  Longer will tarry;
But putting to the main,
At Caux, the mouth of Seine,
With all his martial train
  Landed King Harry.

And taking many a fort,
Furnish'd in warlike sort,
Marcheth tow'rds Agincourt
  In happy hour;
Skirmishing day by day
With those that stopp'd his way,
Where the French gen'ral lay
  With all his power.

Which, in his height of pride,
King Henry to deride,
His ransom to provide
   Unto him sending;
Which he neglects the while
As from a nation vile,
Yet with an angry smile
   Their fall portending.

And turning to his men,
Quoth our brave Henry then,
'Though they to one be ten
   Be not amazèd:
Yet have we well begun;
Battles so bravely won
Have ever to the sun
   By fame been raisèd.

'And for myself' (quoth he)
'This my full rest shall be:
England ne'er mourn for me
   Nor more esteem me:
Victor I will remain
Or on this earth lie slain,
Never shall she sustain
   Loss to redeem me.

'Poitiers and Cressy tell,
When most their pride did swell,
Under our swords they fell:
   No less our skill is
Than when our grandsire great,
Claiming the regal seat,
By many a warlike feat
   Lopp'd the French lilies.'

The Duke of York so dread
The eager vaward led;
With the main Henry sped
    Among his henchmen.
Excester had the rear,
A braver man not there;
O Lord, how hot they were
    On the false Frenchmen!

They now to fight are gone,
Armour on armour shone,
Drum now to drum did groan
    To hear was wonder;
That with the cries they make
The very earth did shake:
Trumpet to trumpet spake,
    Thunder to thunder.

Well it thine age became,
O noble Erpingham,
Which didst the signal aim
    To our hid forces!
When from a meadow by,
Like a storm suddenly
The English archery
    Stuck the French horses.

With Spanish yew so strong,
Arrows a cloth-yard long
That like to serpents stung,
    Piercing the weather;
None from his fellow starts,
But playing manly parts,
And like true English hearts
    Stuck close together.

When down their bows they threw,
And forth their bilbos drew,
And on the French they flew,
   Not one was tardy;
Arms were from shoulders sent,
Scalps to the teeth were rent,
Down the French peasants went—
   Our men were hardy!

This while our noble king,
His broadsword brandishing,
Down the French host did ding
   As to o'erwhelm it;
And many a deep wound lent,
His arms with blood besprent,
And many a cruel dent
   Bruisèd his helmet.

Gloster, that duke so good,
Next of the royal blood,
For famous England stood
   With his brave brother;
Clarence, in steel so bright,
Though but a maiden knight,
Yet in that furious fight
   Scarce such another.

Warwick in blood did wade,
Oxford the foe invade,
And cruel slaughter made
   Still as they ran up;
Suffolk his axe did ply,
Beaumont and Willoughby
Bare them right doughtily,
   Ferrers and Fanhope.

March and Battle

Upon Saint Crispin's Day
Fought was this noble fray,
Which fame did not delay
   To England to carry.
O when shall English men
With such acts fill a pen?
Or England breed again
   Such a King Harry?

MICHAEL DRAYTON

Some years of late, in eighty-eight
   As I do well remember,
It was, some say, the tenth of May,
   And, some say, in September,
   And, some say, in September.

The Spanish train launch'd forth amain,
   With many a fine bravado,
Their (as they thought, but it proved not)
   Invincible Armado,
   Invincible Armado.

There was a little man, that dwelt in Spain,
   Who shot well in a gun-a,
Don Pedro hight, as black a wight
   As the Knight of the Sun-a,
   As the Knight of the Sun-a.

King Philip made him Admiral,
   And bid him not to stay-a,
But to destroy both man and boy,
   And so to come away-a,
   And so to come away-a.

Their navy was well victualled
   With biscuit, pease, and bacon;
They brought two ships, well fraught with whips,
   But I think they were mistaken,
   But I think they were mistaken.

Their men were young, munition strong,
   And, to do us more harm-a,
They thought it meet to join the fleet,
   All with the Prince of Parma,
   All with the Prince of Parma.

They coasted round about our land,
   And so came in by Dover;
But we had men set on them then
   And threw the rascals over,
   And threw the rascals over.

The Queen was then at Tilbury,
   What more could we desire-a?
And Sir Francis Drake, for her sweet sake,
   Did set them all on fire-a,
   Did set them all on fire-a.

Then, straight, they fled, by sea and land,
   That one man killed threescore-a;
And had not they all ran away,
   In truth he had killed more-a,
   In truth he had killed more-a.

Then let them neither brag nor boast,
   But if they come agen-a,
Let them take heed, they do not speed
   As they did, you know when-a,
   As they did, you know when-a.

ANON

THE ARMADA

Attend, all ye who list to hear our noble England's praise;
I tell of the thrice famous deeds she wrought in ancient
  days,
When that great fleet invincible against her bore in vain
The richest spoils of Mexico, the stoutest hearts of Spain.

It was about the lovely close of a warm summer day,
There came a gallant merchant-ship full sail to Plymouth
  Bay;
Her crew hath seen Castile's black fleet, beyond Aurigny's
  isle,
At earliest twilight, on the waves lie heaving many a mile.
At sunrise she escaped their van, by God's especial grace;
And the tall Pinta, till the noon, had held her close in chase.
Forthwith a guard at every gun was placed along the wall;
The beacon blazed upon the roof of Edgecumbe's lofty hall;
Many a light fishing-bark put out to pry along the coast,
And with loose rein and bloody spur rode inland many a
  post.
With his white hair unbonneted, the stout old sheriff comes;
Behind him march the halberdiers; before him sound the
  drums;
His yeomen round the market cross make clear an ample
  space;
For there behoves him to set up the standard of Her Grace.
And haughtily the trumpets peal, and gaily dance the bells,
As slow upon the labouring wind the royal blazon swells.
Look how the Lion of the sea lifts up his ancient crown,
And underneath his deadly paw treads the gay lilies down.
So stalked he when he turned to flight, on that famed Picard
  field,
Bohemia's plume, and Genoa's bow, and Caesar's eagle
  shield.

So glared he when at Agincourt in wrath he turned to bay,
And crushed and torn beneath his claws the princely hunters
lay.
Ho! strike the flagstaff deep, Sir Knight: ho! scatter flowers,
fair maids:
Ho! gunners, fire a loud salute: ho! gallants, draw your
blades:
Thou sun, shine on her joyously; ye breezes, waft her wide;
Our glorious SEMPER EADEM, the banner of our pride.
The freshening breeze of eve unfurled that banner's massy
fold;
The parting gleam of sunshine kissed that haughty scroll of
gold;
Night sank upon the dusky beach, and on the purple sea,
Such night in England ne'er had been, nor e'er again shall
be.
From Eddystone to Berwick bounds, from Lynn to Milford
Bay,
That time of slumber was as bright and busy as the day;
For swift to east and swift to west the ghastly war-flame
spread,
High on St Michael's Mount it shone: it shone on Beachy
Head.
Far on the deep the Spaniard saw, along each southern shire,
Cape beyond cape, in endless range those twinkling points of
fire.
The fisher left his skiff to rock on Tamar's glittering waves:
The rugged miners poured to war from Mendip's sunless
caves:
O'er Longleat's towers, o'er Cranbourne's oaks, the fiery
herald flew:
He roused the shepherds of Stonehenge, the rangers of Beau-
lieu.
Right sharp and quick the bells all night rang out from
Bristol town,

And ere the day three hundred horse had met on Clifton
     down;
The sentinel on Whitehall gate looked forth into the night,
And saw o'erhanging Richmond Hill the streak of blood-red
     light.
Then bugle's note and cannon's roar the deathlike silence
     broke,
And with one start, and with one cry, the royal city woke.
At once on all her stately gates arose the answering fires;
At once the wild alarum clashed from all her reeling spires;
From all the batteries of the Tower pealed loud the voice of
     fear;
And all the thousand masts of Thames sent back a louder
     cheer:
And from the furthest wards was heard the rush of hurrying
     feet,
And the broad streams of pikes and flags rushed down each
     roaring street;
And broader still became the blaze, and louder still the din,
As fast from every village round the horse came spurring in:
And eastward straight from wild Blackheath the warlike
     errand went,
And roused in many an ancient hall the gallant squires of
     Kent.
Southward from Surrey's pleasant hills flew those bright
     couriers forth;
High on bleak Hampstead's swarthy moor they started for
     the north;
And on, and on, without a pause, untired they bounded still:
All night from tower to tower they sprang; they sprang from
     hill to hill:
Till the proud peak unfurled the flag o'er Darwin's rocky
     dales,
Till like volcanoes flared to heaven the stormy hills of
     Wales,

Till twelve fair counties saw the blaze on Malvern's lonely
      height,
Till streamed in crimson on the wind the Wrekin's crest of
      light,
Till broad and fierce the star came forth on Ely's stately fane,
And tower and hamlet rose in arms o'er all the boundless
      plain;
Till Belvoir's lordly terraces the sign to Lincoln sent,
And Lincoln sped the message on o'er the wide vale of
      Trent;
Till Skiddaw saw the fire that burned on Gaunt's embattled
      pile,
And the red glare on Skiddaw roused the burghers of
      Carlisle.

LORD MACAULAY

DRAKE'S DRUM

Drake he's in his hammock an' a thousand mile away,
   (Capten, art tha sleepin' there below?),
Slung atween the round shot in Nombre Dios Bay,
   An' dreamin' arl the time o' Plymouth Hoe.
Yarnder lumes the Island, yarnder lie the ships,
   Wi' sailor lads a dancin' heel-an'-toe,
An' the shore-lights flashin', an' the night-tide dashin',
   He sees et arl so plainly as he saw et long ago.

Drake he was a Devon man, an' rüled the Devon seas,
   (Capten, art tha sleepin' there below?),
Rovin' tho' his death fell, he went wi' heart at ease,
   An' dreamin' arl the time o' Plymouth Hoe.
'Take my drum to England, hang et by the shore,
   Strike et when your powder's runnin' low;

If the Dons sight Devon, I'll quit the port o' Heaven,
  An' drum them up the Channel as we drummed them long
    ago.'

Drake he's in his hammock till the great Armadas come,
  (Capten, art tha sleepin' there below?),
Slung atween the round shot, listenin' for the drum,
  An' dreamin' arl the time o' Plymouth Hoe.
Call him on the deep sea, call him up the Sound,
  Call him when ye sail to meet the foe;
Where the old trade's plyin' an' the old flag flyin'
  They shall find him ware an' wakin', as they found him
    long ago!

SIR HENRY NEWBOLT

THE *REVENGE*

At Flores in the Azores Sir Richard Grenville lay,
And a pinnace, like a flutter'd bird, came flying from far
      away:
'Spanish ships of war at sea! we have sighted fifty-three!'
Then sware Lord Thomas Howard: ' 'Fore God I am no
      coward;
But I cannot meet them here, for my ships are out of gear,
And the half my men are sick. I must fly, but follow quick.
We are six ships of the line; can we fight with fifty-three?'

Then spake Sir Richard Grenville: 'I know you are no
      coward;
You fly them for a moment to fight with them again.
But I've ninety men and more that are lying sick ashore.
I should count myself the coward if I left them, my Lord
      Howard,
To these Inquisition dogs and the devildoms of Spain.'

247

So Lord Howard past away with five ships of war that day,
Till he melted like a cloud in the silent summer heaven;
But Sir Richard bore in hand all his sick men from the land
Very carefully and slow,
Men of Bideford in Devon,
And we laid them on the ballast down below;
For we brought them all aboard,
And they blest him in their pain, that they were not left to
    Spain,
To the thumbscrew and the stake, for the glory of the Lord.

He had only a hundred seamen to work the ship and to fight,
And he sailed away from Flores till the Spaniard came in
    sight,
With his huge sea-castles heaving upon the weather-bow.
'Shall we fight or shall we fly?
Good Sir Richard, tell us now,
For to fight is but to die!
There'll be little of us left by the time this sun be set.'
And Sir Richard said again: 'We be all good English men.
Let us bang these dogs of Seville, the children of the devil,
For I never turn'd my back upon Don or devil yet.'

Sir Richard spoke and he laugh'd, and we roar'd a hurrah,
    and so
The little *Revenge* ran on sheer into the heart of the foe,
With her hundred fighters on deck, and her ninety sick
    below;
For half of their fleet to the right and half to the left were
    seen,
And the little *Revenge* ran on thro' the long sea-lane between.

Thousands of their soldiers look'd down from their decks
    and laugh'd,
Thousands of their seamen made mock at the mad little craft

Running on and on, till delay'd
By their mountain-like San Philip that, of fifteen hundred
　　tons,
And up-shadowing high above us with her yawning tiers of
　　guns,
Took the breath from our sails, and we stay'd.

And while now the great San Philip hung above us like a
　　cloud
Whence the thunderbolt will fall
Long and loud,
Four galleons drew away
From the Spanish fleet that day,
And two upon the larboard and two upon the starboard lay,
And the battle-thunder broke from them all.

But anon the great San Philip, she bethought herself and
　　went
Having that within her womb that had left her ill content;
And the rest they came aboard us, and they fought us hand to
　　hand,
For a dozen times they came with their pikes and mus-
　　queteers,
And a dozen times we shook 'em off as a dog that shakes his
　　ears
When he leaps from the water to the land.

And the sun went down, and the stars came out far over the
　　summer sea,
But never a moment ceased the fight of the one and the fifty-
　　three.
Ship after ship, the whole night long, their high-built
　　galleons came,
Ship after ship, the whole night long, with her battle-thunder
　　and flame;

Ship after ship, the whole night long, drew back with her
      dead and her shame.
For some were sunk and many were shatter'd, and so could
      fight us no more—
God of battles, was ever a battle like this in the world before?

For he said 'Fight on! fight on!'
Tho' his vessel was all but a wreck;
And it chanced that, when half of the short summer night
      was gone,
With a grisly wound to be drest he had left the deck,
But a bullet struck him that was dressing it suddenly dead,
And himself he was wounded again in the side and the head,
And he said 'Fight on! fight on!'

And the night went down, and the sun smiled out far over
      the summer sea,
And the Spanish fleet with broken sides lay round us all in a
      ring;
But they dared not touch us again, for they fear'd that we
      still could sting,
So they watch'd what the end would be.
And we had not fought them in vain,
But in perilous plight were we,
Seeing forty of our poor hundred were slain,
And half of the rest of us maim'd for life
In the crash of the cannonades and the desperate strife;
And the sick men down in the hold were most of them stark
      and cold,
And the pikes were all broken or bent, and the powder was
      all of it spent;
And the masts and the rigging were lying over the side;
But Sir Richard cried in his English pride,
'We have fought such a fight for a day and a night
As may never be fought again!

We have won great glory, my men!
And a day less or more
At sea or ashore,
We die—does it matter when?
Sink me the ship, Master Gunner—sink her, split her in
      twain!
Fall into the hands of God, not into the hands of Spain!'
And the gunner said 'Ay, ay,' but the seamen made reply:
'We have children, we have wives,
And the Lord hath spared our lives.
We will make the Spaniard promise, if we yield, to let us go;
We shall live to fight again and to strike another blow.'
And the lion there lay dying, and they yielded to the foe.

And the stately Spanish men to their flagship bore him then,
Where they laid him by the mast, old Sir Richard caught at
      last,
And they praised him to his face with their courtly foreign
      grace;
But he rose upon their decks, and he cried:
'I have fought for Queen and Faith like a valiant man and
      true;
I have only done my duty as a man is bound to do:
With a joyful spirit I Sir Richard Grenville die!'
And he fell upon their decks, and he died.

And they stared at the dead that had been so valiant and true,
And had holden the power and glory of Spain so cheap
That he dared her with one little ship and his English few;
Was he devil or man? He was devil for aught they knew,
But they sank his body with honour down into the deep,
And they mann'd the *Revenge* with a swarthier alien crew,
And away she sail'd with her loss and long'd for her own;
When a wind from the lands they had ruin'd awoke from
      sleep,

And the water began to heave and the weather to moan,
And or ever that evening ended a great gale blew,
And a wave like the wave that is raised by an earthquake
     grew,
Till it smote on their hulls and their sails and their masts and
     their flags,
And the whole sea plunged and fell on the shot-shatter'd
     navy of Spain,
And the little *Revenge* herself went down by the island crags
To be lost evermore in the main.

LORD TENNYSON

BONNY DUNDEE

To the Lords of Convention 'twas Claver'se who spoke,
'Ere the King's crown shall fall there are crowns to be broke;
So let each Cavalier who loves honour and me,
Come follow the bonnet of Bonny Dundee.

    'Come fill up my cup, come fill up my can,
    Come saddle your horses, and call up your men;
    Come open the West Port, and let me gang free,
    And it's room for the bonnets of Bonny Dundee!'

Dundee he is mounted, he rides up the street,
The bells are rung backward, the drums they are beat;
But the Provost, douce man, said 'Just e'en let him be,
The Gude Town is weel quit of that Deil of Dundee.'
       Come fill up my cup, &c.

As he rode down the sanctified bends of the Bow,
Ilk carline was flyting and shaking her pow;
But the young plants of grace they look'd couthie and slee,
Thinking, 'Luck to thy bonnet, thou Bonny Dundee!'

252

With sour-featured Whigs the Grassmarket was cramm'd
As if half the West had set tryst to be hang'd;
There was spite in each look, there was fear in each e'e,
As they watch'd for the bonnets of Bonny Dundee.

These cowls of Kilmarnock had spits and had spears,
And lang-hafted gullies to kill Cavaliers;
But they shrunk to close-heads, and the causeway was free,
At the toss of the bonnet of Bonny Dundee.

He spurr'd to the foot of the proud Castle rock,
And with the gay Gordon he gallantly spoke;
'Let Mons Meg and her marrows speak twa words or three,
For the love of the bonnet of Bonny Dundee.'

The Gordon demands of him which way he goes—
'Where'er shall direct me the shade of Montrose!
Your Grace in short space shall hear tidings of me,
Or that low lies the bonnet of Bonny Dundee.

'There are hills beyond Pentland, and lands beyond Forth,
If there's lords in the Lowlands, there's chiefs in the North;
There are wild Duniewassals, three thousand times three,
Will cry *hoigh!* for the bonnet of Bonny Dundee.

'There's brass on the target of barken'd bull-hide;
There's steel in the scabbard that dangles beside;
The brass shall be burnish'd, the steel shall flash free,
At a toss of the bonnet of Bonny Dundee.

'Away to the hills, to the caves, to the rocks—
Ere I own an usurper, I'll couch with the fox;
And tremble, false Whigs, in the midst of your glee,
You have not see the last of my bonnet and me!'

He waved his proud hand, and the trumpets were blown,
The kettle-drums clash'd, and the horsemen rode on,
Till on Ravelston's cliffs and on Clermiston's lee,
Died away the wild war-notes of Bonny Dundee.

Come fill up my cup, come fill up my can,
Come saddle the horses and call up the men,
Come open your gates, and let me gae free,
For it's up with the bonnets of Bonny Dundee!

SIR WALTER SCOTT

THE DESTRUCTION OF SENNACHERIB

The Assyrian came down like the wolf on the fold,
And his cohorts were gleaming in purple and gold;
And the sheen of their spears was like stars on the sea,
When the blue wave rolls nightly on deep Galilee.

Like the leaves of the forest when Summer is green,
That host with their banners at sunset were seen:
Like the leaves of the forest when Autumn hath blown,
That host on the morrow lay wither'd and strown.

For the Angel of Death spread his wings on the blast,
And breathed in the face of the foe as he pass'd;
And the eyes of the sleepers wax'd deadly and chill,
And their hearts but once heaved, and for ever grew still!

And there lay the steed with his nostril all wide,
But through it there roll'd not the breath of his pride;
And the foam of his gasping lay white on the turf,
And cold as the spray of the rock-beating surf.

And there lay the rider distorted and pale,
With the dew on his brow, and the rust on his mail:
And the tents were all silent, the banners alone,
The lances unlifted, the trumpet unblown.

And the widows of Ashur are loud in their wail
And the idols are broke in the temple of Baal;
And the might of the Gentile, unsmote by the sword,
Hath melted like snow in the glance of the Lord!

LORD BYRON

THE WAR SONG OF DINAS VAWR

The mountain sheep are sweeter,
But the valley sheep are fatter;
We therefore deemed it meeter
To carry off the latter.
We made an expedition;
We met a host and quelled it;
We forced a strong position,
And killed the men who held it.

On Dyfed's richest valley,
Where herds of kine were browsing,
We made a mighty sally,
To furnish our carousing.
Fierce warriors rushed to meet us;
We met them and o'erthrew them:
They struggled hard to beat us;
But we conquered them, and slew them.

As we drove our prize at leisure,
The king marched forth to catch us;

His rage surpassed all measure,
But his people could not match us.
He fled to his hall pillars;
And, ere our force we led off,
Some sacked his house and cellars,
While others cut his head off.

We there, in strife bewildering,
Spilt blood enough to swim in:
We orphaned many children,
And widowed many women.
The eagles and the ravens
We glutted with our foemen:
The heroes and the cravens,
The spearmen and the bowmen.

We brought away from battle,
And much their land bemoaned them,
Two thousand head of cattle,
And the head of him who owned them:
Edynfed, King of Dyfed,
His head was borne before us;
His wine and beasts supplied our feasts,
And his overthrow, our chorus.

THOMAS LOVE PEACOCK

HOHENLINDEN

On Linden, when the sun was low,
All bloodless lay the untrodden snow;
And dark as winter was the flow
    Of Iser, rolling rapidly.

March and Battle

But Linden saw another sight,
When the drum beat at dead of night
Commanding fires of death to light
    The darkness of her scenery.

By torch and trumpet fast arrayed
Each horseman drew his battle-blade,
And furious every charger neighed
    To join the dreadful revelry.

Then shook the hills with thunder riven;
Then rushed the steed, to battle driven;
And louder than the bolts of Heaven
    Far flashed the red artillery.

But redder yet that light shall glow
On Linden's hills of stainèd snow;
And bloodier yet the torrent flow
    Of Iser, rolling rapidly.

'Tis morn; but scarce yon level sun
Can pierce the war-clouds, rolling dun,
Where furious Frank and fiery Hun
    Shout in their sulphurous canopy.

The combat deepens. On, ye Brave,
Who rush to glory or the grave!
Wave, Munich! all thy banners wave,
    And charge with all thy chivalry.

Few, few shall part, where many meet!
The snow shall be their winding-sheet,
And every turf beneath their feet
    Shall be a soldier's sepulchre.

THOMAS CAMPBELL

THE NIGHT OF TRAFALGÁR

In the wild October night-time, when the wind raved round
   the land,
And the Back-sea met the Front-sea, and our doors were
   blocked with sand,
And we heard the drub of Dead-man's Bay, where bones of
   thousands are,
We knew not what the day had done for us at Trafalgár.
     Had done,
     Had done,
    For us at Trafalgár!

'Pull hard, and make the Nothe, or down we go!' one says,
   says he.
We pulled; and bedtime brought the storm; but snug at
   home slept we.
Yet all the while our gallants after fighting through the day,
Were beating up and down the dark, sou'-west of Cadiz Bay.
     The dark,
     The dark,
    Sou'-west of Cadiz Bay!

The victors and the vanquished then the storm it tossed and
   tore,
As hard they strove, those worn-out men, upon that surly
   shore;
Dead Nelson and his half-dead crew, his foes from near and
   far,
Were rolled together on the deep that night at Trafalgár!
     The deep
     The deep,
    That night at Trafalgár!

       THOMAS HARDY

THE EVE OF WATERLOO

There was a sound of revelry by night,
And Belgium's capital had gather'd then
Her Beauty and her Chivalry, and bright
The lamps shone o'er fair women and brave men;
A thousand hearts beat happily; and when
Music arose with its voluptuous swell,
Soft eyes look'd love to eyes which spake again,
And all went merry as a marriage bell;
But hush! hark! a deep sound strikes like a rising knell!

Did ye not hear it?—No; 'twas but the wind,
Or the car rattling o'er the stony street;
On with the dance! let joy be unconfined;
No sleep till morn, when Youth and Pleasure meet
To chase the glowing Hours with flying feet—
But hark!—that heavy sound breaks in once more,
As if the clouds its echo would repeat;
And nearer, clearer, deadlier than before!
Arm! Arm! it is—it is—the cannon's opening roar!

And there was mounting in hot haste: the steed,
The mustering squadron, and the clattering car,
Went pouring forward with impetuous speed,
And swiftly forming in the ranks of war;
And the deep thunder peal on peal afar;
And near, the beat of the alarming drum
Roused up the soldier ere the morning star;
While throng'd the citizens with terror dumb,
Or whispering, with white lips—'The foe! they come! they
        come!'

And wild and high the 'Cameron's gathering' rose!
The war-note of Lochiel, which Albyn's hills

Have heard, and heard, too, have her Saxon foes:—
How in the noon of night that pibroch thrills,
Savage and shrill! But with the breath which fills
Their mountain-pipe, so fill the mountaineers
With the fierce native daring which instils
The stirring memory of a thousand years,
And Evan's, Donald's fame rings in each clansman's ears!

And Ardennes waves above them her green leaves,
Dewy with nature's tear-drops as they pass,
Grieving, if aught inanimate e'er grieves,
Over the unreturning brave,—alas!
Ere evening to be trodden like the grass
Which now beneath them, but above shall grow
In its next verdure, when this fiery mass
Of living valour, rolling on the foe
And burning with high hope shall moulder cold and low.

Last noon beheld them full of lusty life,
Last eve in Beauty's circle proudly gay,
The midnight brought the signal-sound of strife,
The morn the marshalling in arms,—the day
Battle's magnificently stern array!
The thunder-clouds close o'er it, which when rent
The earth is cover'd thick with other clay,
Which her own clay shall cover, heap'd and pent,
Rider and horse,—friend, foe,—in one red burial blent!

LORD BYRON

THE FIELD OF WATERLOO

Yea, the coneys are scared by the thud of hoofs,
And their white scuts flash at their vanishing heels,
And swallows abandon the hamlet-roofs.

March and Battle

The mole's tunnelled chambers are crushed by wheels,
The lark's eggs scattered, their owners fled;
And the hedgehog's household the sapper unseals.

The snail draws in at the terrible tread,
But in vain; he is crushed by the felloe-rim;
The worm asks what can be overhead,

And wriggles deep from a scene so grim,
And guesses him safe; for he does not know
What a foul red flood will be soaking him!

Beaten about by the heel and toe
Are butterflies, sick of the day's long rheum,
To die of a worse than the weather-foe.

Trodden and bruised to a miry tomb
Are ears that have greened but will never be gold,
And flowers in the bud that will never bloom.

THOMAS HARDY

All the hills and vales along
Earth is bursting into song,
And the singers are the chaps
Who are going to die perhaps.
    O sing, marching men,
    Till the valleys ring again.
    Give your gladness to earth's keeping,
    So be glad, when you are sleeping.

Cast away regret and rue,
Think what you are marching to.
Little live, great pass.
Jesus Christ and Barabbas

Were found the same day.
This died, that went his way.
  So sing with joyful breath,
  For why, you are going to death.
  Teeming earth will surely store
  All the gladness that you pour.

Earth that never doubts nor fears,
Earth that knows of death, not tears,
Earth that bore with joyful ease
Hemlock for Socrates,
Earth that blossomed and was glad
'Neath the cross that Christ had,
Shall rejoice and blossom too
When the bullet reaches you.
  Wherefore, men marching
  On the road to death, sing!
  Pour your gladness on earth's head,
  So be merry, so be dead.

From the hills and valleys earth
Shouts back the sound of mirth,
Tramp of feet and lilt of song
Ringing all the road along.
All the music of their going,
Ringing swinging glad song-throwing,
Earth will echo still, when foot
Lies numb and voice mute.
  On, marching men, on
  To the gates of death with song.
  Sow your gladness for earth's reaping,
  So you may be glad, though sleeping.
  Strew your gladness on earth's bed,
  So be merry, so be dead.

CHARLES SORLEY

THE UNCONCERNED

Now that the world is all in a maze,
Drums, and trumpets rending Heav'ns,
Wounds a-bleeding, mortals dying,
Widows and orphans piteously crying;
Armies marching, towns in a blaze,
Kingdoms and states at sixes and sevens:
What should an honest fellow do,
Whose courage and fortunes run equally low!
Let him live, say I, till his glass be run,
As easily as he may;
Let the wine and the sand of his glass flow together,
For life's but a Winter's day.
Alas from sun to sun,
The time's very short, very dirty the weather,
And we silently creep away.
Let him nothing do, he could wish undone;
And keep himself safe from the noise of gun.

THOMAS FLATMAN

DIRGES, CORONACHS AND ELEGIES

A LYKE-WAKE DIRGE

This ae nighte, this ae nighte,
   Every nighte and alle,
Fire, and sleet, and candle-lighte;
   And Christe receive thye saule.

When thou from hence away art paste,
   Every nighte and alle,
To Whinny-muir thou comest at laste;
   And Christe receive thye saule.

If ever thou gavest hosen and shoon,
   Every nighte and alle,
Sit thee down and put them on;
   And Christe receive thye saule.

If hosen and shoon thou ne'er gavest nane,
   Every nighte and alle,
The whinnes shall pinch thee to the bare bane;
   And Christe receive thye saule.

From Whinny-muir when thou mayst passe,
   Every nighte and alle,
To Brig o' Dread thou comest at laste;
   And Christe receive thye saule.

From Brig o' Dread when thou mayst passe,
   Every nighte and alle,
To purgatory fire thou comest at laste;
   And Christe receive thye saule.

If ever thou gavest meate or drinke,
    Every nighte and alle,
The fire sall never make thee shrinke;
    And Christe receive thye saule.

If meate or drinke thou gavest nane,
    Every nighte and alle,
The fire will burn thee to the bare bane;
    And Christe receive thye saule.

This ae nighte, this ae nighte,
    Every nighte and alle,
Fire, and sleet, and candle-lighte;
    And Christe receive thye saule.

ANON

Call for the robin-redbreast and the wren,
Since o'er shady groves they hover,
And with leaves and flowers do cover
The friendless bodies of unburied men.
Call unto his funeral dole
The ant, the field-mouse, and the mole,
To rear him hillocks that shall keep him warm,
And (when gay tombs are robb'd) sustain no harm;
But keep the wolf far thence, that's foe to men,
For with his nails he'll dig them up again.

JOHN WEBSTER

FIDELE'S DIRGE

Fear no more the heat o' the sun,
    Nor the furious winter's rages;
Thou thy worldly task hast done,
    Home art gone, and ta'en thy wages.
Golden lads and girls all must,
As chimney-sweepers, come to dust.

265

Fear no more the frown o' the great,
   Thou art past the tyrant's stroke;
Care no more to clothe and eat,
   To thee the reed is as the oak.
The sceptre, learning, physic, must
All follow this, and come to dust.

Fear no more the lightning-flash,
   Nor the all-dreaded thunder-stone;
Fear not slander, censure rash;
   Thou hast finished joy and moan.
All lovers young, all lovers must
Consign to thee, and come to dust.

No exorciser harm thee!
Nor no witchcraft charm thee!
Ghost unlaid forbear thee!
Nothing ill come near thee!
Quiet consummation have,
And renowned be thy grave!

WILLIAM SHAKESPEARE

THE TWA CORBIES

As I was walking all alane,
I heard twa corbies making a mane:
The tane unto the tither did say,
'Whar sall we gang and dine the day?'

'—In behint yon auld fail dyke
I wot there lies a new-slain knight;
And naebody kens that he lies there
But his hawk, his hound, and his lady fair.

corbies, ravens   *fail*, turf

'His hound is to the hunting gane,
His hawk to fetch the wild-fowl hame,
His lady's ta'en another mate,
So we may mak' our dinner sweet.

'Ye'll sit on his white hause-bane,
And I'll pike out his bonny blue e'en:
Wi' ae lock o' his gowden hair
We'll theek our nest when it grows bare.

'Mony a one for him maks mane,
But nane sall ken whar he is gane:
O'er his white banes, when they are bare,
The wind sall blaw for evermair.'

ANON

hause, neck   *theek*, thatch

Proud Maisie is in the wood,
    Walking so early;
Sweet Robin sits on the bush,
    Singing so rarely.

'Tell me, thou bonny bird,
    When shall I marry me?'
'When six braw gentlemen
    Kirkward shall carry ye.'

Who makes the bridal bed,
    Birdie, say truly?'
'The grey-headed sexton
    That delves the grave duly.

The glow-worm o'er grave and stone
    Shall light thee steady
The owl from the steeple sing,
    "Welcome, proud lady".'

SIR WALTER SCOTT

'I heard a cow low, a bonnie cow low,
    And a cow low down in yon glen:
Lang, lang will my young son greet
    Or his mither bid him come ben!

'I heard a cow low, a bonnie cow low,
    And a cow low down in yon fauld:
Lang, lang will my young son greet
    Or his mither take him frae cauld!'

ANON

  greet, cry *ben*, to the inner room

Full fathom five thy father lies;
    Of his bones are coral made;
Those are pearls that were his eyes:
    Nothing of him that doth fade,
But doth suffer a sea-change
Into something rich and strange:
Sea nymphs hourly ring his knell.
    Ding-dong!
    Hark! now I hear them,
    Ding-dong, bell!
WILLIAM SHAKESPEARE

TWEED AND TILL

Tweed said to Till,
    'What gars ye rin sae still?'—
Till said to Tweed,
    'Though ye rin wi' speed,
    And I rin slaw,
Where ye droun ae man,
    I droun twa.'

ANON

THE FLOWERS OF THE FOREST

I've heard the lilting at our yowe-milking,
　　Lasses a-lilting before the dawn o' day;
But now they are moaning in ilka green loaning:
　　'The Flowers of the Forest are a' wede away.'

At buchts, in the morning, nae blythe lads are scorning;
　　The lasses are lonely, and dowie, and wae;
Nae daffin', nae gabbin', but sighing and sabbing;
　　Ilk ane lifts her leglen, and hies her away.

In hairst, at the shearing, nae youths now are jeering,
　　The bandsters are lyart, and runkled and grey;
At fair or at preaching, nae wooing, nae fleeching:
　　The Flowers of the Forest are a' wede away.

At e'en, in the gloaming, nae swankies are roaming
　　'Bout stacks wi' the lasses at bogle to play,
But ilk ane sits drearie, lamenting her dearie:
　　The Flowers of the Forest are a' wede away.

Dule and wae for the order sent our lads to the Border;
　　The English, for ance, by guile won the day:
The Flowers of the Forest, that foucht aye the foremost,
　　The prime o' our land, are cauld in the clay.

We'll hear nae mair lilting at the yowe-milking,
　　Women and bairns are heartless and wae;
Sighing and moaning on ilka green loaning;
　　'The Flowers of the Forest are a' wede away.'

JEAN ELLIOT

yowe, ewe; *loaning*, lane; *wede*, withered; *buchts*, sheepfolds; *daffin'*, romping; *leglen*, milk-pail; *hairst*, harvest; *bandsters*, binders; *lyart*, grizzled; *runkled*, wrinkled; *fleeching*, flattering; *swankies*, smart lads; *bogle*, hide-and-seek; *dule*, sorrow.

AN IRISH AIRMAN FORESEES HIS DEATH

I know that I shall meet my fate
Somewhere among the clouds above;
Those that I fight I do not hate,
Those that I guard I do not love;
My country is Kiltartan Cross,
My countrymen Kiltartan's poor,
No likely end could bring them loss
Or leave them happier than before.
Nor law, nor duty bade me fight,
Nor public men, nor cheering crowds,
A lonely impulse of delight
Drove to this tumult in the clouds;
I balanced all, brought all to mind,
The years to come seemde waste of breath,
A waste of breath the years behind
In balance with this life, this death.

W. B. YEATS

THE BONNIE EARL OF MORAY

Ye Highlands and ye Lawlands,
    Oh! where hae ye been?
They hae slain the Earl of Moray,
    And hae laid him on the green.

Now wae be to thee, Huntly,
    And wherefore did you sae?
I bade you bring him wi' you,
    But forbade you him to slay.

He was a braw gallant,
　　And he rid at the ring;
And the bonnie Earl of Moray,
　　Oh! he might hae been a king.

He was a braw gallant,
　　And he play'd at the ba';
And the bonnie Earl of Moray
　　Was the flower amang them a'.

He was a braw gallant,
　　And he play'd at the glove;
And the bonnie Earl of Moray,
　　Oh! he was the Queen's luve.

Oh! lang will his lady
　　Look owre the castle Doune,
Ere she see the Earl of Moray
　　Come sounding thro' the toun.

ANON

THE KNIGHT'S TOMB

Where is the grave of Sir Arthur O'Kellyn?
Where may the grave of that good man be?—
By the side of a spring, on the breast of Helvellyn,
Under the twigs of a young birch tree!
The oak that in summer was sweet to hear,
And rustled its leaves in the fall of the year,
And whistled and roared in the winter alone,
Is gone,—and the birch in its stead is grown.—
The Knight's bones are dust,
And his good sword rust;—
His soul is with the saints, I trust.

S. T. COLERIDGE

ON THE UNIVERSITY CARRIER

who sickn'd in the time of his vacancy, being forbid to
go to London, by reason of the Plague

Here lies old *Hobson*, Death hath broke his girt,
And here alas, hath laid him in the dirt,
Or else the ways being foul, twenty to one,
He's here stuck in a slough, and ogerthrown.
'Twas such a shifter, that if truth were known,
Death was half glad when he had got him down;
For he had any time this ten yeers full,
Dodged with him, betwixt *Cambridge* and the Bull.
And surely, Death could never have pregailed,
Had not his weekly course of carriage failed;
But lately finding him so long at home,
And thinking now his journey's end was come,
And that he had taken up his latest Inn,
In the kind office of a Chamberlin
Shewed him his room where he must lodge that night,
Pulled off his Boots, and took away the light:
If any ask for him, it shall be said,
Hobson has supped, and's newly gone to bed.

JOHN MILTON

UPON A MAID

Here she lies (in bed of spice)
Fair as Eve in Paradise:
For her beauty it was such
Poets could not praise too much.
Virgins come, and in a ring
Her supremest requiem sing;
Then depart, but see ye tread
Lightly, lightly o'er the dead.

ROBERT HERRICK

A slumber did my spirit seal;
   I had no human fears:
She seemed a thing that could not feel
   The touch of earthly years.

No motion has she now, no force;
   She neither hears nor sees;
Rolled round in earth's diurnal course,
   With rocks, and stones, and trees.

WILLIAM WORDSWORTH

DE CŒNATIONE MICÆ

Look round: You see a little supper room;
But from my window, lo! great Caesar's tomb!
And the great dead themselves, with jovial breath
Bid you be merry and remember death.

MARTIAL: translated from the
Latin by R. L. STEVENSON

PLATO'S TOMB

Eagle! why soarest thou above that tomb?
To what sublime and star-ypaven home
   Floatest thou?—
I am the image of swift Plato's spirit,
Ascending heaven; Athens doth inherit
   His corpse below.

ANON: translated from the
Greek by P. B. SHELLEY

273

IN PLAGUE TIME

Adieu, farewell earth's bliss,
This world uncertain is;
Fond are life's lustful joys,
Death proves them all but toys,
None from his darts can fly.
I am sick, I must die.
      Lord, have mercy on us!

Rich men, trust not in wealth,
Gold cannot buy you health;
Physic himself must fade,
All things to end are made.
The plague full swift goes by.
I am sick, I must die.
      Lord, have mercy on us!

Beauty is but a flower
Which wrinkles will devour;
Brightness falls from the air,
Queens have died young and fair,
Dust hath closed Helen's eye.
I am sick, I must die.
      Lord, have mercy on us!

Strength stoops unto the grave,
Worms feed on Hector brave,
Swords may not fight with fate,
Earth still holds ope her gate.
Come! come! the bells do cry.
I am sick, I must die.
      Lord, have mercy on us!

Wit with his wantonness
Tasteth death's bitterness;

Hell's executioner
Hath no ears for to hear
What vain art can reply.
I am sick, I must die.
  Lord, have mercy on us!

Haste, therefore, each degree,
To welcome destiny.
Heaven is our heritage,
Earth but a player's stage;
Mount we unto the sky.
I am sick, I must die.
  Lord, have mercy on us!

       THOMAS NASHE

WAKE ALL THE DEAD! WHAT HO! WHAT HO!

Wake all the dead! what ho! what ho!
How soundly they sleep whose pillows lie low,
They mind not poor lovers who walk above
On the decks of the world in storms of love.
 No whisper now, nor glance can pass
 Through wickets or through panes of glass;
For our windows and doors are shut and barred.
Lie close in the church, and in the churchyard.
 In every grave make room, make room!
 The world's at an end, and we come, we come.

      SIR WILLIAM DAVENANT

MARVELS AND RIDDLES

The man in the wilderness said to me,
How many strawberries grow in the sea?
I answered him as I thought good,
As many red herrings as grow in the wood.

ANON

I saw a peacock with a fiery tail
I saw a blazing comet drop down hail
I saw a cloud wrapped with ivy round
I saw an oak creep upon the ground
I saw a pismire swallow up a whale
I saw the sea brimful of ale
I saw a Venice glass full fifteen feet deep
I saw a well full of men's tears that weep
I saw red eyes all of a flaming fire
I saw a house bigger than the moon and higher
I saw the sun at twelve o'clock at night
I saw the man that saw this wondrous sight.

ANON

WONDERS

The Andalusian merchant, that returns
   Laden with cochineal and china dishes,
Reports in Spain how strangely Fogo burns
   Amidst an ocean full of flying fishes:
These things seem wondrous, yet more wondrous I,
Whose heart with fear doth freeze, with love doth fry.

ANON

THE GREAT PANJANDRUM

So she went into the garden
to cut a cabbage-leaf
to make an apple-pie;
and at the same time
a great she-bear, coming down the street,
pops its head into the shop.
What! no soap?
So he died,
and she very imprudently married the Barber:
and there were present
the Picninnies,
and the Joblillies,
And the Garyulies,
and the g   ·t Panjandrum himself,
with the litt' round button at top;
and they all fell to playing the game of catch-as-catch-can,
till the gunpowder ran out at the heels of their boots.

SAMUEL FOOTE

THE WHITE KNIGHT'S SONG

I'll tell thee everything I can;
    There's little to relate.
I saw an aged aged man,
    A-sitting on a gate.
'Who are you, aged man?' I said.
    'And how is it you live?'
And his answer trickled through my head,
    Like water through a sieve.

He said 'I look for butterflies
    That sleep among the wheat:
I make them into mutton-pies,
    And sell them in the street.
I sell them unto men,' he said,
    'Who sail the stormy seas;
And that's the way I get my bread—
    A trifle, if you please.'

But I was thinking of a plan
    To dye one's whiskers green,
And always use so large a fan
    That they could not be seen.
So, having no reply to give
    To what the old man said,
I cried 'Come, tell me how you live!'
    And thumped him on the head.

His accents mild took up the tale:
    He said 'I go my ways,
And when I find a mountain-rill,
    I set it in a blaze;
And thence they make a stuff they call
    Rowland's Macassar-Oil—
Yet twopence-halfpenny is all
    They give me for my toil'.

But I was thinking of a way
    To feed oneself on batter,
And so go on from day to day
    Getting a little fatter.
I shook him well from side to side,
    Until his face was blue:
'Come, tell me how you live,' I cried,
    'And what it is you do!'

He said 'I hunt for haddocks' eyes
    Among the heather bright,
And work them into waistcoat-buttons
    In the silent night.
And these I do not sell for gold
    Or coin of silvery shine,
But for a copper halfpenny,
    And that will purchase nine.

'I sometimes dig for buttered rolls,
    Or set limed twigs for crabs;
I sometimes search the grassy knolls
    For wheels of Hansom-cabs.
And that's the way' (he gave a wink)
    'By which I get my wealth—
And very gladly will I drink
    Your Honour's noble health.'

I heard him then, for I had just
    Completed my design
To keep the Menai bridge from rust
    By boiling it in wine.
I thanked him much for telling me
    The way he got his wealth,
But chiefly for his wish that he
    Might drink my noble health.

And now, if e'er by chance I put
    My fingers into glue,
Or madly squeeze a right-hand foot
    Into a left-hand shoe,
Or if I drop upon my toe
    A very heavy weight,
I weep, for it reminds me so
Of that old man I used to know—

Whose look was mild, whose speech was slow,
Whose hair was whiter than the snow,
Whose face was very like a crow,
With eyes, like cinders, all aglow,
Who seemed distracted with his woe,
Who rocked his body to and fro,
And muttered mumblingly and low,
As if his mouth were full of dough,
Who snorted like a buffalo—
That summer evening long ago
   A-sitting on a gate.

LEWIS CARROLL

Tam o' the linn cam up the gait,
Wi twenty puddens on a plate,
An ilka pudden had a pin,
'We'll eat them a,' quo' Tam o' the linn.

Tam o' the linn had nae breeks tae wear,
He coft him a sheepskin tae mak him a pair,
The fleshy side oot, the woolly side in,
'It's fine summer cleedin,' quo' Tam o' the linn.

Tam o' the linn, he had three bairns,
They fell in the fire, in each ither's airms;
'Oh,' quo the bunemost, 'I've got a het skin.'
'It's hetter below,' quo' Tam o' the linn.

Tam o' the linn gae tae the moss,
Tae seek a stable tae his horse;
The moss was open, an Tam fell in.
'I've stabled mysel,' quo' Tam o' the linn.

ANON

THE RIDDLING KNIGHT

There were three sisters fair and bright,
   Jennifer, Gentle and Rosemary,
And they three loved one valiant knight—
   As the dow flies over the mulberry-tree.

The eldest sister let him in,
And barr'd the door with a silver pin.

The second sister made his bed,
And placed soft pillows under his head.

The youngest sister that same night
Was resolved for to wed wi' this valiant knight.

'And if you can answer questions three,
O then, fair maid, I'll marry wi' thee.

'O what is louder nor a horn,
Or what is sharper nor a thorn?

'Or what is heavier nor the lead,
Or what is better nor the bread?

'Or what is longer nor the way,
Or what is deeper nor the sea?'—

'O shame is louder nor a horn,
And hunger is sharper nor a thorn.

'O sin is heavier nor the lead,
The blessing's better nor the bread.

'O the wind is longer nor the way
And love is deeper nor the sea.'

                dow, dove

'You have answer'd aright my questions three',
  Jennifer, Gentle and Rosemary;
'And now, fair maid, I'll marry wi' thee',
  As the dow flies over the mulberry-tree.

ANON

Oh send to me an apple that hasn't any kernel,
And send to me a capon without a bone or feather,
And send to me a ring that has no twist or circlet,
And send to me a baby that's all grace and good temper.

How could there be an apple that hasn't any kernel?
How could there be a capon without a bone or feather?
How could there be a ring that has no twist or circlet?
How could there be a baby that's all grace and good temper?

The apple in its blossom hadn't any kernel;
And when the hen was sitting there was no bone or feather;
And when the ring was melting it had no twist or circlet;
And when we were in love there was grace and good temper.

ANON: translated from the
Welsh by GWYN WILLIAMS

THE SONG OF THE MAD PRINCE

Who said, 'Peacock Pie'?
  The old King to the sparrow:
Who said, 'Crops are ripe'?
  Rust to the harrow:
Who said, 'Where sleeps she now?
  Where rests she now her head,
Bathed in eve's loveliness'?—
  That's what I said.

Who said, 'Ay, mum's the word'?;
   Sexton to willow:
Who said, 'Green dusk for dreams,
   Moss for a pillow'?
Who said, 'All Time's delight
   Hath she for narrow bed;
Life's troubled bubble broken'?—
   That's what I said.

WALTER DE LA MARE

VOYAGING AND TRAVEL

How many miles to Babylon?
  Three score miles and ten.
Can I get there by candle-light?
  Yes, and back again.

ANON

There was a naughty Boy
  A naughty Boy was he
He would not stop at home
He could not quiet be—
      He took
      In his Knapsack
      A Book
      Full of vowels
      And a shirt
      With some towels—
      A slight cap
      For night cap—
      A hair brush
      Comb ditto
      New Stockings
      For old ones
      Would split O!
      This Knapsack
      Tight at 's back
      He rivetted close
And follow'd his Nose
      To the North
      To the North
And follow'd his nose
      To the North.

There was a naughty Boy
   And a naughty Boy was he
He ran away to Scotland
   The people for to see—
     There he found
     That the ground
     Was as hard
     That a yard
     Was as long,
     That a song
     Was as merry,
     That a cherry
     Was as red—
     That lead
     Was as weighty
     That forescore
     Was as eighty
     That a door
     Was as wooden
     As in England—
     So he stood in
     His shoes
     And he wonder'd
     He stood in his
     Shoes and he wonder'd.

JOHN KEATS

SKIMBLESHANKS: THE RAILWAY CAT

There's a whisper down the line at 11.39
When the Night Mail's ready to depart,
Saying 'Skimble where is Skimble has he gone to hunt the
     thimble?
We must find him or the train can't start.'
All the guards and all the porters and the stationmaster's
     daughters

They are searching high and low,
Saying 'Skimble where is Skimble for unless he's very nimble
Then the Night Mail just can't go.'
At 11.42 then the signal's nearly due
And the passengers are frantic to a man—
Then Skimble will appear and he'll saunter to the rear:
He's been busy in the luggage van!
  He gives one flash of his glass-green eyes
   And the signal goes 'All Clear!'
   And we're off at last for the northern part
    Of the Northern Hemisphere!

You may say that by and large it is Skimble who's in charge
Of the Sleeping Car Express.
From the driver and the guards to the bagmen playing cards
He will supervise them all, more or less.
Down the corridor he paces and examines all the faces
Of the travellers in the First and in the Third;
He establishes control by a regular patrol
And he'd know at once if anything occurred.
He will watch you without winking and he sees what you are
   thinking
And it's certain that he doesn't approve
Of hilarity and riot, so the folk are very quiet
Whem Skimble is about and on the move.
  You can play no pranks with Skimbleshanks!
   He's a Cat that cannot be ignored;
   So nothing goes wrong on the Northern Mail
    When Skimbleshanks is aboard.

Oh it's very pleasant when you have found your little den
With your name written up on the door.
And the berth is very neat with a newly folded sheet
And there's not a speck of dust on the floor.
There is every sort of light—you can make it dark or bright;

There's a handle that you turn to make a breeze.
There's a funny little basin you're suppose to wash your face
    in
And a crank to shut the window if you sneeze.
Then the guard looks in politely and will ask you very
        brightly
'Do you like your morning tea weak or strong?'
But Skimble's just behind him and was ready to remind him,
For Skimble won't let anything go wrong.
     And when you creep into your cosy berth
        And pull up the counterpane,
     You ought to reflect that it's very nice
     To know that you won't be bothered by mice—
     You can leave all that to the Railway Cat,
        The Cat of the Railway Train!

In the watches of the night he is always fresh and bright;
Every now and then he has a cup of tea
With perhaps a drop of Scotch while he's keeping on the
        watch,
Only stopping here and there to catch a flea.
You were fast asleep at Crewe and so you never knew
That he was walking up and down the station;
You were sleeping all the while he was busy at Carlisle,
Where he greets the stationmaster with elation.
But you saw him at Dumfries, where he speaks to the police
If there's anything they ought to know about:
When you get to Gallowgate there you do not have to
        wait—
For Skimbleshanks will help you to get out!
     He gives you a wave of his long brown tail
        Which says: 'I'll see you again!
     You'll meet without fail on the Midnight Mail
        The Cat of the Railway Train.'

                          T. S. ELIOT

BERMUDAS

Where the remote Bermudas ride
In the ocean's bosom unespied,
From a small boat that rowed along,
The listening winds received this song:
   'What should we do but sing His praise
That led us through the watery maze,
Unto an isle so long unknown,
And yet far kinder than our own?
Where He the huge sea-monsters wracks
That lift the deep upon their backs,
He lands us on a grassy stage,
Safe from the storm's, and prelate's rage.
He gave us this eternal spring,
Which here enamels everything,
And sends the fowls to us in care,
On daily visits through the air;
He hangs in shades the orange bright,
Like golden lamps in a green night,
And does in the pomegranates close
Jewels more rich than Ormus shows;
He makes the figs our mouths to meet,
And throws the melons at our feet;
But apples plants of such a price,
No tree could ever bear them twice.
With cedars chosen by His hand,
From Lebanon, He stores the land,
And makes the hollow seas that roar,
Proclaim the ambergris on shore;
He cast (of which we rather boast)
The Gospel's pearl upon our coast,
And in these rocks for us did frame
A temple where to sound His name.
Oh! let our voice His praise exalt

Till it arrive at Heaven's vault,
Which, thence (perhaps) rebounding, may
Echo beyond the Mexique Bay.'

Thus sung they in the English boat
An holy and a cheerful note;
And all the way, to guide their chime,
With falling oars they kept the time.

ANDREW MARVELL

TRADE WINDS

In the harbour, in the island, in the Spanish Seas,
Are the tiny white houses and the orange-trees,
And day-long, night-long, the cool and pleasant breeze
    Of the steady Trade Winds blowing.

There is the red wine, the nutty Spanish ale,
The shuffle of the dancers, the old salt's tale,
The squeaking fiddle, and the soughing in the sail
    Of the steady Trade Winds blowing.

And o' nights there's fire-flies and the yellow moon,
And in the ghostly palm-trees the sleepy tune
Of the quiet voice calling me, the long low croon
    Of the steady Trade Winds blowing.

JOHN MASEFIELD

ST GERVAIS

Coming out of the mountains of a summer evening,
travelling alone;
Coming out of the mountains
singing,

Coming among men, and limousines,
and elegant tall women, and hotels
with private decorative gardens,
Coming among dust,

After the distant cowbells, bringing
memory of mule-tracks, slithering snow,
wild pansies, and the sudden
loose clattering of rock,

I remembered Sunday evenings, church bells and cinemas
and clumsy trams
searching interminable streets
for quiet slums, the slums where I

remembering St Gervais and the gorges, linger, bringing
in the worn shell of air, the pines,
the white-cloud-vision of Mont Blanc, and up
beyond Les Contamines, the seven shrines.

MICHAEL ROBERTS

SAILING HOMEWARD

Cliffs that rise a thousand feet
Without a break,
Lake that stretches a hundred miles
Without a wave,
Sands that are white through all the year
Without a stain,
Pine-tree woods, winter and summer
Ever-green,
Streams that for ever flow and flow
Without a pause,
Trees that for twenty thousand years

Your vows have kept,
You have suddenly healed the pain of a traveller's heart,
And moved his brush to write a new song.

CHAN FANG-SHĒNG: *trans-
lated from the Chinese by*
ARTHUR WALEY

WHERE LIES THE LAND

Where lies the land to which the ship would go?
Far, far ahead, is all her seamen know.
And where the land she travels from? Away,
Far, far behind, is all that they can say.

On sunny noons upon the deck's smooth face,
Linked arm in arm, how pleasant here to pace;
Or, o'er the stern reclining, watch below
The foaming wake far widening as we go.

On stormy nights when wild north-westers rave,
How proud a thing to fight with wind and wave!
The dripping sailor on the reeling mast
Exults to bear, and scorns to wish it past.

Where lies the land to which the ship would go?
Far, far ahead, is all her seamen know.
And where the land she travels from? Away,
Far, far behind, is all that they can say.

A. H. CLOUGH

THE ROAD NOT TAKEN

Two roads diverged in a yellow wood,
And sorry I could not travel both
And be one traveller, long I stood
And looked down one as far as I could
To where it bent in the undergrowth;

Then took the other, as just as fair,
And having perhaps the better claim,
Because it was grassy and wanted wear;
Though as for that the passing there
Had worn them really about the same,

And both that morning equally lay
In leaves no step had trodden black.
Oh, I kept the first for another day!
Yet knowing how way leads on to way,
I doubted if I should ever come back.

I shall be telling this with a sigh
Somewhere ages and ages hence:
Two roads diverged in a wood, and I—
I took the one less travelled by,
And that has made all the difference.

ROBERT FROST

THE ROLLING ENGLISH ROAD

Before the Roman came to Rye or out to Severn strode,
The rolling English drunkard made the rolling English road.
A reeling road, a rolling road, that rambles round the shire,
And after him the parson ran, the sexton and the squire;
A merry road, a mazy road, and such as we did tread
The night we went to Birmingham by way of Beachy Head.

I knew no harm of Bonaparte and plenty of the Squire,
And for to fight the Frenchman I did not much desire;
But I did bash their baggonets because they came arrayed
To straighten out the crooked road an English drunkard
  made,
Where you and I went down the lane with ale-mugs in our
  hands,
The night we went to Glastonbury by way of Goodwin
  Sands.

His sins they were forgiven him; or why do flowers run
Behind him, and the hedges all strengthening in the sun?
The wild thing went from left to right and knew not which
  was which,
But the wild rose was above him when they found him in the
  ditch.
God pardon us, nor harden us; we did not see so clear
The night we went to Bannockburn by way of Brighton Pier.

My friends, we will not go again or ape an ancient rage,
Or stretch the folly of our youth to be the shame of age,
But walk with clearer eyes and ears this path that wandereth,
And see undrugged in evening light the decent inn of death;
For there is good news yet to hear and fine things to be seen,
Before we go to Paradise by way of Kensal Green.

                                        G. K. CHESTERTON

A long time ago
I went on a journey,
Right to the corner
Of the Eastern Ocean.
The road there
Was long and winding,

And stormy waves
Barred my path.
What made me
Go this way?
Hunger drove me
Into the World.
I tried hard
To fill my belly,
And even a little
Seemed a lot.
But this was clearly
A bad bargain,
So I went home
And lived in idleness.

T'AO CH'IEN: *translated from*
the Chinese by ARTHUR WALEY

EPILOGUE

'O where are you going?' said reader to rider,
'That valley is fatal when furnaces burn,
Yonder's the midden whose odours will madden,
That gap is the grave where the tall return.'

'O do you imagine,' said fearer to farer,
'That dusk will delay on your path to the pass,
Your diligent looking discover the lacking
Your footsteps feel from granite to grass?'

'O what was that bird,' said horror to hearer,
'Did you see that shape in the twisted trees?
Behind you swiftly the figure comes softly,
The spot on your skin is a shocking disease?'

Voyaging and Travel

'Out of this house'—said rider to reader
'Yours never will'—said farer to fearer
'They're looking for you'—said hearer to horror
As he left them there, as he left them there.

W. H. AUDEN

Jog on, jog on, the footpath way,
    And merrily hent the stile-a;
A merry heart goes all the day,
    Your sad tires in a mile-a.

WILLIAM SHAKESPEARE

THE SEA

SIR PATRICK SPENS

The king sits in Dunfermline town,
    Drinking the blood-red wine:
'O where will I get a skeely skipper,
    To sail this new ship of mine?'

O up and spake an eldern knight,
    Sat at the king's right knee:
'Sir Patrick Spens is the best sailor
    That ever sail'd the sea.'

Our king has written a braid letter,
    And seal'd it with his hand,
And sent it to Sir Patrick Spens,
    Was walking on the strand.

'To Noroway, to Noroway,
    To Noroway o'er the faem;
The king's daughter of Noroway,
    'Tis thou maun bring her hame.'

The first word that Sir Patrick read,
    Sae loud, loud laughèd he;
The neist word that Sir Patrick read,
    The tear blinded his e'e.

'O wha is this has done this deed,
    And tauld the king o' me,
To send me out at this time of the year
    To sail upon the sea?

Be it wind, be it weet, be it hail, be it sleet,
    Our ship must sail the faem;
The king's daughter of Noroway,
    'Tis we must fetch her hame.'

They hoysed their sails on Monenday morn,
    Wi' a' the speed they may;
They hae landed in Noroway,
    Upon a Wodensday.

They hadna been a week, a week
    In Noroway but twae,
When that the lords o' Noroway
    Began aloud to say:

'Ye Scottishmen spend a' our king's goud,
    And a' our queenis fee!'
'Ye lie, ye lie, ye liars loud,
    Fu' loud I hear ye lie!

For I brought as much white monie
    As gane my men and me,
And I brought a half fou o' gude red goud
    Out o'er the sea wi' me.

Make ready, make ready, my merry men a',
    Our gude ship sails the morn:'
'Now, ever alake! my master dear,
    I fear a deadly storm!

I saw the new moon late yestreen,
    Wi' the auld moon in her arm;
And if we gang to sea, master,
    I fear we'll come to harm.'

The Sea

They hadna sailed a league, a league,
    A league but barely three,
When the lift grew dark, and the wind blew loud,
    And gurly grew the sea.

The ankers brak, and the topmasts lap,
    It was sic a deadly storm,
And the waves came o'er the broken ship,
    Till a' her sides were torn.

'O where will I get a gude sailor,
    To take my helm in hand,
Till I get up to the tall topmast,
    To see if I can spy land?'

'O here am I, a sailor gude,
    To take the helm in hand,
Till you go up to the tall topmast,
    But I fear you'll ne'er spy land.'

He hadna gane a step, a step,
    A step but barely ane,
When a bout flew out of our goodly ship,
    And the salt sea it cam in.

'Gae fetch a web o' the silken claith,
    Another o' the twine,
And wap them into our ship's side,
    And let na the sea come in.'

They fetched a web o' the silken claith,
    Another o' the twine,
And they wapped them roun' that gude ship's side,
    But still the sea cam in.

O laith, laith were our gude Scots lords
   To weet their cork-heel'd shoon;
But lang or a' the play was play'd,
   They wat their hats aboon.

And mony was the feather-bed
   That flottered on the faem,
And mony was the gude lord's son
   That never mair cam hame.

The ladies wrang their fingers white,
   The maidens tore their hair,
A' for the sake of their true loves,
   For them they'll see nae mair.

O lang, lang may the ladies sit,
   Wi' their fans into their hand,
Before they see Sir Patrick Spens
   Come sailing to the strand.

And lang, lang may the maidens sit,
   Wi' their goud kames in their hair,
A' waiting for their ain dear loves,
   For them they'll see nae mair.

Half owre, half owre to Aberdour
   'Tis fifty fathoms deep,
And there lies gude Sir Patrick Spens,
   Wi' the Scots lords at his feet.

ANON

SPANISH LADIES

Farewell and adieu to you, Fair Spanish Ladies,
  Farewell and adieu to you, Ladies of Spain.
For we've received orders to sail for old England,
  But we hope in a short time to see you again.
    We'll rant and we'll roar, all o'er the wild ocean,
    We'll rant and we'll roar, all o'er the wild seas,
Until we strike soundings in the Channel of Old England,
From Ushant to Scilly is thirty-five leagues.

We hove our ship to, with the wind at sou-west, boys,
  We hove our ship for to strike soundings clear;
Then filled the main topsail and bore right away, boys,
  And straight up the Channel our course we did steer.
    We'll rant and we'll roar, etc.

The first land we made was a point called the Dodman,
  Next Rame Head off Plymouth, Start, Portland and Wight,
We sailed then by Beachy, by Fairlee and Dung'ness,
  Then bore straight away for the South Foreland Light.

The signal was made for the Grand Fleet to anchor,
  We clewed up our topsails, stuck out tacks and sheets,
We stood by our stoppers, we brailed in our spanker,
  And anchored ahead of the noblest of fleets.

Then let every man here toss off a full bumper,
  Then let every man here toss off his full bowl,
For we will be jolly and drown melancholy,
  With a health to each jovial and true-hearted soul.
    We'll rant and we'll roar, all o'er the wild ocean,
    We'll rant and we'll roar, all o'er the wide seas,
Until we strike soundings in the Channel of Old England,
From Ushant to Scilly is thirty-five leagues.

A<small>NON</small>

THE RIME OF THE ANCIENT MARINER

PART I

It is an ancient Mariner,
And he stoppeth one of three.
'By thy long grey beard and glittering eye,
Now wherefore stopp'st thou me?

*An ancient
Mariner
meeteth three
gallants bidden
to a wedding
feast, and
detaineth one.*

'The Bridegroom's doors are opened wide,
And I am next of kin;
The guests are met, the feast is set:
May'st hear the merry din.'

He holds him with his skinny hand,
'There was a ship,' quoth he.
'Hold off! unhand me, grey-beard loon!'
Eftsoons his hand dropt he.

He holds him with his glittering eye—
The Wedding-Guest stood still,
And listens like a three years' child:
The Mariner hath his will.

*The Wedding
Guest is spell-
bound by the
eye of the old
seafaring man
and
constrained to
hear his tale.*

The Wedding-Guest sat on a stone:
He cannot choose but hear;
And thus spake on that ancient man,
The bright-eyed Mariner.

'The ship was cheer'd, the harbour clear'd,
Merrily did we drop
Below the kirk, below the hill,
Below the lighthouse top.

*The Mariner
tells how the
ship sailed
southward
with a good
wind and fair
weather, till it
reached the
Line.*

'The Sun came up upon the left,
Out of the sea came he!
And he shone bright, and on the right
Went down into the sea.

301

'Higher and higher every day,
Till over the mast at noon—'
The Wedding-Guest here beat his breast,
For he heard the loud bassoon.

The Wedding-
Guest heareth
the bridal
music; but
the Mariner
continueth
his tale.

The bride hath paced into the hall,
Red as a rose is she;
Nodding their heads before her goes
The merry minstrelsy.

The Wedding-Guest he beat his breast,
Yet he cannot choose but hear;
And thus spake on that ancient man,
The bright-eyed Mariner.

The ship
driven by a
storm toward
the South
Pole.

'And now the Storm-blast came, and he
Was tyrannous and strong:
He struck with his o'ertaking wings,
And chased us south along.

'With sloping masts and dipping prow,
As who pursued with yell and blow
Still treads the shadow of his foe,
And forward bends his head,
The ship drove fast, loud roar'd the blast,
And southward aye we fled.

'And now there came both mist and snow,
And it grew wondrous cold:
And ice, mast-high, came floating by,
As green as emerald.

The land of
ice, and of
fearful sounds,
where no
living thing
was to be seen.

'And through the drifts the snowy clifts
Did send a dismal sheen:
Nor shapes of men nor beasts we ken—
The ice was all between.

'The ice was here, the ice was there,
The ice was all around:
It crack'd and growl'd, and roar'd and howl'd,
Like noises in a swound!

'At length did cross an Albatross,
Thorough the fog it came;
As if it had been a Christian soul,
We hail'd it in God's name.

Till a great sea-bird, called the Albatross, came through the snow-fog and was received with great joy and hospitality.

'It ate the food it ne'er had eat,
And round and round it flew.
The ice did split with a thunder-fit;
The helmsman steer'd us through!

'And a good south wind sprung up behind;
The Albatross did follow,
And every day, for food or play,
Came to the mariners' hollo!

And lo! the Albatross proveth a bird of good omen, and followeth the ship as it returned northward through fog and floating ice.

'In mist or cloud, on mast or shroud,
It perched for vespers nine;
Whiles all the night, through fog-smoke white,
Glimmered the white Moon-shine'.

'God save thee, ancient Mariner,
From the fiends, that plague thee thus!—
Why look'st thou so?'—'With my cross-bow
I shot the Albatross.

The ancient Mariner inhospitably killeth the pious bird of good omen.

PART II

'The Sun now rose upon the right:
Out of the sea came he,
Still hid in mist, and on the left
Went down into the sea.

'And the good south wind still blew behind,
But no sweet bird did follow,
Nor any day for food or play
Came to the mariners' hollo!

His ship-mates cry out against the ancient Mariner for killing the bird of good luck.

'And I had done a hellish thing,
And it would work 'em woe:
For all averred I had killed the bird
That made the breeze to blow.
Ah wretch! said they, the bird to slay,
That made the breeze to blow!

But when the fog cleared off, they justify the same, and thus make themselves accomplices in the crime.

'Nor dim nor red, like God's own head,
The glorious Sun uprist:
Then all averred I had killed the bird
That brought the fog and mist.
'Twas right, said they, such birds to slay,
That bring the fog and mist.

The fair breeze continues; the ship enters the Pacific Ocean, & sails north-ward, even till it reaches the Line.
The ship hath been suddenly becalmed.

'The fair breeze blew, the white foam flew,
The furrow follow'd free;
We were the first that ever burst
Into that silent sea.

'Down dropt the breeze, the sails dropt down,
'Twas sad as sad could be;
And we did speak only to break
The silence of the sea!

'All in a hot and copper sky,
The bloody Sun, at noon,
Right up above the mast did stand,
No bigger than the Moon.

'Day after day, day after day,
We stuck, nor breath nor motion;

The Sea

As idle as a painted ship
Upon a painted ocean.

'Water, water, every where,
And all the boards did shrink:
Water, water every where
Nor any drop to drink.

And the Albatross begins to be avenged.

'The very deep did rot: O Christ!
That ever this should be!
Yea, slimy things did crawl with legs
Upon the slimy sea.

'About, about, in reel and rout
The death-fires danced at night;
The water, like a witch's oils,
Burnt green, and blue, and white.

'And some in dreams assurèd were
Of the Spirit that plagued us so;
Nine fathom deep he had follow'd us
From the land of mist and snow.

A Spirit had followed them, one of the invisible inhabitants of this planet, neither departed soul nor angels; concerning whom the learned Jew, Josephus, and the Platonic Constantinopolitan, Michael Psellus, may be consulted. They are very numerous, and there is no climate or element without one or more.

'And every tongue, through utter drought,
Was wither'd at the root;
We could not speak, no more than if
We had been choked with soot.

'Ah! well a-day! what evil looks
Had I from old and young!
Instead of the cross, the Albatross
About my neck was hung.

The shipmates in their sore distress, would fain throw the whole guilt on the ancient Mariner: in sign whereof they hang the dead sea-bird round his neck.

305

The Sea

'There passed a weary time. Each throat
Was parch'd, and glazed each eye.
A weary time! a weary time!
How glazed each weary eye!

Mariner
beholdeth a
sign in the
element afar
off.

When looking westward, I beheld
A something in the sky.

'At first it seem'd a little speck,
And then it seem'd a mist;
It moved and moved, and took at last
A certain shape, I wist.

'A speck, a mist, a shape, I wist!
And still it near'd and near'd:
As if it dodged a water-sprite,
It plunged, and tack'd and veer'd.

approach, it
seemeth him
to be a ship;
and at a dear
ransom be
freeth his
speech from
the bonds of
thirst.

'With throats unslaked, with black lips baked,
We could nor laugh nor wail;
Through utter drought all dumb we stood!
I bit my arm, I suck'd the blood,
And cried, A sail! a sail!

'With throats unslaked, with black lips baked,
Agape they heard me call:

A flash of joy;

Gramercy! they for joy did grin,
And all at once their breath drew in,
As they were drinking all.

follows. For
can it be a ship
that comes
onward without
wind or tide?

'See! see! (I cried) she tacks no more!
Hither to work us weal;
Without a breeze, without a tide,
She steadies with upright keel!

'The western wave was all a-flame.
The day was well nigh done!
Almost upon the western wave
Rested the broad, bright Sun;
When that strange shape drove suddenly
Betwixt us and the Sun.

'And straight the Sun was fleck'd with bars,
(Heaven's Mother send us grace!)
As if through a dungeon-grate he peer'd
With broad and burning face.

*It seemeth
him but the
skeleton of a
ship.*

'Alas! (thought I, and my heart beat loud)
How fast she nears and nears!
Are those *her* sails that glance in the Sun,
Like restless gossameres?

*And its ribs
are seen as
bars on the
face of the
setting Sun.*

'Are those *her* ribs through which the Sun
Did peer, as through a grate?
And is that Woman all her crew?
Is that a Death? and are there two?
Is Death that woman's mate?

*The Spectre-
Woman and
her Death-
mate, and no
other, on
board the
skeleton ship.
Like vessel
like crew!
Death and
Life-in-
Death have
diced for the
ship's crew,
and she (the
latter) win-
neth the
ancient
Mariner.*

'*Her* lips were red, *her* looks were free,
Her locks were yellow as gold:
Her skin was as white as leprosy,
The Night-mare Life-in-Death was she,
Who thicks man's blood with cold.

'The naked hulk alongside came,
And the twain were casting dice;
"The game is done! I've won! I've won!"
Quoth she, and whistles thrice.

'The Sun's rim dips; the stars rush out:
At one stride comes the dark;
With far-heard whisper, o'er the sea,
Off shot the spectre-bark.

*No twilight
within the
courts of the
Sun.*

The Sea

*At the rising
of the Moon.*

'We listen'd and look'd sideways up!
Fear at my heart, as at a cup,
My life-blood seem'd to sip!
The stars were dim, and thick the night,
The steersman's face by his lamp gleam'd white;
From the sails the dew did drip—
Till clomb above the eastern bar
The hornèd Moon, with one bright star
Within the nether tip.

*One after
another.*

'One after one, by the star-dogg'd Moon,
Too quick for groan or sigh,
Each turn'd his face with a ghastly pang,
And curs'd me with his eye.

*His ship-
mates drop
down dead.*

'Four times fifty living men
(And I heard nor sigh nor groan)
With heavy thump, a lifeless lump,
They dropp'd down one by one.

*But Life-in-
Death begins
her work on
the ancient
Mariner.*

'The souls did from their bodies fly,—
They fled to bliss or woe!
And every soul, it pass'd me by,
Like the whizz of my cross-bow!'

PART IV

*The
Wedding-
Guest
feareth that
a Spirit is
talking to
him;*

'I fear thee, ancient Mariner!
I fear thy skinny hand!
And thou art long, and lank, and brown,
As is the ribb'd sea-sand.

*But the
ancient
Mariner
assureth him
of his bodily*

'I fear thee, and thy glittering eye,
And thy skinny hand so brown.'—
'Fear not, fear not, thou Wedding-Guest!
This body dropt not down.

life, and proceedeth to relate his horrible penance.

'Alone, alone, all, all alone,
Alone on a wide, wide sea!
And never a saint took pity on
My soul in agony.

'The many men, so beautiful!
And they all dead did lie:
And a thousand thousand slimy things
Lived on; and so did I.

He despiseth the creatures of the calm.

'I look'd upon the rotting sea,
And drew my eyes away;
I look'd upon the rotting deck,
And there the dead men lay.

And envieth that they should live, and so many lie dead.

'I look'd to heaven and tried to pray;
But or ever a prayer had gusht,
A wicked whisper came, and made
My heart as dry as dust.

'I closed my lids, and kept them close,
And the balls like pulses beat;
But the sky and the sea, and the sea and the sky,
Lay like a load on my weary eye,
And the dead were at my feet.

'The cold sweat melted from their limbs,
Nor rot nor reek did they:
The look with which they look'd on me
Had never pass'd away.

But the curse liveth for him in the eye of the dead men.

'An orphan's curse would drag to hell
A spirit from on high;
But oh! more horrible than that
Is the curse in a dead man's eye!
Seven days, seven nights, I saw that curse,
And yet I could not die.

The Sea

In his lone-
liness and
fixedness he
yearneth
towards the
journeying
Moon, and
the stars that
still sojourn,
yet still move
onward; and
everywhere
the blue sky
belongs to
them, and is

'The moving Moon went up the sky,
And no where did abide:
Softly she was going up,
And a star or two beside—

'Her beams bemock'd the sultry main,
Like April hoar-frost spread;
But where the ship's huge shadow lay,
The charmed water burnt alway
A still and awful red.

their appointed rest and their native country and their own natural homes, which they
enter unannounced, as lords that are certainly expected, and yet there is a silent joy at
their arrival.

By the light
of the Moon
he beholdeth
God's
creatures of
the great
calm.

'Beyond the shadow of the ship,
I watched the water-snakes:
They moved in tracks of shining white,
And when they rear'd, the elfish light
Fell off in hoary flakes.

'Within the shadow of the ship
I watch'd their rich attire:
Blue, glossy green, and velvet black,
They coil'd and swam; and every track
Was a flash of golden fire.

Their beauty
and their
happiness.

He blesseth
them in his
heart.

'O happy living things! no tongue
Their beauty might declare:
A spring of love gush'd from my heart,
And I blessed them unaware;
Sure my kind saint took pity on me,
And I bless'd them unaware.

The spell
begins to
break.

'The selfsame moment I could pray;
And from my neck so free
The Albatross fell off, and sank
Like lead into the sea.

The Sea

PART V

'O sleep! It is a gentle thing,
Beloved from pole to pole!
To Mary Queen the praise be given!
She sent the gentle sleep from Heaven,
That slid into my soul.

'The silly buckets on the deck,
That had so long remain'd,
I dreamt that they were filled with dew;
And when I awoke, it rain'd.

By grace of the holy Mother, the ancient Mariner is refreshed with rain.

'My lips were wet, my throat was cold,
My garments all were dank;
Sure I had drunken in my dreams,
And still my body drank.

'I moved, and could not feel my limbs:
I was so light—almost
I thought that I had died in sleep,
And was a blessed ghost.

'And soon I heard a roaring wind:
It did not come anear;
But with its sound it shook the sails,
That were so thin and sere.

He heareth sounds and seeth strange sights and commotions in the sky and the element.

'The upper air burst into life!
And a hundred fire-flags sheen,
To and fro they were hurried about!
And to and fro, and in and out,
The wan stars danced between.

'And the coming wind did roar more loud,
And the sails did sigh like sedge;
And the rain pour'd down from one black cloud;
The Moon was at its edge.

311

'The thick black cloud was cleft, and still
The Moon was at its side:
Like waters shot from some high crag,
The lightning fell with never a jag,
A river steep and wide.

*The bodies of
the ship's
crew are in-
spirited, and the
ship moves on;*
'The loud wind never reach'd the ship,
Yet now the ship moved on!
Beneath the lightning and the Moon
The dead men gave a groan.

'They groan'd, they stirr'd, they all uprose,
Nor spake, nor moved their eyes;
It had been strange, even in a dream,
To have seen those dead men rise.

'The helmsman steer'd, the ship moved on;
Yet never a breeze up-blew;
The mariners all 'gan work the ropes,
Where they were wont to do;
They raised their limbs like lifeless tools—
We were a ghastly crew.

'The body of my brother's son
Stood by me, knee to knee:
The body and I pull'd at one rope,
But he said naught to me.'

*But not by
the souls of
the men, nor
by demons of
earth or
middle air, but
by a blessed
troop of
angelic
spirits, sent
down by the
invocation of
the guardian
saint.*
'I fear thee, ancient Mariner!'
'Be calm, thou Wedding-Guest!
'Twas not those souls that fled in pain,
Which to their corses came again,
But a troop of spirits blest:

'For when it dawn'd—they dropp'd their arms,
And cluster'd round the mast;
Sweet sounds rose slowly through their mouths,
And from their bodies pass'd.

'Around, around, flew each sweet sound,
Then darted to the Sun;
Slowly the sounds came back again,
Now mix'd, now one by one.

'Sometimes a-dropping from the sky
I heard the skylark sing;
Sometimes all little birds that are,
How they seem'd to fill the sea and air
With their sweet jargoning!

'And now 'twas like all instruments,
Now like a lonely flute;
And now it is an angel's song,
That makes the Heavens be mute.

'It ceased; yet still the sails made on
A pleasant noise till noon,
A noise like of a hidden brook
In the leafy month of June,
That to the sleeping woods all night
Singeth a quiet tune.

'Till noon we quietly sailèd on,
Yet never a breeze did breathe:
Slowly and smoothly went the ship,
Moved onward from beneath.

'Under the keel nine fathom deep,
From the land of mist and snow,
The Spirit slid: and it was he
That made the ship to go.
The sails at noon left off their tune,
And the ship stood still also.

The lonesome Spirit from the South Pole carries on the ship as far as the Line, in obedience to the angelic troop, but still requireth vengeance.

'The Sun, right up above the mast,
Had fix'd her to the ocean:
But in a minute she 'gan stir,
With a short uneasy motion—
Backwards and forwards half her length
With a short uneasy motion.

'Then like a pawing horse let go,
She made a sudden bound:
It flung the blood into my head,
And I fell down in a swound.

*The Polar
Spirit's
fellow-
demons, the
invisible in-
habitants of
the element,
take part in
his wrong;
and two of
them relate
one to the
other, that
penance, long
and heavy for
the ancient
Mariner hath
been accorded
to the Polar
Spirit, who
returneth
southward.*

'How long in that same fit I lay
I have not to declare;
But ere my living life return'd,
I heard, and in my soul discern'd
Two voices in the air.

' "It is he?" quoth one, "is this the man?
By Him who died on cross,
With his cruel bow he laid full low
The harmless Albatross.

' "The spirit who bideth by himself
In the land of mist and snow,
He loved the bird that loved the man
Who shot him with his bow."

'The other was a softer voice,
As soft as honey-dew:
Quoth he, "The man hath penance done,
And penance more will do."

The Sea

PART VI

First Voice:

' "But tell me, tell me! speak again,
Thy soft response renewing—
What makes that ship drive on so fast?
What is the ocean doing?"

Second Voice:

' "Still as a slave before his lord,
The ocean hath no blast;
His great bright eye most silently
Up to the moon is cast—

' "If he may know which way to go;
For she guides him smooth or grim,
See, brother, see! how graciously
She looketh down on him."

First Voice:

' "But why drives on that ship so fast,
Without or wave or wind?"

Second Voice:

' "The air is cut away before,
And closes from behind.

' "Fly, brother, fly! more high, more high!
Or we shall be belated:
For slow and slow that ship will go,
When the Mariner's trance is abated."

'I woke, and we were sailing on
As in a gentle weather:
'Twas night, calm night, the Moon was high;
The dead men stood together.

The Mariner hath been cast into a trance; for the angelic power causeth the vessel to drive northward faster than human life could endure.

The supernatural motion is retarded; the Mariner awakes, and his penance begins anew.

315

'All stood together on the deck,
For a charnel-dungeon fitter:
All fix'd on me their stony eyes,
That in the Moon did glitter.

'The pang, the curse, with which they died,
Had never pass'd away:
I could not draw my eyes from theirs,
Nor turn them up to pray.

*The curse is
finally
expiated.*

'And now this spell was snapt: once more
I viewed the ocean green,
And look'd far forth, yet little saw
Of what had else been seen—

Like one, that on a lonesome road
Doth walk in fear and dread,
And having once turn'd round, walks on
And turns no more his head;
Because he knows a frightful fiend
Doth close behind him tread.

'But soon there breathed a wind on me,
Nor sound nor motion made:
Its path was not upon the sea,
In ripple or in shade.

'It raised my hair, it fann'd my cheek
Like a meadow-gale of spring—
It mingled strangely with my fears,
Yet it felt like a welcoming.

'Swiftly, swiftly flew the ship,
Yet she sail'd softly too:
Sweetly, sweetly blew the breeze—
On me alone it blew.

'Oh! dream of joy! is this indeed
The lighthouse top I see?
Is this the hill? is this the kirk?
Is this mine own countree?

*And the an-
cient Mariner
beholdeth his
native
country.*

'We drifted o'er the harbour-bar,
And I with sobs did pray—
O let me be awake, my God!
Or let me sleep alway.

'The harbour-bar was clear as glass,
So smoothly it was strewn!
And on the bay the moonlight lay,
And the shadow of the Moon.

'The rock shone bright, the kirk no less
That stands above the rock:
The moonlight steep'd in silentness
The steady weathercock.

'And the bay was white with silent light
Till rising from the same,
Full many shapes, that shadows were,
In crimson colours came.

*The angelic
spirits leave
the dead
bodies,*

'A little distance from the prow
Those crimson shadows were:
I turn'd my eyes upon the deck—
Oh, Christ! what saw I there!

*And appear in
their own
form soft light.*

'Each corse lay flat, lifeless and flat,
And, by the holy rood!
A man all light, a seraph-man,
On every corse there stood.

'This seraph-band, each waved his hand:
It was a heavenly sight!
They stood as signals to the land,
Each one a lovely light;

'This seraph-band, each waved his hand,
No voice did they impart—
No voice, but oh! the silence sank
Like music on my heart.

'But soon I heard the dash of oars,
I heard the Pilot's cheer;
My head was turn'd perforce away,
And I saw a boat appear.

'The Pilot and the Pilot's boy,
I heard them coming fast:
Dear Lord in Heaven! it was a joy
The dead men could not blast.

'I saw a third—I heard his voice:
It is the Hermit good!
He singeth loud his godly hymns
That he makes in the wood.
He'll shrieve my soul, he'll wash away
The Albatross's blood.

PART VII

*The Hermit
of the Wood.*

'This Hermit good lives in that wood
Which slopes down to the sea.
How loudly his sweet voice he rears!
He loves to talk with marineres
That come from a far countree.

He kneels at morn, and noon, and eve—
He hath a cushion plump.
It is the moss that wholly hides
The rotted old oak-stump.

'The skiff-boat near'd; I heard them talk,
"Why this is strange, I trow!
Where are those lights so many and fair,
That signal made but now?"

' "Strange, by my faith!" the Hermit said—
"And they answer'd not our cheer!
The planks look warp'd! and see those sails,
How thin they are and sere!
I never saw aught like to them,
Unless perchance it were

*Approacheth
the ship with
wonder.*

' "Brown skeletons of leaves that lag
My forest-brook along;
When the ivy-tod is heavy with snow,
And the owlet whoops to the wolf below,
That eats the she-wolf's young."

' "Dear Lord! it hath a fiendish look—
(The Pilot made reply)
I am a-feared,"—"Push on, push on!"
Said the Hermit cheerily.

'The boat came closer to the ship,
But I nor spake nor stirr'd;
The boat came close beneath the ship;
And straight a sound was heard.

The ship sud-
denly
sinketh.

'Under the water it rumbled on,
Still louder and more dread:
It reach'd the ship, it split the bay;
The ship went down like lead.

The ancient
Mariner is
saved in the
Pilot's boat.

'Stunned by that loud and dreadful sound,
Which sky and ocean smote,
Like one that hath been seven days drown'd
My body lay afloat;
But swift as dreams, myself I found
Within the Pilot's boat.

'Upon the whirl, where sank the ship,
The boat spun round and round;
And all was still, save that the hill
Was telling of the sound.

'I moved my lips—the Pilot shriek'd
And fell down in a fit;
The holy Hermit raised his eyes,
And pray'd where he did sit.

'I took the oars: the Pilot's boy,
Who now doth crazy go,
Laugh'd loud and long, and all the while
His eyes went to and fro.
"Ha! ha!" quoth he, "full plain I see
The Devil knows how to row."

'And now, all in my own countree,
I stood on the firm land!
The Hermit stepp'd forth from the boat,
And scarcely he could stand.

' "O shrieve me, shrieve me, holy man!"
The Hermit cross'd his brow.
"Say quick," quoth he, "I bid thee say—
What manner of man art thou?"

*The ancient
Mariner
earnestly en-
treateth the
Hermit to
shrieve him;
and the pen-
ance of life
falls on him.*

'Forthwith this frame of mine was wrench'd
With a woful agony,
Which forced me to begin my tale;
And then it left me free.

'Since then, at an uncertain hour,
That agony returns:
And till my ghastly tale is told,
This heart within me burns.

*And ever and
anon through-
out his future
life an agony
constraineth
him to travel
from land to
land;*

'I pass, like night, from land to land;
I have strange power of speech;
That moment that his face I see,
I know the man that must hear me:
To him my tale I teach.

'What loud uproar bursts from that door!
The wedding-guests are there:
But in the garden-bower the bride
And bride-maids singing are:
And hark, the little vesper bell,
Which biddeth me to prayer!

'O Wedding-Guest! this soul hath been
Alone on a wide, wide sea;
So lonely 'twas, that God Himself
Scarce seemed there to be.

The Sea

'O sweeter than the marriage feast,
'Tis sweeter far to me,
To walk together to the kirk
With a goodly company!—

'To walk together to the kirk,
And all together pray,
While each to his great Father bends,
Old men, and babes, and loving friends,
And youths and maidens gay!

And to teach,
by his own
example,
love and
reverence to
all things
that God
made and
loveth.

'Farewell, farewell! but this I tell
To thee, thou Wedding-Guest!
He prayeth well, who loveth well
Both man and bird and beast.

'He prayeth best, who loveth best
All things both great and small;
For the dear God who loveth us,
He made and loveth all.'

The Mariner, whose eye is bright,
Whose beard with age is hoar,
Is gone: and now the Wedding-Guest
Turn'd from the bridegroom's door.

He went like one that hath been stunned,
And is of sense forlorn:
A sadder and a wiser man
He rose the morrow morn.

S. T. COLERIDGE

THE LAST CHANTEY

'And there was no more sea.'

Thus said the Lord in the Vault above the Cherubim,
   Calling to the Angels and the Souls in their degree:
     'Lo! Earth has passed away
     On the smoke of Judgment Day.
That Our word may be established shall We gather up the
     sea?'

Loud sang the souls of the jolly, jolly mariners:
   'Plague upon the hurricane that made us furl and flee!
     But the war is done between us,
     In the deep the Lord hath seen us—
Our bones we'll leave the barracout', and God may sink
     the sea!'

Then said the soul of Judas that betrayèd Him:
   'Lord, hast Thou forgotten Thy covenant with me?
     How once a year I go
     To cool me on the floe?
And Ye take my day of mercy if Ye take away the sea.'

Then said the soul of the Angel of the Off-shore Wind:
   (He that bits the thunder when the bull-mouthed breakers
     flee):
     'I have watch and ward to keep
     O'er Thy wonders on the deep,
And Ye take mine honour from me if Ye take away the
     sea!'

Loud sang the souls of the jolly, jolly mariners:
   'Nay, but we were angry, and a hasty folk are we.
     If we worked the ship together
     Till she foundered in foul weather,

Are we babes that we should clamour for a vengeance on
 the sea?'

Then said the souls of the slaves that men threw overboard:
 'Kennelled in the picaroon a weary band were we;
  But Thy arm was strong to save,
  And it touched us on the wave,
 And we drowsed the long tides idle till Thy Trumpets
  tore the sea.'

Then cried the soul of the stout Apostle Paul to God:
 'Once we frapped a ship, and she laboured woundily.
  There were fourteen score of these,
  And they blessed Thee on their knees,
 When they learned Thy Grace and Glory under Malta by
  the sea!'

Loud sang the souls of the jolly, jolly mariners,
 Plucking at their harps, and they plucked unhandily:
  'Our thumbs are rough and tarred,
  And the tune is something hard—
 May we lift a Deepsea Chantey such as seamen use at sea?'

Then said the souls of the gentlemen-adventurers—
 Fettered wrist to bar all for red iniquity:
  'Ho, we revel in our chains
  O'er the sorrow that was Spain's!
 Heave or sink it, leave or drink it, we were masters of the
  sea!'

Up spake the soul of a grey Gothavn 'speckshioner—
 (He that led the flenching in the fleets of fair Dundee):
  'Oh, the ice-blink white and near,
  And the bowhead breaching clear!
 Will Ye whelm them all for wantonness that wallow in the
  sea?'

The Sea

Loud sang the souls of the jolly, jolly mariners,
 Crying: 'Under Heaven, here is neither lead nor lee!
  Must we sing for evermore
  On the windless, glassy floor?
 Take back your golden fiddles and we'll beat to open sea!'

Then stooped the Lord and He called the good sea up to
       Him,
 And 'stablishèd its borders unto all eternity,
  That such as have no pleasure
  For to praise the Lord by measure,
 They may enter into galleons and serve Him on the sea.

Sun, Wind, and Cloud shall fail not from the face of it,
 Stinging, ringing spindrift, nor the fulmar flying free;
  And the ships shall go abroad
  To the Glory of the Lord
 Who heard the silly sailor-folk and gave them back their sea!
                                        RUDYARD KIPLING

THE FORSAKEN MERMAN

Come, dear children, let us away;
Down and away below!
Now my brothers call from the bay,
Now the great winds shoreward blow,
Now the salt tides seaward flow;
Now the wild white horses play,
Champ and chafe and toss in the spray.
Children dear, let us away!
This way, this way!

Call her once before you go—
Call once yet!
In a voice that she will know:
'Margaret! Margaret!'
Children's voices should be dear
(Call once more) to a mother's ear;
Children's voices, wild with pain—
Surely she will come again!
Call her once and come away;
This way, this way!
'Mother dear, we cannot stay!
The wild white horses foam and fret.'
Margaret! Margaret!

Come, dear children, come away down;
Call no more!
One last look at the white-wall'd town,
And the little grey church on the windy shore;
Then come down!
She will not come though you call all day;
Come away, come away!

Children dear, was it yesterday
We heard the sweet bells over the bay?
In the caverns where we lay,
Through the surf and through the swell,
The far-off sound of a silver bell?
Sand-strewn caverns, cool and deep,
Where the winds are all asleep;
Where the spent lights quiver and gleam,
Where the salt weed sways in the stream,
Where the sea-beasts, ranged all round,
Feed in the ooze of their pasture-ground;
Where the sea-snakes coil and twine,
Dry their mail and bask in the brine;
Where great whales come sailing by,

Sail and sail, with unshut eye,
Round the world for ever and aye?
When did music come this way?
Children dear, was it yesterday?

Children dear, was it yesterday
(Call yet once) that she went away?
Once she sate with you and me,
On a red gold throne in the heart of the sea,
And the youngest sate on her knee.
She comb'd its bright hair, and she tended it well,
When down swung the sound of a far-off bell.
She sigh'd, she look'd up through the clear green sea;
She said: 'I must go, for my kinsfolk pray
In the little grey church on the shore to-day.
'Twill be Easter-time in the world—ah me!
And I lose my poor soul, Merman! here with thee.'
I said: 'Go up, dear heart, through the waves;
Say thy prayer, and come back to the kind sea-caves!'
She smiled, she went up through the surf in the bay.
Children dear, was it yesterday?

   Children dear, were we long alone?
'The sea grows stormy, the little ones moan;
Long prayers,' I said, 'in the world they say;
Come!' I said; and we rose through the surf in the bay
We went up the beach, by the sandy down
Where the sea-stocks bloom, to the white-wall'd town;
Through the narrow paved streets, where all was still,
To the little grey church on the windy hill.
From the church came a murmur of folk at their prayers,
But we stood without in the cold blowing airs.
We climb'd on the graves, on the stones worn with rains,
And we gazed up the aisle through the small leaded panes.
She sate by the pillar; we saw her clear:

'Margaret, hist! come quick, we are here!
Dear heart,' I said, 'we are long alone;
The sea grows stormy, the little ones moan.'
But, ah, she gave me never a look,
For her eyes were seal'd to the holy book!
Loud prays the priest; shut stands the door.
Come away, children, call no more!
Come away, come down, call no more!

    Down, down, down!
Down to the depths of the sea!
She sits at her wheel in the humming town,
Singing most joyfully.
Hark what she sings: 'O joy, O joy,
For the humming street, and the child with its toy!
For the priest, and the bell, and the holy well;
For the wheel where I spun,
And the blessed light of the sun!'
And so she sings her fill,
Singing most joyfully,
Till the spindle drops from her hand,
And the whizzing wheel stands still.
She steals to the window, and looks at the sand,
And over the sand at the sea;
And her eyes are set in a stare;
And anon there breaks a sigh,
And anon there drops a tear,
From a sorrow-clouded eye,
And a heart sorrow-laden,
A long, long sigh;
For the cold strange eyes of a little Mermaiden
And the gleam of her golden hair.

    Come away, away children;
Come children, come down!

The Sea

The hoarse wind blows coldly;
Lights shine in the town.
She will start from her slumber
When gusts shake the door;
She will hear the winds howling,
Will hear the waves roar.
We shall see, while above us
The waves roar and whirl,
A ceiling of amber,
A pavement of pearl.
Singing: 'Here came a mortal,
But faithless was she!
And alone dwell for ever
The kings of the sea.'

But, children, at midnight,
When soft the winds blow,
When clear falls the moonlight,
When spring-tides are low;
When sweet airs come seaward
From heaths starr'd with broom,
And high rocks throw mildly
On the blanch'd sands a gloom;
Up the still, glistening beaches,
Up the creeks we will hie,
Over banks of bright seaweed
The ebb-tide leaves dry.
We will gaze, from the sand-hills,
At the white, sleeping town;
At the church on the hill-side—
And then come back down.
Singing: 'There dwells a loved one,
But cruel is she!
She left lonely for ever
The kings of the sea.'   MATTHEW ARNOLD

SUNK LYONESSE

In sea-cold Lyonesse,
When the Sabbath eve shafts down
On the roofs, walls, belfries
Of the foundered town,
The Nereids pluck their lyres
Where the green translucency beats,
And with motionless eyes at gaze
Make minstrelsy in the streets.
And the ocean water stirs
In salt-worn casemate and porch.
Plies the blunt-snouted fish
With fire in his skull for torch.
And the ringing wires resound;
And the unearthly lovely weep,
In lament of the music they make
In the sullen courts of sleep:
Whose marble flowers bloom for aye:
And—lapped by the moon-guiled tide—
Mock their carver with heart of stone,
Caged in his stone-ribbed side.

WALTER DE LA MARE

All day I hear the noise of waters
    Making moan,
Sad as the seabird is when going
    Forth alone
He hears the winds cry to the waters'
    Monotone.

The grey winds, the cold winds are blowing
    Where I go.

The Sea

I hear the noise of many waters
    Far below.
All day, all night, I hear them flowing
    To and fro.

JAMES JOYCE

LOVE

LOVE WILL FIND OUT THE WAY

Over the mountains
   And over the waves,
Under the fountains
   And under the graves;
Under floods that are deepest,
   Which Neptune obey,
Over rocks that are steepest,
   Love will find out the way.

When there is no place
   For the glow-worm to lie,
When there is no space
   For receipt of a fly;
When the midge dares not venture
   Lest herself fast she lay,
If Love come, he will enter
   And will find out the way.

You may esteem him
   A child for his might;
Or you may deem him
   A coward for his flight;
But if she whom Love doth honour
   Be concealed from the day—
Set a thousand guards upon her,
   Love will find out the way.

Some think to lose him
   By having him confined;
And some do suppose him,
   Poor heart! to be blind;

Love

But if ne'er so close ye wall him,
    Do the best that ye may,
Blind Love, if so ye call him,
    He will find out the way.

You may train the eagle
    To stoop to your fist;
Or you may inveigle
    The Phoenix of the east;
The lioness, you may move her
    To give over her prey;
But you'll ne'er stop a lover—
    He will find out the way.

If the earth it should part him,
    He would gallop it o'er;
If the seas should o'erthwart him,
    He would swim to the shore;
Should his Love become a swallow,
    Through the air to stray,
Love will lend wings to follow,
    And will find out the way.

There is no striving
    To cross his intent;
There is no contriving
    His plots to prevent;
But if once the message greet him
    That his True Love doth stay,
If Death should come and meet him,
    Love will find out the way!

ANON

THE SEEDS OF LOVE

I sowed the seeds of love,
And I sowed them in the spring,
I gathered them up in the morning so soon
While the small birds so sweetly sing.

My garden was planted well,
With flowers everywhere:
But I had not the liberty to choose for myself
Of the flowers that I love so dear.

The gardener was standing by
And I asked him to choose for me.
He chose for me the violet, the lily, and the pink,
But these I refused all three.

The violet I did not like
Because it bloomed so soon.
The lily and the pink I really overthink,
So I vowed I would wait till June.

In June there was a red rose bud,
And that is the flower for me.
I oftentimes have plucked that red rose bud,
Till I gained the willow tree.

The willow tree may twist,
And the willow tree may twine,
I oftentimes have wished I were in that young man's arms
That once had the heart of mine.

Come all you false young men,
Do not leave me here to complain,
For the grass that has oftentimes been trampled under foot,
Give it time, it will rise up again.

ANON

Have you seen but a bright lily grow
    Before rude hands have touch'd it?
Have you mark'd but the fall of the snow
    Before the soil hath smutch'd it?
Have you felt the wool of beaver,
        Or swan's down ever?
Or have smelt o' the bud o' the brier,
        Or the nard in the fire?
Or have tasted the bag of the bee?
O so white, O so soft, O so sweet is she!

BEN JONSON

O, MY LUVE IS LIKE A RED, RED ROSE

O, my luve is like a red, red rose,
    That's newly sprung in June:
O, my luve is like the melodie
    That's sweetly played in tune.

As fair art thou, my bonnie lass,
    So deep in luve am I;
And I will luve thee still, my dear,
    Till a' the seas gang dry.

Till a' the seas gang dry, my dear,
    And the rocks melt wi' the sun:
And I will luve thee still, my dear,
    While the sands o' life shall run.

And fare thee weel, my only luve,
    And fare thee weel a while!
And I will come again, my luve,
    Tho' it were ten thousand mile!

ROBERT BURNS

WALSINGHAME

'As you came from the holy land
    Of Walsinghame,
Met you not with my true love
    By the way as you came?'

'How shall I know your true love,
    That have met many one
As I went to the holy land,
    That have come, that have gone?'

'She is neither white nor brown,
    But as the heavens fair,
There is none hath a form so divine
    In the earth or the air.'

'Such an one did I meet, good Sir,
    Such an angelic face,
Who like a queen, like a nymph did appear
    By her gait, by her grace.'

'She hath left me here all alone,
    All alone as unknown,
Who sometimes did me lead with herself,
    And me loved as her own.'

'What's the cause that she leaves you alone
    And a new way doth take,
Who loved you once as her own
    And her joy did you make?'

'I have loved her all my youth,
    But now old as you see,
Love likes not the falling fruit
    From the withered tree.

Love

'Know that Love is a careless child,
    And forgets promise past;
He is blind, he is deaf when he list
    And in faith never fast.

'His desire is a dureless content
    And a trustless joy;
He is won with a world of despair
    And is lost with a toy.

'Of womenkind such indeed is the love
    Or the word love abused,
Under which many childish desires
    And conceits are excused.

'But love is a durable fire
    In the mind ever burning;
Never sick, never old, never dead,
    From itself never turning.'

SIR WALTER RALEGH

When in the chronicle of wasted time
    I see descriptions of the fairest wights,
And beauty making beautiful old rhyme,
    In praise of Ladies dead and lovely Knights,
Then, in the blazon of sweet beauty's best,
    Of hand, of foot, of lip, of eye, of brow,
I see their antique pen would have exprest
    Even such a beauty as you master now.
So all their praises are but prophecies
    Of this our time, all you prefiguring;
And, for they look'd but with divining eyes,
    They had not skill enough your worth to sing:
        For we, which now behold these present days,
        Have eyes to wonder, but lack tongues to praise.

WILLIAM SHAKESPEARE

A NEW COURTLY SONNET OF THE LADY GREENSLEEVES

Greensleeves was all my joy,
Greensleeves was my delight;
Greensleeves was my heart of gold,
And who but Lady Greensleeves.

Alas, my Love! ye do me wrong
  To cast me off discourteously;
And I have loved you so long,
  Delighting in your company.
    Greensleeves was all my joy, etc.

I have been ready at your hand,
  To grant whatever you would crave;
I have both waged life and land,
  Your love and goodwill for to have.

I bought thee kerchers to thy head,
  That were wrought fine and gallantly;
I kept thee both at board and bed,
  Which cost my purse well favouredly.

I bought thee petticoats of the best,
  The cloth so fine as fine might be;
I gave thee jewels for thy chest,
  And all this cost I spent on thee.

Thy purse and eke thy gay gilt knives,
  Thy pincase gallant to the eye;
No better wore the burgess wives,
  And yet thou wouldst not love me.

Thy gown was of the grassy green,
  Thy sleeves of satin hanging by,

waged, risked

338

Which made thee be our harvest queen,
    And yet thou wouldst not love me.

My gayest gelding I thee gave,
    To ride wherever liked thee;
No lady ever was so brave,
    And yet thou wouldst not love me.

My men were clothed all in green,
    And they did ever wait on thee;
All this was gallant to be seen,
    And yet thou wouldst not love me.

For every morning when thou rose,
    I sent thee dainties orderly,
To cheer thy stomach from all woes,
    And yet thou wouldst not love me.

Well, I will pray to God on high,
    That thou my constancy mayst see,
And that yet once before I die,
    Thou wilt vouchsafe to love me.

Greensleeves, now farewell! adieu!
    God I pray to prosper thee;
For I am still thy lover true.
    Come once again and love me.
      Greensleeves was all my joy,
        Greensleeves was my delight;
      Greensleeves was my heart of gold,
        And who but Lady Greensleeves.

ANON

YOUNG BEKIE

Young Bekie was as brave a knight
    As ever sail'd the sea;
And he's doen him to the court of France,
    To serve for meat and fee.

He had nae been i' the court of France
    A twelvemonth nor sae long,
Til he fell in love with the king's daughter,
    And was thrown in prison strong.

The king he had but ae daughter,
    Burd Isbel was her name;
And she has to the prison-house gane,
    To hear the prisoner's mane.

'O gin a lady wou'd borrow me,
    At her stirrup-foot I wou'd rin;
Or gin a widow wou'd borrow me,
    I wou'd swear to be her son.

'Or gin a virgin wou'd borrow me,
    I wou'd wed her wi' a ring;
I'd gie her ha's, I'd gie her bowers,
    The bonny towrs o' Linne.'

O barefoot, barefoot gaed she but,
    And barefoot came she ben;
It was no for want o' hose and shoone,
    Nor time to put them on;

But a' for fear that her father dear
    Had heard her making din:
She's stown the keys o' the prison-house door
    And latten the prisoner gang,

borrow, ransom   *but*, out   *ben*, in

Love

O whan she saw him, Young Bekie,
    Her heart was wondrous sair!
For the mice but and the bold rottons
    Had eaten his yallow hair.

She's gi'en him a shaver for his beard,
    A comber till his hair,
Five hunder pound in his pocket,
    To spen' and nae to spair.

She's gi'en him a steed was good in need,
    An' a saddle o' royal bone,
A leash o' hounds o' ae litter,
    And Hector callèd one.

Atween this twa a vow was made,
    'T was made full solemnly,
That or three years was come an' gane,
    Well married they should be.

He had nae been in 's ain country
    A twelvemonth till an end,
Till he's forc'd to marry a duke's daughter,
    Or than lose a' his land.

'Ohon, alas!' says Young Bekie,
    'I know not what to dee;
For I canno win to Burd Isbel,
    An' she kensnae to come to me.'

O it fell once upon a day
    Burd Isbel fell asleep,
And up its starts the Billy Blind,
    And stood at her bed-feet.

rottons, rats   *royal bone*, ivory   *Or than*, Or else
    Billy Blind, a friendly household fairy

Love

'O waken, waken, Burd Isbel,
  How can you sleep so soun',
Whan this is Bekie's wedding day,
  An' the marriage gaein on?

'Ye do ye to your mither's bowr,
  Think neither sin nor shame;
An' ye tak twa o' your mither's marys,
  To keep ye frae thinking lang.

'Ye dress yoursel' in the red scarlet,
  An' your marys in dainty green,
An' ye pit girdles abour your middles
  Wou'd buy an earldome.

'O ye gang down by yon sea-side,
  An' down by yon sea-stran';
Sae bonny will the Hollan's boats
  Come rowin' till your han'.

'Ye set your milke-white foot abord,
  Cry, Hail ye, Domine!
An' I shal be the steerer o't,
  To row you o'er the sea.'

She's tane her till her mither's bowr,
  Thought neither sin nor shame,
An she took twa o' her mither's marys,
  To keep her frae thinking lang.

She dress'd hersel' i' the red scarlet,
  Her marys i' dainty green,
And they pat girdles about their middles
  Would buy an earldome.

marys, maids

342

And they gid down by yon sea-side,
   And down by yon sea-stran';
Sae bonny did the Hollan's boats
   Come rowin' to their han'.

She set her milke-white foot on board,
   Cried, Hail ye, Domine!
And the Billy Blind was the steerer o't,
   To row her o'er the sea.

Whan she came to young Bekie's gate,
   She heard the music play;
Sae well she kent frae a' she heard,
   It was his wedding day.

She's pitten her han' in her pocket,
   Gi'en the porter guineas three;
'Hae, tak ye that, ye proud portèr,
   Bid the bride-groom speake to me.'

O whan that he cam up the stair,
   He fell low down on his knee:
He hail'd the king, and he hail'd the queen,
   And he hail'd him, Young Bekie.

'O, I've been porter at your gates
   This thirty years an' three;
But there's three ladies at them now,
   Their like I never did see.

'There's ane o' them dress'd in red scarlet,
   An' twa in dainty green,
An' they hae girdles about their middles
   Wou'd buy an earldome.'

Love

Then out it spake the bierly bride,
    Was a' goud to the chin;
'Gin she be braw without,' she says,
    'We's be as braw within.'

Then up it starts him, Young Bekie,
    And the tears was in his e'e:
'I'll lay my life it's Burd Isbel,
    Come o'er the sea to me.'

O quickly ran he down the stair,
    And when he saw 't was shee,
He kindly took her in his arms,
    And kiss'd her tenderly.

'O hae ye forgotten, Young Bekie,
    The vow ye made to me,
Whan I took you out o' the prison strong,
    Whan ye was condemn'd to die?

'I gae you a steed was good in need,
    An' a saddle o' royal bone,
A leash o' hounds o' ae litter,
    An' Hector callèd one.'

It was well kent what the lady said,
    That it wasnae a lee,
For at ilka word the lady spake,
    The hound fell at her knee.

'Tak hame, tak hame your daughter dear,
    A blessing gae her wi'!
For I maun marry my Burd Isbel,
    That's come o'er the sea to me.'

bierly, stately

Love

'Is this the custom o' your house,
   Or the fashion o' your lan',
To marry a maid in a May mornin',
   An' to send her back at even?'

ANON

THE DESPAIRING LOVER

Distracted with care
For Phyllis the fair,
Since nothing could move her,
Poor Damon, her lover,
Resolves in despair
No longer to languish,
Nor bear so much anguish:
But, mad with his love,
To a precipice goes,
Where a leap from above
Would soon finish his woes.

When in rage he came there,
Beholding how steep
The sides did appear,
And the bottom how deep;
His torments projecting,
And sadly reflecting,
That a lover forsaken
A new love may get,
But a neck, when once broken,
Can never be set:
And, that he could die

Love

Whenever he would,
But, that he could live
But as long as he could:
How grievous soever
The torment might grow,
He scorn'd to endeavour
To finish it so.
But bold, unconcern'd
At thoughts of the pain,
He calmly return'd
To his cottage again.

WILLIAM WALSH

LOST LOVE

His eyes are quickened so with grief,
He can watch a grass or leaf
Every instant grow; he can
Clearly through a flint wall see,
Or watch the startled spirit flee
From the throat of a dead man.
  Across two counties he can hear
And catch your words before you speak.
The woodlouse or the maggot's weak
Clamour rings in his sad ear,
And noise so slight it would surpass
Credence—drinking sound of grass,
Worm talk, clashing jaws of moth
Chumbling holes in cloth;
The groan of ants who undertake
Gigantic loads for honour's sake,
(Their sinews creak, their breath comes thin);
Whir of spiders when they spin,

And minute whispering, mumbling, sighs
Of idle grubs and flies.
    This man is quickened so with grief,
He wanders god-like or like thief
Inside and out, below, above,
Without relief seeking lost love.

ROBERT GRAVES

O, OPEN THE DOOR TO ME, O!

O, open the door, some pity to show,
    If love it may na be, O!
Tho' thou hast been false, I'll ever prove true,
    O, open the door to me, O!

Cauld is the blast upon my pale cheek,
    But caulder thy love for me, O!
The frost that freezes the life at my heart
    Is naught to my pains frae thee, O!

The wan moon is setting behind the white wave,
    And Time is setting with me, O!
False friends, false love, farewell! for mair
    I'll ne'er trouble them nor thee, O!

She has open'd the door, she has open'd it wide;
    She sees the pale corse on the plain, O!
My true love! she cried, and sank down by his side
    Never to rise again, O!

ROBERT BURNS

JACK AND JOAN

Jack and Joan they think no ill,
But loving live, and merry still;
Do their week-days' work, and pray
Devoutly on the holy day;
Skip and trip it on the green,
And help to choose the Summer Queen;
Lash out at a country feast
Their silver penny with the best.

Well can they judge of nappy ale,
And tell at large a winter tale;
Climb up to the apple loft,
And turn the crabs till they be soft.
Tib is all the father's joy,
And little Tom the mother's boy.
All their pleasure is content,
And care to pay their yearly rent.

Joan can call by name her cows,
And deck her windows with green boughs;
She can wreaths and tutties make,
And trim with plums a bridal cake.
Jack knows what brings gain or loss,
And his long flail can stoutly toss;
Make the hedge which others break,
And ever thinks what he doth speak.

Now you courtly dames and knights,
That study only st ange delights,
Though you scorn the home-spun gray
And revel in your rich array;
Though your tongues dissemble deep
And can your heads from danger keep:
Yet for all your pomp and train,
Securer lives the silly swain.

THOMAS CAMPION

348

THE SIMPLE PLOUGHBOY

O the Ploughboy was a-ploughing
With his horses on the plain,
   And was singing of a song as on went he:
'Since that I have fall'n in love,
If the parents disapprove,
   'Tis the first thing that will send me to the sea.'

When the parents came to know
That their daughter loved him so,
   Then they sent a gang, and press'd him for the sea.
And they made of him a tar,
To be slain in cruel war;
   Of the simple Ploughboy singing on the lea.

The maiden sore did grieve,
And without a word of leave,
   From her father's house she fled secretlie,
In male attire dress'd,
With a star upon her breast,
   All to seek her simple Ploughboy on the sea.

Then she went o'er hill and plain,
And she walked in wind and rain,
   Till she came to the brink of the blue sea,
Saying, 'I am forced to rove,
For the loss of my true love,
   Who is but a simple Ploughboy from the lea.'

Now the first she did behold,
O it was a sailor bold,
   'Have you seen my simple Ploughboy?' then said she.
'They have press'd him to the fleet,
Sent him tossing on the deep,
   Who is but a simple Ploughboy from the lea.'

Then she went to the Captain,
And to him she made complain,
   'O a silly Ploughboy's run away from me!'
Then the Captain smiled and said,
'Why Sir! surely you're a maid!
   So the Ploughboy I will render up to thee.'

Then she pullèd out a store,
Of five hundred crowns and more,
   And she strew'd them on the deck, did she.
Then she took him by the hand,
And she row'd him to the land,
   Where she wed the simple Ploughboy back from sea.

ANON

LEEZIE LINDSAY

'Will you gang wi' me, Leezie Lindsay,
   Will ye gang to the Highlands wi' me?
Will ye gang wi' me, Leezie Lindsay,
   My bride and my darling to be?'

'To gang to the Highlands wi' you, sir,
   I dinna ken how that may be;
For I ken nae the land that ye live in,
   Nor ken I the lad I'm gaun wi'.'

'O Leezie, lass, ye maun ken little,
   If sae be ye dinna ken me;
For my name is Lord Ronald Macdonald,
   A chieftain o' high degree.'

She has kilted her coats o' green satin,
   She has kilted them up to the knee,
And she's aff wi' Lord Ronald Macdonald,
   His bride and his darling to be.

ANON

BROWN PENNY

I whispered, 'I am too young,'
And then, 'I am old enough';
Wherefore I threw a penny
To find out if I might love.
'Go and love, go and love, young man,
If the lady be young and fair.'
Ah, penny, brown penny, brown penny,
I am looped in the loops of her hair.

O love is the crooked thing,
There is nobody wise enough
To find out all that is in it,
For he would be thinking of love
Till the stars had run away
And the shadows eaten the moon.
Ah, penny, brown penny, brown penny,
One cannot begin it too soon.

W. B. YEATS

Western wind, when will thou blow
   The small rain down can rain?
Christ, if my love were in my arms
   And I in my bed again!

ANON

PRAISE THE LORD

Let us with a gladsome mind
Praise the Lord, for he is kind,
For his mercies aye endure,
Ever faithful, ever sure.

Let us blaze His Name abroad,
For of gods he is the God;

That by His wisdom did create
The painted Heav'ns so full of state.

That did the solid Earth ordain
To rise above the watery plain.

And caused the Golden-tressèd Sun,
All the day long his course to run.

The hornèd Moon to shine by night,
Amongst her spangled sisters bright.

All living creatures He doth feed,
And with full hand supplies their need.

Let us therefore warble forth
His mighty Majesty and worth.

That His mansion hath on high
Above the reach of mortal eye.
For his mercies aye endure,
Ever faithful, ever sure.

JOHN MILTON

THE LAMB

Little Lamb, who made thee?
    Dost thou know who made thee?
Gave thee life, and bid thee feed
By the stream and o'er the mead;
Gave thee clothing of delight,
Softest clothing, woolly, bright;
Gave thee such a tender voice,
Making all the vales rejoice?
    Little Lamb, who made thee?
    Dost thou know who made thee?

Little Lamb, I'll tell thee,
    Little Lamb, I'll tell thee:
He is called by thy name,
For he calls himself a Lamb,
He is meek, and he is mild;
He became a little child.
I a child, and thou a lamb,
We are called by his name.
    Little Lamb, God bless thee!
    Little Lamb, God bless thee!

WILLIAM BLAKE

THE ELIXIR

Teach me, my God and King,
    In all things thee to see,
And what I do in any thing,
    To do it as for thee:

Not rudely as a beast,
    To run into an action;
But still to make thee prepossest,
    And give it his perfection.

God and Heaven

A man that looks on glass,
   On it may stay his eye;
Or if he pleaseth, through it pass
   And then the heaven espy.

All may of thee partake:
   Nothing can be so mean,
Which with his tincture (for thy sake)
   Will not grow bright and clean.

A servant with this clause
   Makes drudgery divine:
Who sweeps a room, as for thy laws,
   Makes that and the action fine.

This is the famous stone
   That turneth all to gold:
For that which God doth touch and own
   Cannot for less be told.

GEORGE HERBERT

I sing of a maiden
   That is makeless;
King of all kings
   To her son she chose.

He came all so still
   There his mother was,
As dew in April
   That falleth on the grass.

makeless, matchless

He came all so still
   To his mother's bower,
As dew in April
   That falleth on the flower.

He came all so still
   There his mother lay,
As dew in April
   That falleth on the spray.

Mother and maiden
   Was never none but she;
Well may such a lady
   God's mother be.

ANON

ON THE MORNING OF CHRIST'S NATIVITY

But peaceful was the night
Wherein the Prince of light
   His reign of peace upon the earth began:
The Winds with wonder whist,
Smoothly the waters kissed,
   Whispering new joys to the mild Ocean,
Who now hath quite forgot to rave,
While Birds of Calm sit brooding on the charmed wave.

The Stars with deep amaze
Stand fixed in stedfast gaze,
   Bending one way their precious influence,
And will not take their flight,
For all the morning light,
   Or *Lucifer* that often warned them thence;

355

But in their glimmering Orbs did glow,
Until their Lord himself bespake, and bid them go.

And through the shady gloom
Had given day her room,
 The Sun himself with-held his wonted speed,
And his head for shame,
As his inferior flame,
 The new enlightened world no more should need;
He saw a greater Sun appear
Then his bright Throne, or burning Axletree could bear.

The Shepherds on the Lawn,
Or ere the point of dawn,
 Sate simply chatting in a rustick row;
Full little thought they than,
That the mighty *Pan*
 Was kindly come to live with them below;
Perhaps their loves, or else their sheep,
Was all that did their silly thoughts so busy keep.

When such musick sweet
Their hearts and ears did greet,
 As never was by mortal finger strook,
Divinely-warbled voice
Answering the stringed noise,
 As all their souls in blisful rapture took:
The Air such pleasure loth to lose,
With thousand echoes still prolongs each heavenly close.

Nature that heard such sound
Beneath the hollow round
 Of *Cynthia's* seat, the Airy region thrilling,
Now was almost won
To think her part was done,
 And that her reign had here its last fulfilling;

God and Heaven

She knew such harmony alone
Could hold all Heaven and Earth in happier union.

At last surrounds their sight
A Globe of circular light,
   That with long beams the shame-faced night arrayed,
The helmed Cherubim
And sworded Seraphim,
   Are seen in glittering ranks with wings displayed,
Harping in loud and solemn quire,
With unexpressive notes to Heaven's new-born Heir.

Such Musick (as 'tis said)
Before was never made,
   But when of old the sons of morning sung,
While the Creator Great
His constellations set,
   And the well-balanced world on hinges hung,
And cast the dark foundations deep,
And bid the weltering waves their oozy channel keep.

Ring out ye Crystal sphears,
Once bless our human ears,
   (If ye have power to touch our senses so)
And let your silver chime
Move in melodious time;
   And let the Bass of Heaven's deep Organ blow,
And with your ninefold harmony
Make up full consort to th'Angelic symphony.

JOHN MILTON

THE BURNING BABE

As I in hoary winter's night stood shivering in the snow,
Surprised I was with sudden heat which made my heart to
      glow;
And lifting up a fearful eye to view what fire was near,
A pretty Babe all burning bright did in the air appear;
Who, scorched with excessive heat, such floods of tears did
      shed,
As though his floods should quench his flames which with
      his tears were fed.
'Alas!' quoth he, 'but newly born in fiery heats I fry,
Yet none approach to warm their hearts or feel my fire but I.
My faultless breast the furnace is, the fuel wounding thorns;
Love is the fire, and sighs the smoke, the ashes shame and
      scorns;
The fuel justice layeth on, and mercy blows the coals;
The metal in this furnace wrought are men's defiled souls:
For which, as now on fire I am to work them to their good,
So will I melt into a bath to wash them in my blood.'
With this he vanished out of sight and swiftly shrunk away,
And straight I called unto mind that it was Christmas Day.

ROBERT SOUTHWELL

CAROL

There was a Boy bedded in bracken,
Like to a sleeping snake all curled he lay;
On his thin navel turned this spinning sphere,
Each feeble finger fetched seven suns away.
He was not dropped in good-for-lambing weather,
He took no suck when shook buds sing together,
But he is come in cold-as-workhouse weather,
      Poor as a Salford child.

JOHN SHORT

JOURNEY OF THE MAGI

'A cold coming we had of it,
Just the worst time of the year
For a journey, and such a long journey:
The ways deep and the weather sharp,
The very dead of winter.'
And the camels galled, sore-footed, refractory,
Lying down in the melting snow.
There were times we regretted
The summer palaces on slopes, the terraces,
And the silken girls bringing sherbet.
Then the camel men cursing and grumbling
And running away, and wanting their liquor and women,
And the night-fires going out, and the lack of shelters,
And the cities hostile and the towns unfriendly
And the villages dirty and charging high prices:
A hard time we had of it.
At the end we preferred to travel all night,
Sleeping in snatches,
With the voices singing in our ears, saying
That this was all folly.

Then at dawn we came down to a temperate valley,
Wet, below the snow line, smelling of vegetation;
With a running stream and a water-mill beating the darkness,
And three trees on the low sky,
And an old white horse galloped away in the meadow.
Then we came to a tavern with vine-leaves over the lintel,
Six hands at an open door dicing for pieces of silver,
And feet kicking the empty wine-skins.
But there was no information, and so we continued
And arrived at evening, not a moment too soon
Finding the place; it was (you may say) satisfactory.

All this was a long time ago, I remember,
And I would do it again, but set down
This set down
This: were we led all that way for
Birth or Death? There was a Birth, certainly,
We had evidence and no doubt. I had seen birth and death
But had thought they were different; this Birth was
Hard and bitter agony for us, like Death, our death.
We returned to our places, these Kingdoms,
But no longer at ease here, in the old dispensation,
With an alien people clutching their gods.
I should be glad of another death.

T. S. ELIOT

THE HOLY WELL

As it fell out one May morning,
    And upon one bright holiday,
Sweet Jesus asked of his dear mother,
    If he might go to play.

'To play, to play, sweet Jesus shall go,
    And to play pray get you gone;
And let me hear of no complaint
    At night when you come home.'

Sweet Jesus went down to yonder town,
    As far as the Holy Well,
And there did see as fine children
    As any tongue can tell.

He said, 'God bless you every one,
    And your bodies Christ save and see:
Little children, shall I play with you,
    And you shall play with me?'

But they made answer to him, 'No:
    They were lords and ladies all;
And he was but a maiden's child,
    Born in an ox's stall.'

Sweet Jesus turned him around,
    And he neither laughed nor smiled,
But the tears came trickling from his eyes
    To be but a maiden's child.

Sweet Jesus turnèd him about,
    To his mother's dear home went he,
And said, 'I have been in yonder town,
    As far as you can see.

'I have been down in yonder town
    As far as the Holy Well,
There did I meet as fine children
    As any tongue can tell.

'I bid God bless them every one,
    And their bodies Christ save and see:
Little children, shall I play with you,
    And you shall play with me?

'But they made answer to me, No:
    They were lords and ladies all;
And I was but a maiden's child,
    Born in an ox's stall.'—

'Though you are but a maiden's child,
    Born in an ox's stall,
Thou art the Christ, the King of heaven,
    And the Saviour of them all.

'Sweet Jesus, go down to yonder town
　　As far as the Holy Well,
And take away those sinful souls,
　　And dip them deep in hell.'

'Nay, nay,' sweet Jesus said,
　　'Nay, nay, that may not be;
For there are too many sinful souls
　　Crying out for the help of me.'

ANON

EASTER

I got me flowers to straw Thy way,
　　I got me boughs off many a tree,
But Thou wast up by break of day,
　　And brought'st Thy sweets along with Thee.

The Sun arising in the East,
　　Though he give light, and th' East perfume,
If they should offer to contest
　　With Thy arising, they presume.

Can there be any day but this,
　　Though many suns to shine endeavour?
We count three hundred, but we miss;
　　There is but one, and that one ever.

GEORGE HERBERT

Glorious the sun in mid career;
Glorious th' assembled fires appear;
　　Glorious the comet's train:
Glorious the trumpet and alarm;
Glorious th' Almighty's stretched-out arm;
　　Glorious th' enraptured main:

Glorious the northern lights a-stream;
Glorious the song, when God's the theme;
   Glorious the thunder's roar:
Glorious Hosanna from the den;
Glorious the catholic Amen;
   Glorious the martyr's gore:

Glorious,—more glorious—is the crown
Of Him that brought salvation down,
   By meekness called thy Son:
Thou that stupendous truth believed;—
And now the matchless deed's achieved,
   DETERMINED, DARED, and DONE!

CHRISTOPHER SMART

LIGHT SHINING OUT OF DARKNESS

God moves in a mysterious way,
   His wonders to perform;
He plants His footsteps in the sea,
   And rides upon the storm.

Deep in unfathomable mines
   Of never failing skill,
He treasures up His bright designs,
   And works His sovereign will.

Ye fearful saints, fresh courage take,
   The clouds ye so much dread
Are big with mercy, and shall break
   In blessings on your head.

Judge not the Lord by feeble sense,
   But trust Him for His grace;
Behind a frowning providence,
   He hides a smiling face.

God and Heaven

His purposes will ripen fast,
    Unfolding every hour;
The bud may have a bitter taste,
    But sweet will be the flower.

Blind unbelief is sure to err,
    And scan His work in vain;
God is His own interpreter,
    And He will make it plain.

WILLIAM COWPER

Yet if His Majesty, our sovereign Lord,
Should of his own accord
Friendly himself invite,
And say 'I'll be your guest to-morrow night,'
How should we stir ourselves, call and command
All hands to work! 'Let no man idle stand!
'Set me fine Spanish tables in the hall;
See they be fitted all;
Let there be room to eat
And order taken that there want no meat.
See every sconce and candlestick made bright,
That without tapers they may give a light.
'Look to the presence: are the carpets spread,
The dazie o'er the head,
The cushions in the chairs,
And all the candles lighted on the stairs?
Perfume the chambers, and in any case
Let each man give attendance in his place!'
Thus, if a king were coming, would we do;
And 'twere good reason too;
For 'tis a duteous thing

To show all honour to an earthly king,
And after all our travail and our cost,
So he be pleased, to think no labour lost.

But at the coming of the King of Heaven
All's set at six and seven;
We wallow in our sin,
Christ cannot find a chamber in the inn.
We entertain Him always like a stranger,
And, as at first, still lodge Him in the manger.

ANON

EXPECTANS EXPECTAVI

From morn to midnight, all day through,
I laugh and play as others do,
I sin and chatter, just the same
As others with a different name.

And all year long upon the stage
I dance and tumble and do rage
So vehemently, I scarcely see
The inner and eternal me.

I have a temple I do not
Visit, a heart I have forgot,
A self that I have never met,
A secret shrine—and yet, and yet

This sanctuary of my soul
Unwitting I keep white and whole,
Unlatched and lit, if Thou should'st care
To enter or to tarry there.

With parted lips and outstretched hands
And listening ears Thy servant stands,
Call Thou early, call Thou late,
To Thy great service dedicate.

Charles Sorley

ST. PATRICK'S BREASTPLATE

I bind unto myself today
The strong Name of the Trinity,
By invocation of the same,
The Three in One, and One in Three.

I bind this day to me for ever,
By power of faith, Christ's Incarnation;
His baptism in the Jordan river;
His death on Cross for my salvation;
His bursting from the spicèd tomb;
His riding up the heavenly way;
His coming at the day of doom:
I bind unto myself today.

I bind unto myself today
The virtues of the starlit heaven,
The glorious sun's life-giving ray,
The whiteness of the moon at even,
The flashing of the lightning free,
The whirling wind's tempestuous shocks,
The stable earth, the deep salt sea
Around the old eternal rocks.

I bind unto myself today
The power of God to hold and lead,
His eye to watch, His might to stay,
His ear to hearken to my need,

God and Heaven

The wisdom of my God to teach,
His hand to guide, His shield to ward,
The word of God to give me speech,
His heavenly host to be my guard.

Christ be with me, Christ within me,
Christ behind me, Christ before me,
Christ beside me, Christ to win me,
Christ to comfort and restore me,
Christ beneath me, Christ above me,
Christ in quiet, Christ in danger,
Christ in hearts of all that love me,
Christ in mouth of friend and stranger.

I bind unto myself the Name,
The strong Name of the Trinity;
By invocation of the same,
The Three in One, and One in Three,
Of whom all nature hath creation,
Eternal Father, Spirit, Word,
Praise to the Lord of my salvation:
Salvation is of Christ the Lord.

*Ascribed to St. Patrick: translated
from the Irish by* C. F. ALEXANDER

THANKSGIVINGS FOR THE BEAUTY OF HIS PROVIDENCE

These sweeter far than lilies are,
No roses may with these compare!
How these excel
No tongue can tell!
Which he that well and truly knows
With praise and joy he goes.

God and Heaven

How great and happy's he that knows his ways,
    To be divine and heavenly joys!
    To whom each city is more brave
Than walls of pearl, and streets which gold doth pave;
    Whose open eyes
    Behold the skies;
Who loves their wealth and beauty more
    Than kings love golden ore!

Who sees the heavenly ancient ways
Of God the Lord, with joy and praise;
    More than the skies,
    With open eyes
Doth prize them all; yea, more than gems,
    And regal diadems.
That more esteemeth mountains as they are,
    Than if they gold and silver were:
To whom the sun more pleasure brings,
Than crowns and thrones and palaces to kings;
    That knows his ways
    To be the joys
And way of God. These things who knows
    With joy and praise he goes!

THOMAS TRAHERNE

PEACE

My Soul, there is a Country
    Afar beyond the stars,
Where stands a wingèd sentry
    All skilful in the wars,
There, above noise and danger,
    Sweet peace sits crown'd with smiles,
And One born in a Manger
    Commands the Beauteous files.

He is thy gracious friend
    And (O my Soul awake!)
Did in pure love descend,
    To die here for thy sake.
If thou canst get but thither,
    There grows the flower of peace,
The Rose that cannot wither,
    Thy fortress, and thy ease.
Leave then thy foolish ranges;
    For none can thee secure,
But One, who never changes,
    Thy God, thy Life, thy Cure.

HENRY VAUGHAN

Christ hath a garden walled around,
A Paradise of fruitful ground,
Chosen by love and fenced by grace
From out the world's wide wilderness.

Like trees of spice His servants stand,
There planted by His mighty hand;
By Eden's gracious streams, that flow
To feed their beauty where they grow.

Awake, O wind of heaven, and bear
Their sweetest perfume through the air;
Stir up, O south, the boughs that bloom,
Till the belovèd Master come;

That He may come and linger yet
Among the trees that He hath set;
That He may evermore be seen
To walk amid the springing green.

ISAAC WATTS

JERUSALEM

Jerusalem, my happy home,
　　When shall I come to thee?
When shall my sorrows have an end,
　　Thy joys when shall I see?

O happy harbour of the saints,
　　O sweet and pleasant soil,
In thee no sorrow may be found,
　　No grief, no care, no toil.

There lust and lucre cannot dwell,
　　There envy bears no sway;
There is no hunger, heat, nor cold,
　　But pleasure every way.

Thy walls are made of precious stones,
　　Thy bulwarks diamonds square;
Thy gates are of right orient pearl,
　　Exceeding rich and rare.

Thy turrets and thy pinnacles
　　With carbuncles do shine;
Thy very streets are paved with gold,
　　Surpassing clear and fine.

Ah, my sweet home, Jerusalem,
　　Would God I were in thee!
Would God my woes were at an end,
　　Thy joys that I might see!

Thy gardens and thy gallant walks
　　Continually are green;
There grows such sweet and pleasant flowers
　　As nowhere else are seen.

Quite through the streets, with silver sound,
  The flood of life doth flow;
Upon whose banks on every side
  The wood of life doth grow.

There trees for evermore bear fruit,
  And evermore do spring;
There evermore the angels sit,
  And evermore do sing.

Our Lady sings *Magnificat*
  With tune surpassing sweet;
And all the virgins bear their part,
  Sitting about her feet.

Jerusalem, my happy home,
  Would God I were in thee!
Would God my woes were at an end,
  Thy joys that I might see!

ANON

Matthew, Mark, Luke and John,
Bless the bed that I lie on.
  Four corners to my bed,
  Four angels round my head;
  One to watch and one to pray
  And two to bear my soul away.

ANON

EPIGRAMS AND REFLECTIONS

A ROUND

Hey nonny no!
Men are fools that wish to die!
Is't not fine to dance and sing
When the bells of death do ring?
Is't not fine to swim in wine,
And turn upon the toe,
And sing hey nonny no!
When the winds blow and the seas flow?
Hey nonny no!

ANON

THE BONNIE BROUKIT BAIRN

Mars is braw in crammasy,
Venus in a green silk goun,
The auld mune shak's her gowden feathers,
Their starry talk's a wheen o' blethers,
Nane for thee a thochtie sparin',
Earth, thou bonnie broukit bairn!
—*But greet, an' in your tears ye'll droun*
The haill clanjamfrie!

HUGH MACDIARMID

Crammasy, crimson; *wheen o' blethers*, pack of nonsense; *broukit*, pale-faced; *greet*, weep; *clanjamfrie*, collection.

372

FARA DIDDLE DYNO

Ha ha! ha ha! This world doth pass
    Most merrily I'll be sworn,
For many an honest Indian ass
    Goes for a unicorn.
                Fara diddle dyno,
                This is idle fyno.

Tie hie! tie hie! O sweet delight!
    He tickles this age that can
Call Tullia's ape a marmasyte
    And Leda's goose a swan.
                Fara diddle dyno,
                This is idle fyno.

So so! so so! Fine English days!
    For false play is no reproach,
For he that doth the coachman praise
    May safely use the coach.
                Fara diddle dyno,
                This is idle fyno.

                        THOMAS WEELKES

MEDITATIO

When I carefully consider the curious habits of dogs
I am compelled to conclude
That man is the superior animal.

When I consider the curious habits of man
I confess, my friend, I am puzzled.

                        EZRA POUND

THE BOUNTY OF OUR AGE

To see a strange outlandish fowl,
A quaint baboon, an ape, an owl,
A dancing bear, a giant's bone,
A foolish engine move alone,
A morris dance, a puppet-play,
Mad Tom to sing a roundelay,
A woman dancing on a rope,
Bull-baiting also at the *Hope*,
A rhymer's jests, a juggler's cheats,
A tumbler showing cunning feats,
Or players acting on the stage,—
There goes the bounty of our age:
But unto any pious motion
There's little coin and less devotion.

HENRY FARLEY

THE HARDSHIP OF ACCOUNTING

Never ask of money spent
Where the spender thinks it went.
Nobody was ever meant
To remember or invent
What he did with every cent.

ROBERT FROST

TELL ME NOW

'Tell me now, what should a man want
But to sit alone, sipping his cup of wine?'
I should like to have visitors come and discuss philosophy
And not to have the tax-collector coming to collect taxes;

374

My three sons married into good families
And my five daughters wedded to steady husbands.
Then I could jog through a happy five-score years
And, at the end, need no Paradise.

WANG CHI: *translated from the
Chinese by* ARTHUR WALEY

The hart he loves the high wood,
　　The hare she loves the hill;
The knight he loves his bright sword,
　　The lady loves her will.

ANON

THE FALSE HEART

I said to Heart, 'How goes it?' Heart replied:
'Right as a Ribstone Pippin!' But it lied.

HILAIRE BELLOC

WISHES OF AN ELDERLY MAN

I wish I loved the Human Race;
I wish I loved its silly face;
I wish I liked the way it walks;
I wish I liked the way it talks;
And when I'm introduced to one
I wish I thought *What Jolly Fun!*

SIR WALTER RALEIGH

THE FORT OF RATHANGAN

The fort over against the oak-wood,
Once it was Bruidge's, it was Cathal's,
It was Aed's, it was Ailill's,
It was Conaing's, it was Cuiline's,
And it was Maeldúin's;
The fort remains after each in his turn—
And the kings asleep in the ground.

ANON: *translated from the
Irish by* KUNO MEYER

THE PAST

The debt is paid,
The verdict said,
The Furies laid,
The plague is stayed,
All fortunes made;
Turn the key and bolt the door,
Sweet is death forevermore.
Nor haughty hope, nor swart chagrin,
Nor murdering hate, can enter in.
All is now secure and fast;
Not the gods can shake the Past;
Flies-to the adamantine door
Bolted down forevermore.
None can reënter there,—
No thief so politic,
No Satan with a royal trick
Steal in by window, chink, or hole,

History and Time

To bind or unbind, add what lacked,
Insert a leaf, or forge a name,
New-face or finish what is packed,
Alter or mend eternal Fact.

R. W. EMERSON

THE WAY THROUGH THE WOODS

They shut the road through the woods
Seventy years ago.
Weather and rain have undone it again,
And now you would never know
There was once a road through the woods
Before they planted the trees.
It is underneath the coppice and heath,
And the thin anemones.
Only the keeper sees
That, where the ring-dove broods,
And the badgers roll at ease,
There was once a road through the woods.

Yet, if you enter the woods
Of a summer evening late,
When the night-air cools on the trout-ringed pools
Where the otter whistles his mate,
(They fear not men in the woods,
Because they see so few.)
You will hear the beat of a horse's feet,
And the swish of a skirt in the dew,
Steadily cantering through
The misty solitudes,
As though they perfectly knew
The old lost road through the woods. . . .
But there is no road through the woods.

RUDYARD KIPLING

TWO HOUSES

Between a sunny bank and the sun
The farmhouse smiles
On the riverside plat:
No other one
So pleasant to look at
And remember, for many miles,
So velvet hushed and cool under the warm tiles.

Not far from the road it lies, yet caught
Far out of reach
Of the road's dust
And the dusty thought
Of passers-by, though each
Stops, and turns, and must
Look down at it like a wasp at the muslined peach.

But another house stood there long before:
And as if above graves
Still the turf heaves
Above its stones:
Dark hangs the sycamore,
Shadowing kennel and bones
And the black dog that shakes his chain and moans.

And when he barks, over the river
Flashing fast,
Dark echoes reply,
And the hollow past
Half yields the dead that never
More than half hidden lie:
And out they creep and back again for ever.

EDWARD THOMAS

THE OLD MEN ADMIRING THEMSELVES
IN THE WATER

I heard the old, old men say,
'Everything alters,
And one by one we drop away.'
They had hands like claws, and their knees
Were twisted like the old thorn-trees
By the waters.
I heard the old, old men say,
'All that's beautiful drifts away
Like the waters.'

W. B. YEATS

THE AUTUMN WIND

Autumn wind rises; white clouds fly.
Grass and trees wither; geese go south.
Orchids, all in bloom; chrysanthemums smell sweet;
I think of my lovely lady; I never can forget.
Floating-pagoda boat crosses Fên River;
Across the mid-stream white waves rise.
Flute and drum keep time to sound of rowers' song;
Amidst revel and feasting sad thoughts come;
Youth's years how few, age how sure!

EMPEROR WU-TI: *translated from
the Chinese by* ARTHUR WALEY

ALL HUSHED AND STILL WITHIN THE HOUSE

All hushed and still within the house;
   Without—all wind and driving rain;
But something whispers to my mind
Through rain and through the wailing wind,
      Never again.
Never again? Why not again?
Memory has power as real as thine.

EMILY BRONTË

A MEMENTO FOR MORTALITY

*Taken from the view of Sepulchres of so many Kings
and Nobles, as lie interred in the Abbey of Westminster.*

Mortality, behold and fear!
What a change of flesh is here!
Think how many royal bones
Sleep within this heap of stones,
Hence removed from beds of ease,
Dainty fare, and what might please,
Fretted roofs, and costly shows,
To a roof that flats the nose:
Which proclaims all flesh is grass,
How the world's fair glories pass;
That there is no trust in health,
In youth, in age, in greatness, wealth:
For if such could have reprieved,
Those had been immortal lived.
Know from this the world a snare,
How that greatness is but care,
How all pleasures are but pain,
And how short they do remain:

For here they lie had realms and lands,
That now want strength to stir their hands;
Where from their pulpits seeled with dust
They preach, 'In greatness is no trust.'
Here's an acre sown indeed
With the richest royal'st seed
That the earth did e'er suck in
Since the first man died for sin:
Here the bones of birth have cried
'Though Gods they were, as men they died.'
Here are sands, ignoble things,
Dropped from the ruined sides of Kings;
With whom the poor man's earth being shown,
The difference is not easily known.
Here's a world of pomp and state
Forgotten, dead, disconsolate.

WILLIAM BASSE (?)

MAN'S MORTALITY

Like as the damask rose you see,
Or like the blossom on the tree,
Or like the dainty flower of May,
Or like the morning to the day,
Or like the sun, or like the shade,
Or like the gourd which Jonas had—
Even such is man, whose thread is spun,
Drawn out, and cut, and so is done.
The rose withers, the blossom blasteth,
The flower fades, the morning hasteth,
The sun sets, the shadow flies,
The gourd consumes; and man he dies

Like to the grass that's newly sprung,
Or like a tale that's new begun,
Or like the bird that's here to-day.
Or like the pearlèd dew of May,
Or like an hour, or like a span,
Or like the singing of a swan—
Even such is man, who lives by breath,
Is here, now there: so life, and death.
The grass withers, the tale is ended,
The bird is flown, the dew's ascended,
The hour is short, the span not long,
The swan's near death; man's life is done.

Like to the bubble in the brook,
Or, in a glass, much like a look,
Or like a shuttle in weaver's hand,
Or like a writing on the sand,
Or like a thought, or like a dream,
Or like the gliding of the stream—
Even such is man, who lives by breath,
Is here, now there: so life, and death.
The bubble's cut, the look's forgot,
The shuttle's flung, the writing's blot,
The thought is past, the dream is gone,
The water glides; man's life is done.

Like to an arrow from the bow,
Or like swift course of watery flow,
Or like the time 'twixt flood and ebb,
Or like the spider's tender web,
Or like a race, or like a goal,
Or like the dealing of a dole—
Even such is man, whose brittle state
Is always subject unto fate.

The arrow's shot, the flood soon spent,
The time no time, the web soon rent,
The race soon run, the goal soon won,
The dole soon dealt; man's life first done.

Like to the lightning from the sky,
Or like a post that quick doth hie,
Or like a quaver in short song,
Or like a journey three days long,
Or like the snow when summer's come,
Or like the pear, or like the plum—
Even such is man, who heaps up sorrow,
Lives but this day and dies to-morrow.
The lightning's past, the post must go,
The song is short, the journey's so,
The pear doth rot, the plum doth fall,
The snow dissolves, and so must all.

Like to the seed put in earth's womb,
Or like dead Lazarus in his tomb,
Or like Tabitha being asleep,
Or Jonas-like within the deep,
Or like the night, or stars by day
Which seem to vanish clean away:
Even so this death man's life bereaves,
But, being dead, man death deceives.
The seed it springeth, Lazarus standeth,
Tabitha wakes, and Jonas landeth,
The night is past, the stars remain;
So man that dies shall live again.

ANON

SONG

Who can say
Why Today
Tomorrow will be yesterday?
Who can tell
Why to smell
The violet, recalls the dewy prime
Of youth and buried time?
The cause is nowhere found in rhyme.

LORD TENNYSON

When that I was and a little tiny boy,
   With hey, ho, the wind and the rain;
A foolish thing was but a toy,
   For the rain it raineth every day.

But when I came to man's estate,
   With hey, ho, the wind and the rain;
'Gainst knaves and thieves men shut their gate,
   For the rain it raineth every day.

But when I came, alas! to wive,
   With hey, ho, the wind and the rain;
By swaggering could I never thrive,
   For the rain it raineth every day.

But when I came unto my beds,
   With hey, ho, the wind and the rain;
With toss-pots still had drunken heads,
   For the rain it raineth every day.

A great while ago the world begun,
   With hey, ho, the wind and the rain;
But that's all one, our play is done,
   And we'll strive to please you every day.

WILLIAM SHAKESPEARE

FURTHER INFORMATION

POETRY, MUSIC AND DANCING

p. 34. *On First Looking into Chapman's Homer.* George Chapman, the Elizabethan poet, published a translation of *The Iliad* in 1611 and *The Odyssey* in 1614.

p. 36. *The Splendour Falls.* One of the lyrics in *The Princess*.

p. 42. *Song for a Dance.* From The Masque of the Inner Temple and Grays Inn, acted in 1612.

NIGHT AND DAY, SEASONS AND WEATHERS

p. 47. *Hark! Hark!* Song from *Cymbeline*.

p. 48. *The Star that Bids the Shepherd Fold.* Speech from *Comus*, a masque presented at Ludlow Castle in 1634. This speech was spoken by the twelve-year-old Lord Brackley, who with his younger brother and sister took the main parts.

p. 49. *Song of the Water.* From *Death's Jest Book*, a five-act play.

p. 52. *When daffodils begin to peer.* Song from *A Winter's Tale*.

p. 53. *When as the rye reach to the chin.* Song from *The Old Wives Tale*.

p. 56. *Fall, leaves, fall.* Song written for one of the characters in the imaginary country Gondal to which many of Emily Brontë's poems refer.

p. 56. *Hiems.* Song from *Love's Labour's Lost*.

p. 57. *On the Frozen Lake.* From Part I of a long autobiographical poem, *The Prelude*.

p. 59. *A Song to the Wind.* This poem is a riddle supposed to have been put by Taliessin, the legendary Welsh poet, to an assembly of aged bards.

BEASTS AND BIRDS

p. 63. *Auguries of Innocence.* The first part of a long poem of this name.

p. 64. *A Lark's Nest.* One of Smart's *Hymns for the Amusement of Children*.

CHILDREN

VICTUALS AND DRINK

SOME PEOPLE

p. 117. *Meg Merrilies*. Meg Merrilies is a character in Scott's *Guy Mannering*, a story about Galloway. Keats wrote this poem while on a walking-tour in that part of Scotland, and sent it in a letter to his younger sister Fanny.

p. 118. *An Old Man*. In Wordsworth's *Poems* this has the title *Animal Tranquillity and Decay*.

FOUR COUNTRIES

p. 126. *Jerusalem*. These four verses appear in the Preface to Blake's *Milton: a poem in two books*.

p. 126. *The New London*. The closing stanzas of a long poem—*Annus Mirabilis*—on the sea-fights against the Dutch in 1665 and 1666, and the Fire of London in 1666.

p. 128. *Westminster Bridge*. The sonnet was composed on top of a coach; Wordsworth was on his way to France.

p. 129. *Puck's Song*. An enlarged version of the poem in *Puck of Pook's Hill*.

p. 132. *Canadian Boat Song*. Thousands of people emigrated from the Highlands to Canada in the late 1700's and in the 1800's. Many of them were forced to go by their landlords, who wanted their land for sheep.

KINGS, QUEENS AND HEROES

p. 136. *When Alysandyr our King*. Written on the death of Alexander III of Scotland in 1285.

p. 137. *A Ditty*. Eliza, Queen of the Shepherds, is Queen Elizabeth I, whom poets often wrote of as a shepherdess.

p. 139. *Elizabeth of Bohemia*. She was the daughter of James I, and sister of Charles I; wife of the King of Bohemia, and mother of Prince Rupert of the Rhine; often called 'The Queen of Hearts'.

p. 139. *As I was going by Charing Cross*. The statue of Charles I by Hubert Le Sueur, now at the top of Whitehall, was originally erected at Charing Cross.

p. 140. *When the King Enjoys his Own Again*. Written in 1643, to keep up Royalist spirits: much used at the Restoration of Charles II.

p. 141. *O'er the Water to Charlie*. Charles Edward Stuart, 'Bonnie Prince Charlie'.

p. 142. *Freedom*. From a long poem *The Bruce*.

p. 144. *Upon Sir Francis Drake's Return*. Drake returned from sailing round the world in 1581 and was knighted by Queen Elizabeth. Sir Humphrey Gilbert, half-brother of Sir Walter Ralegh, sailed in 1583 to Newfoundland and established there the first British colony in North America.

p. 145. *Of the Great and Famous Sir Francis Drake*. Robert Hayman was a nephew of Sir Walter Ralegh and governor of Newfoundland.

p. 149. *O Captain! my Captain!* The Captain is Abraham Lincoln, President of the United States, who was assassinated in 1865, soon after he had led the North to victory in the American Civil War.

NINE TALES

p. 150. *Horatius*. 31 out of the 70 stanzas of the whole poem have been omitted.

p. 170. *Sir Eglamour*. A parody of an old ballad, from *The Melancholy Knight*, 1615, which is a satire on the romances of the period, including *The Faerie Queene*.

MAGIC

p. 188. *I'll Sail upon the Dog-star*. From the comedy, *A Fool's Preferment*.

p. 188. *Three Men of Gotham*. A catch, sung by Mr Hilary and the Rev. Mr Larynx, two characters in Peacock's novel *Nightmare Abbey*.

p. 189. *O Blest Unfabled Incense Tree*. From *Nepenthe*, a poem in two cantos.

p. 201. *Kubla Khan.* Written on waking from a daytime sleep, just after reading a book about the Great Khan. Coleridge had the impression that he had composed 200–300 lines; but he was interrupted by a visitor after writing down the lines that make the present poem, and after the visitor had gone he could not remember any more.

FAIRIES, NYMPHS AND GODS

p. 205. *The Fairies' Farewell.* The first half of the poem of that title. Bishop Corbet's view was that Fairies were Catholics and ceased to prosper after the Reformation.

p. 216. *Ariel's Song.* From *The Tempest.*

p. 217. *Sabrina Fair.* From *Comus,* a masque presented at Ludlow Castle. *Sabrina* is the nymph of the Severn.

p. 217. *The God of Sheep.* From the play, *The Faithful Shepherdess.*

WITCHES, CHARMS AND SPELLS

p. 221. *Nativity Chant.* Sung by the old gipsy, Meg Merrilies, in Scott's *Guy Mannering.*

p. 224. *Witches' Charm.* The last of three charms, from *The Masque of Queens,* performed in 1609.

p. 226. *Gipsy Song.* From a masque, *The Metamorphosed Gipsies,* performed in 1621.

p. 227. *A Voice Speaks from the Well.* From the play *The Old Wives' Tale.*

p. 229. *Good Wish.* One of the forms once used to bless everyday activities in the Highlands—fishing, going on a journey, hunting, and so on.

MARCH AND BATTLE

p. 252. *Bonny Dundee.* Bonny Dundee was John Graham of Claverhouse, Viscount Dundee, who raised an army in Scotland for the exiled James II. The scene of this episode is Edinburgh. From a poetic drama, *The Doom of Devorgoil*

p. 256. *Hohenlinden*. At Hohenlinden, in Bavaria, the French revolutionary army beat the Austrians in 1800.

p. 258. *The Night of Trafalgar*. Song from *The Dynasts*, a long dramatic poem.

p. 259. *The Eve of Waterloo*. Stanzas from Canto III of *Childe Harold*, a long narrative poem.

p. 260. *The Field of Waterloo*. Chorus from *The Dynasts*.

DIRGES, CORONACHS AND ELEGIES

p. 265. *Call for the robin-redbreast*. From the play *The White Devil*.

p. 265. *Fidele's Dirge*. From *Cymbeline*.

p. 267. *Proud Maisie*. Sung by Madge Wildfire, a madwoman in *The Heart of Midlothian*.

p. 268. *I heard a cow low*. The first two verses, which may have come from an older ballad, of *The Queen of Elfland's Nourric* .

p. 268. *Full Fathom Five*. Sung by Ariel in *The Tempest*.

p. 269. *The Flowers of the Forest*. Lament for the Battle of Flodden, 1513, written more than two centuries later, though the first line and the refrain are traditional and date from the time of the battle.

p. 270. *The Bonnie Earl of Moray*. The Earl of Moray, whose home was at Doune, was murdered in 1592 by the Earl of Huntly who said the King had ordered him to arrest Moray. The Queen is the wife of James VI of Scotland and I of England.

p. 274. *In Plague Time*. From *Summer's Last Will and Testament*.

p. 275. *Wake all the Dead!* The first of two stanzas.

MARVELS AND RIDDLES

p. 276. *Wonders*. The second verse of a poem with this title.

p. 277. *The Great Panjandrum*. Foote was an actor and is said to have written these lines at David Garrick's request for a poem with no meaning.

Further Information

INDEX OF FIRST LINES

INDEX OF TITLES

Index of Titles

INDEX OF AUTHORS